# FROM CYPRUS TO LEPANTO

## GIOVANNI PIETRO CONTARINI

# HISTORIA DELLE COSE SVCCESSE DAL PRINCIPIO DELLA GVERRA MOSSA DA SELIM OTTOMANO A' VENETIANI,

Fino al dì della gran Giornata Vittoriosa contra Turchi,

Descritta non meno particolare che fedelmente da M. Gio. Pietro Contarini Venetiano.

## CON PRIVILEGIO.

IN VENETIA
Appresso Francesco Rampazetto.
MDLXXII.

# FROM CYPRUS TO LEPANTO

### GIOVANNI PIETRO CONTARINI

*History of the Events, Which Occurred from the Beginning of the War Brought against the Venetians by Selim the Ottoman, to the Day of the Great and Victorious Battle against the Turks*

Introduction, Translation, and Notes
by
Kiril Petkov

ITALICA PRESS
New York & Bristol, UK
2019

Copyright © 2019 by Italica Press
ITALICA PRESS, INC.
99 Wall Street, Suite 650
New York, New York 10005
inquiries@italicapress.com

Italica Press Medieval & Renaissance Texts

All rights reserved. No part of this publication may be reproduced, stored in a retrieval system, or transmitted, in any form or by any means, electronic, mechanical, photocopying, recording, or otherwise, without prior permission of Italica Press. It may not be used in a course-pack or any other collection without prior permission of Italica Press.

**Library of Congress Cataloging-in-Publication Data**
Names: Contarini, Giovanni, 1549-1604 or 1605, author. | Petkov, Kiril, 1964- editor, translator, writer of introduction.
Title: From Cyprus to Lepanto : history of the events, which occurred from the beginning of the war brought against the Venetians by Selim the Ottoman, to the day of the great and victorious battle against the Turks / Gianpietro Pietro Contarini ; introduction, translation, and notes by Kiril Petkov.
Other titles: Historia delle cose successe dal principio della guerra mossa da Selim Ottomano a'Venetiani. English
Description: New York : Italica Press, 2019. | Series: Italica Press medieval & Renaissance texts | Translation of: Historia delle cose successe dal principio della guerra mossa da Selim Ottomano a' Venetiani. | Includes bibliographical references and index. | Summary: "'From Cyprus to Lepanto,' translated and edited by Kiril Petkov, is the first English translation of Gianpietro Contarini's 1572 'History...of the War Brought against the Venetians by Selim the Ottoman.' His work is the first and principal narrative of the war between the Holy League and the Ottomans, which began with the conquest of Cyprus and culminated in the battle of Lepanto. It includes Petkov's introduction on the author's sources, style, and above all, philosophy of history, as well as notes, a bibliography and an index"— Provided by publisher.
Identifiers: LCCN 2019022465 (print) | LCCN 2019022466 (ebook) | ISBN 9781599103815 (hardcover) | ISBN 9781599103822 (paperback) | ISBN 9781599103839 (ebook)
Subjects: LCSH: Cyprian War, 1570-1571. | Lepanto, Battle of, Greece, 1571. | Venice (Italy)—History—Turkish Wars, 1453-1571. | Italy—History—16th century. | Cyprus—History—Turkish Conquest, 1570-1571.
Classification: LCC DG678.2 .C6613 2019 (print) | LCC DG678.2 (ebook) | DDC 956.93/01--dc23
LC record available at https://lccn.loc.gov/2019022465
LC ebook record available at https://lccn.loc.gov/2019022466

Cover Illustration: *The Battle of Lepanto*, attributed to Ignazio Danti from a 1572 etching by Fernando Bertelli. Gallery of Maps, Vatican Museums. Wikimedia.

For a Complete List of Titles in Medieval & Renaissance Texts
Visit our Website at: http://www.italicapress.com/index003.html.

# CONTENTS

| | |
|---|---|
| LIST OF ILLUSTRATIONS | VI |
| ACKNOWLEDGEMENTS | VII |
| INTRODUCTION | XI |
| GIOVANNI PIETRO CONTARINI, HISTORY OF THE EVENTS | 1 |
|    PREFACE | 3 |
|    CAUSES OF THE CONFLICT | 7 |
|    PREPARATIONS | 14 |
|    THE BATTLE FOR CYPRUS | 26 |
|    NICOSIA | 29 |
|    FAMAGUSTA | 37 |
|    THE HOLY LEAGUE | 77 |
|    THE FORCES OF THE HOLY LEAGUE | 88 |
|      *Vanguard* | 88 |
|      *Left Wing* | 89 |
|      *Center* | 91 |
|      *Right Wing* | 92 |
|      *Rearguard* | 94 |
|    THE OTTOMAN FORCES | 96 |
|      *Right Wing* | 105 |
|      *Center* | 107 |
|      *Left Wing* | 109 |
|      *Reserve* | 112 |
|    THE BATTLE OF LEPANTO | 113 |
|    AFTERMATH | 126 |
|      *Galleys* | 130 |
|      *Artillery* | 131 |
|      *Slaves* | 131 |
| GLOSSARY | 133 |

BIBLIOGRAPHY 135
    EDITIONS OF THE *HISTORY* AND THE *ELEGANTISSIMA DESCRIPTIO* 135
    EARLY MODERN WORKS IN PRINT AND MANUSCRIPT 136
    MODERN STUDIES AND EDITIONS 138
INDEX 145

## ILLUSTRATIONS

Frontispiece. Title page from Giovanni Pietro Contarini, *Historia delle cose successe dal principio della guerra mossa da Selim Ottomano a' Venetiani, fino al dì della gran giornata vittoriosa contra Turchi, descritta … da M. Gio. Pietro Contarini Venetiano*. In Venetia: Appresso Francesco Rampazetto, 1572     II

Map of the Eastern Mediterranean. From Giovanni Pietro Contarini, *Elegantissima totius Europae, ac partis Asiae, nec non littorum Africae descriptio*. Venice: [s.n.], 1564, plates 16–17     VIII–IX

Caravel. Detail from Contarini, *Elegantissima totius Europae*, plate 10     X

# ACKNOWLEDGEMENTS

The work on this translation was greatly facilitated by grants from the American Philosophical Society in Philadelphia and the Faculty and Academic Staff Development Program of the University of Wisconsin-River Falls. I am deeply grateful to the APhS reviewers and the colleagues on FASDB's Selection Committee for Research Grants for the support. I would like to thank the librarians and staff at Biblioteca Marciana, Venice, Biblioteca Comunale, Treviso, Biblioteca Apostolica Vaticana, and Biblioteca Alessandrina, Rome, for their kind assistance. My most sincere thanks go to Ronald G. Musto and Eileen Gardiner for undertaking this publication and for their outstanding editorial work.

The Author

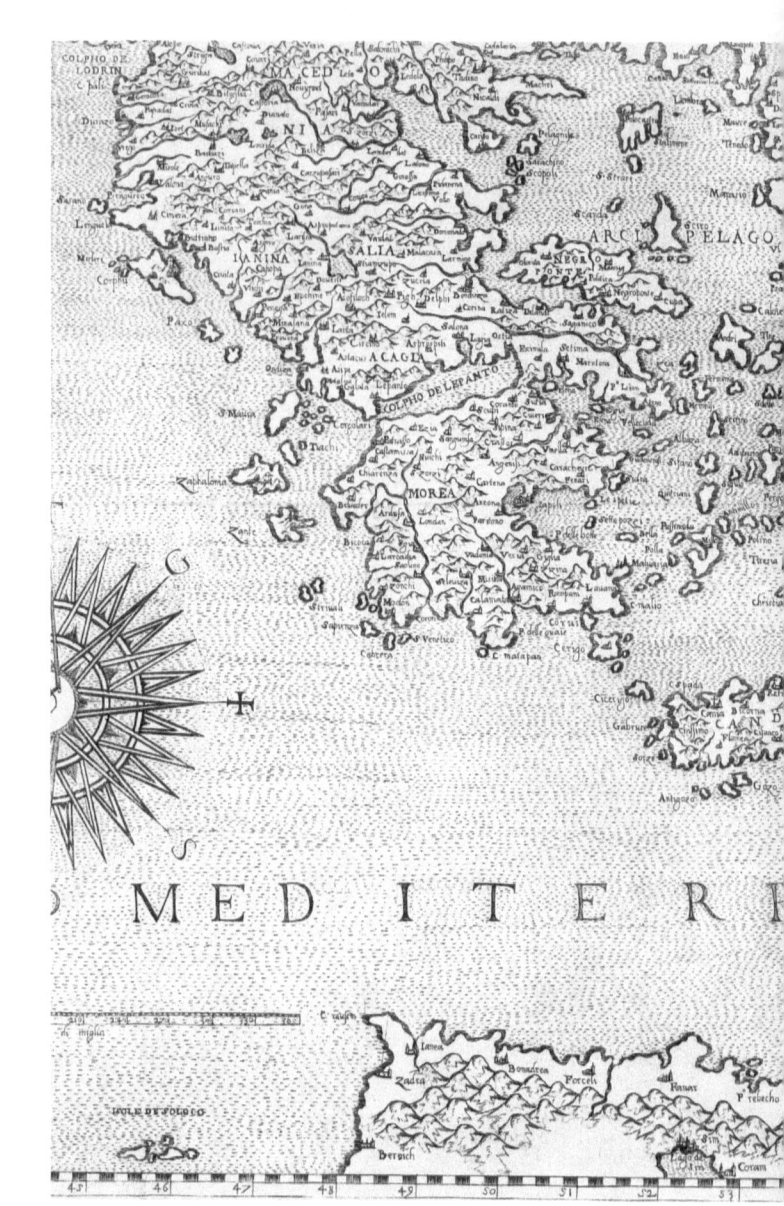

# INTRODUCTION

ON THE MORNING of October 7, 1571, two massive fleets joined battle at the rocks of Curzolari, the ancient Enchinades, seven small islands in the Ionian Sea at the entrance to the Gulf of Patras, off the coast of western Greece. The armada of the Holy League, a coalition of Venetian, Spanish, and papal vessels, augmented with squadrons from the duchies of Tuscany, Savoy, Parma, and Urbino, the Knights Hospitaller of Malta, the Republic of Genoa, and other Christian allies confronted a comparable Ottoman naval force augmented with North African corsair units. More than four hundred and fifty heavily armed galleys with over one hundred and fifty thousand sailors, oarsmen, and soldiers onboard, clashed in a short but fierce fight. Little quarter was sought, or given, by either side. In terms of hardware, manpower, and logistics, it was the largest-ever encounter of oared vessels of the pre-modern world.

The most formidable clash of naval forces in the Mediterranean, it was also one of the most famous naval confrontations in history. By the early afternoon, it was all over. The concerted action of the central and western Mediterranean Catholic powers resulted in a resounding victory over their Ottoman opponents, making up for a series of humiliating defeats during the preceding decades. The Holy League's coalition prevailed, deploying a novel weapon, a squadron of six side-armed, large galleasses, having the advantage of more firearms of all sizes and shapes, and carrying detachments of more seasoned fighting men.

The Ottoman forces, which had counted on their slightly superior numbers, more agile vessels than the Spanish galleys, and the skill of their experienced bowmen, were annihilated. Save for a sizable squadron under the corsair ruler of Algiers, Uluj Ali, who managed to slip away with forty of his galleys intact, the bulk of the Ottoman vessels were captured or sent to the bottom of the sea, their crews and fighters killed or enslaved. The League suffered comparatively few casualties, their triumph only marred by the loss of a disproportionate number of ranking Venetian naval commanders.

The battle of Lepanto, as it came to be known after the name of the chief naval base of the area from which the Ottoman fleet sailed forth to meet their adversaries, was the peak of the war between the Ottomans and the central and western Mediterranean Christian powers in 1570–73. The heroic sacrifice of the flower of the Venetian naval leadership was not accidental. The Republic of Venice bore the brunt of the Ottoman pressure, and it was most instrumental in orchestrating the Holy League to oppose the Ottomans during this episode of ongoing imperial and confessional struggle in the region. After a period of relative calm under the Ottoman Sultan Suleiman the Magnificent (1520–66), tensions between the Ottoman Empire and Venice began to mount with the accession of his son Selim II (1566–74). The Ottomans had developed intense economic and strategic interests in the Eastern Mediterranean, and one of the jewels of the Venetian maritime empire, the island of Cyprus, now sat squarely within their logistic networks.

By late 1569, it had become clear that Venice and the Ottomans were on a collision course. The seizure of two Venetian ships in January 1570 was the opening salvo of the war. Half-hearted diplomatic moves did not prevent the inevitable. In late spring, a large Ottoman expeditionary force led by Lala Mustafa Pasha landed on Cyprus, laid siege to its inadequately defended capital, Nicosia, and shortly captured it. The invading army then moved on to Famagusta, the much better fortified principal maritime base on the island. After several months of fierce resistance and feeble attempts at a rescue by Venetian naval detachments, Famagusta surrendered on August 1, 1571. The success cost the besiegers dearly, prompting the Ottoman commander to unleash grisly reprisals on the surviving defenders. Unable to protect the island, the Venetians focused on halting further Ottoman advance on the open seas. They found a somewhat reluctant ally in the Spanish monarchy, alarmed by the Ottoman momentum and what they considered its emboldening effect on unassimilated Spanish Muslims and on North African Muslim polities. They also found an enthusiastic supporter in Italy, in the person of Pope Pius V.

# INTRODUCTION

The Holy League was proclaimed on May 25, 1571 and opened the second stage of the war, now principally a naval confrontation. Put under the command of Philip II's half-brother, the impetuous Don Juan of Austria, and led by seasoned naval commanders, the League held together despite internal squabbles. It proceeded eastward in orderly fashion, until it happened upon the Ottoman armada under Müezzinzade Ali Pasha, which had been ordered to project the Ottoman success at Cyprus into the central Mediterranean. The League's triumph terminated that project, but Lepanto was both the peak and the end of that phase of the face-off. A third stage set in: the League's fleet dissolved, the allies pursued their separate political interests, and their impetus was lost. The Ottomans rebuilt their naval capabilities and continued their expansion on the European mainland. War-weary, the Venetians cut their losses and concluded a separate peace on March 7, 1573. The Holy League was over and so was the war. Venice acknowledged the loss of Cyprus and made concessions on the mainland. The Ottomans continued their advance in the Mediterranean.[1]

---

1. The war of 1570–73 and the battle of Lepanto have generated a large amount of contemporary reflections and a burgeoning scholarly output. Principal surveys include George Hill, *A History of Cyprus* 3. *The Frankish Period, 1432–1571* (Cambridge: Cambridge University Press, 1948, repr., 2010); Kenneth Setton, *The Papacy and the Levant (1204–1571)* 4. *The Sixteenth Century: From the Reign of Julius III to Pius V* (Philadelphia: American Philosophical Society, 1984); Maddalena Redolfi, *Venezia e la difesa di Levante: Da Lepanto a Candia, 1570–1670* (Venice: Arsenale, 1986); Romano Canossa, *Lepanto: Storia della "Lega Santa" contro i Turchi* (Rome: Sapere, 2000); Niccolò Capponi, *Victory of the West: The Great Christian-Muslim Clash at the Battle of Lepanto* (New York: Da Capo Press, 2007); Manuel Rivero Rodríguez, *La batalla de Lepanto: Cruzada, guerra santa e identidad confesional* (Madrid: Silex Ediciones, 2008); Alessandro Barbero, *Lepanto: La battaglia dei tre imperi* (Bari: Laterza, 2010). There are several shorter surveys in larger works; the most recent short and judicious synthesis is in Noel Malcolm, *Agents of Empire: Knights, Corsairs, Jesuits, and Spies in the Sixteenth-Century Mediterranean World* (Oxford: Oxford University Press, 2016), 101–74, with excellent bibliography.

THE TRIUMPH OF LEPANTO thus gave way to harsh political realities, so much so that modern observers have been hard put to evaluate adequately its significance. For some, Lepanto marked the end of the Ottoman imperial expansion in the central and western Mediterranean. True, Cyprus was lost, Ottoman power was entrenched in the eastern portion of the Middle Sea and North Africa, and during the next century the Ottomans enlarged their dominion in east-central Europe and the Levant, to crown it with the conquest of Crete in 1669. But the back of the formidable Ottoman naval machine was broken at Lepanto. Ottoman successes on the high seas were rare after 1571, mere setbacks for the Western Christian powers than further progress on a menacing trajectory.[2]

Others point out the speedy rebuilding of Ottoman naval capabilities — a strong Ottoman fleet was in operation in the summer of 1573[3] — the loss of sizable Venetian outposts, such as Cyprus, the continuing Ottoman expansion, the conquest of Tunis in 1574, and the failure of the western Christians to pursue concerted action. Lepanto, in that view, was merely a frontier clash, stimulating another decade of conflicts between the Hapsburgs and the Ottomans, until both parties reached their logistic limits, turned their attention away from the Mediterranean, and outsourced the war in the Middle Sea to corsairs. It was only an episode of the final stretch of the imperial and confessional confrontation in the region, which culminated

---

2. See, among others, Cayetano Rosell, *Historia del combate naval de Lepanto y juicio de la importancia y consecuencias de aquel suceso* (Madrid: Imprimeria de la Real Academia de la Historia, 1853); Guido A. Quarti, *La Guerra Contro il Turco in Cipro e a Lepanto, 1570–1571: Storia Documentata* (Venice: Stabilimento Grafico G. Bellini, 1935); Luciano Serrano, *La liga de Lepanto entre España, Venecia, y la Santa Sede (1570–1573): Ensayo historico abase de documentos diplomaticos,* 2 vols. (Madrid: Tipografia de la Revista de Archivos, 1918–20); Michel Lesure, *Lépante: La crise de l'empire Ottoman* (Paris: Julliard, 1972).

3. See Colin Imber, "The Reconstruction of the Ottoman Fleet after the Battle of Lepanto, 1571–1572," in *Studies in Ottoman History and Law*, Colin Imber, ed. (Istanbul: The Isis Press, 1996), 85–102.

in the crusade of Alcazar of 1578 and ended with the Hapsburg-Ottoman peace of 1580.[4]

A third view holds it that Lepanto was more than anything a psychological victory for the western Christians. It demonstrated that the Ottomans were not invincible, even though the war's aftermath underscored the inability of the western powers to ally permanently in the face of the Ottoman pressure, which continued unopposed. Nonetheless, the Christian feeling of inferiority gave way to a new confidence to face the Ottoman military's advance, and this, in time, marked the beginning of Ottoman naval decline.

A fourth view offers a nuance to the theory of Ottoman decline at Lepanto, and considers the League's victory in terms of the debilitating effect it had on Ottoman expert manpower. Success in war at sea and on board Mediterranean fighting vessels depended on the sophisticated skills — honed only after long practice — of sailors, marines, fighting men, and (for the Ottomans) bowmen. At Lepanto, an entire generation of these practitioners, who were indispensable for the adequate manning of the rebuilt Ottoman war fleets, ended up on the bottom of the sea or in shackles at the oars of the League's galleys. The terrible casualties sapped Ottoman military capabilities. While the Ottomans were training their replacements, the technological, political, and strategic conditions in the Mediterranean changed radically, and not to their benefit. Lepanto gave the central and western Mediterranean powers a breather, which the changed realities of early modern naval warfare turned into a permanent advantage.[5]

Modern scholars thus differ in their assessment. Yet the wide roster of interpretations, as well as the continuing re-examination of the war that led to Lepanto, point to a fundamental agreement

---

4. Andrew C. Hess, "The Battle of Lepanto and Its Place in Mediterranean History," *Past & Present* 57 (November 1972): 53–73.

5. John F. Guilmartin, Jr., *Gunpowder and Galleys: Changing Technology and Mediterranean Warfare at Sea in the Sixteenth Century* (Cambridge: Cambridge University Press, 1974).

among interpreters: it was a momentous occurrence. In this, modern scholarship and popular taste are in full agreement with those of the early modern Europeans. Contemporaries, eyewitnesses, and the early modern public in general had no doubt that the war of Cyprus and Lepanto was, above all, an occurrence of tremendous import. The opening of the war, the conquest of Cyprus, the formation of the Holy League, and the victory at Lepanto unleashed a flood of publications. The large output of printed diplomatic correspondence, prose and poetry, political tracts, newsletters and prints of every imaginable form and content, artwork and historical treatises, through which the echo of Lepanto reverberated to the farthest corners of the Europe, testify to the enormous interest in keeping current with the events as they unfolded.[6]

GIVEN SUCH A MARKED INTEREST over the ages, it is somewhat strange that none of the principal contemporary accounts of the war has

---

6. An older but still valuable synopsis of the echo of Lepanto in Italian culture is Carlo Dionissoti, "Lepanto nella cultura italiana del tempo," in Gino Benzoni, ed., *Il Mediterraneo nella seconda metà del '500 alla luce di Lepanto* (Florence: Olschki, 1974), 127–52; in Ottoman sources, Halil Inalcik, "Lepanto in the Ottoman documents," ibid., 185–92; and Manoussos Manoussacas, "Lepanto e i Greci," ibid., 215–42; in Spanish sources, Luciano Serrano, ed., *Correspondencia diplomatica entre España y la Santa Sede durante el pontificado de S. Pio V*, 4 vols. (Madrid: Tipografia de la Revista de Archivos, 1914). For Lepanto and modern memorializing, see Ian Fenlon, "Lepanto: The Arts of Celebration in Renaissance Venice," in *Proceedings of the British Academy* 73 (1987): 221–26; D.E. Rhodes, "La battaglia di Lepanto e la stampa popolare a Venezia: Studio bibliografico," in Alessandro Scarsella, ed., *Metodologia bibliografica e storia del libro: Atti del seminario sul libro antico offerti a Dennis E. Rhodes*, "Miscellanea Marciana" 10–11 (1995–96): 9–63; Umberto Rozzo, "La battaglia di Lepanto nell'editoria dell'epoca e una miscellanea fontaniana," *Rara Volumina* 1–2 (2000): 41–69; Tulio Bulgarelli, "La battaglia di Lepanto e il giornalismo romano del Cinquecento," *Accademie e biblioteche d'Italia* 29 (1961): 231–39; and Anastasia Stouraiti, "Costruendo un luogo della memoria: Lepanto," in *Meditando sull'evento di Lepanto: Odierne interpretazioni e memorie, Convegno storico. Venezia, 8 novembre 2002. Raccolta delle relazioni* (Venice: Studi Veneziani, series Storia di Venezia, 2002).

been rendered in the modern English idiom.[7] The written output on Lepanto is formidable indeed, but it is not difficult to pick a worthy representative.

In the chorus of eyewitness and contemporary accounts of the battle and the events that led to it, Giovanni Pietro Contarini's *History* holds the pride of place. Published in early 1572, a few months after Lepanto, the *History* is the first comprehensive account of the war and the only one to attempt a concise but comprehensive overview of its course and the Holy League's triumph.[8] It was also the first in the barrage of information, where euphoric and critical voices often mingled, to go beyond effluent praise and mere factual reporting to take a stand on the meaning and importance of the events reported. Significantly, it is also the only account by an immediate observer. Despite falling short of the best examples of contemporary history writing in the humanist vein, Contarini blended his straightforward, matter-of-fact narrative with keen and consistent reflections on the political philosophy of war and interfaith conflict in the context of the Ottoman-Catholic confrontation in the early modern Mediterranean.

It is thus disappointing that Contarini's identity is still an enigma. The dedication of the *History* indicates that he was a Venetian. The

---

7. The first compendium of translated primary sources on Lepanto — in this case, Latin poetry — appeared only recently. See Elizabeth White, Sarah Spence, and Andrew Lemons, ed. and trans., *The Battle of Lepanto* (Cambridge, MA: Harvard University Press, 2014).

8. The second early historical narrative is Emilio Maria Manolesso, *Historia Nova, nella qualle si contengono tutti i successi della guerra Turchesca...* (Padua: Lorenzo Pasquari, 1572), but the work actually appeared in the first months of 1573, as the dating is according to the Venetian calendar. Manolesso's treatise is pan-European, however, and the war of Cyprus and Lepanto is only a part of "everything that happened in the world since 1570 to the present." The third immediate historical account is that of Fernando Herrera, *Relación de la guerra de Chipre y suceso de la batalla naval de Lepanto* (Seville: Alonso Escrivano, 1572), modern edition in *Colleción de documentos inéditos para la historia de España* (Madrid: Sociedad de Bibliófilos Andaluces, 1852), 21:243–382.

reverent tone in which he addresses the patron, Patriarch Giovanni Grimani, suggests that he was more likely a commoner than a member of the patriciate. Contarini knew his classics, which implies good education, but his approach to history and his style reflect neither a trained historian nor a humanist. The only other work besides the *History* that can be associated with his name is the *Elegantissima descriptio,* a geographical atlas of Europe, the Mediterranean, and the Near East in sixteen plates, first published in 1564.[9] Both works point to a meticulous mind, carefully balancing detail and larger framework, able to present concisely, visually and verbally, and intimately an agenda without articulating it in the elegant synthesis of the humanist. Contarini is thus a keen but accidental scholar. These are the only certain facts and plausible inferences about him at present; anything else would be pure conjecture.[10]

The *History,* for its part, has a relatively clear genealogy. Two things stand out in this regard. First, the treatise fits squarely into the Venetian chronicling tradition of the period, abounding in amateur worthies with a knack for recording facts but falling short of the analytical and critical standards a humanist historian would uphold.[11] Most of the account is straightforward fact bracketed by dates. The march of time is the *History*'s organizing narrative principle. Here and there, the succinct chronological exposition is punctuated by a few authorial commentaries. Interpretative segments appear on very few occasions, cast in the beloved manner of ancient and Renaissance

---

9. Ioannis Petri Contareni, *Elegantissima totius Europae, ac partis Asiae, nec non littorum Africae descriptio* (Venice: s.n., 1564).

10. Gino Benzoni, "Contarini, Gianpietro," DBI 28 (1983). Online at: http://www.treccani.it/enciclopedia/gianpietro-contarini_(Dizionario-Biografico).

11. The *Diaries* of Marino Sanudo are the best known and most voluminous representative of this genre, populated by scores of Venetian amateur chroniclers. The recently published digest in translation, *Venice, Città Excellentissima: Selections from the Renaissance Diaries of Marin Sanudo,* Patricia H. Labalme and Laura Sanguineti White, ed., Linda L. Carroll, trans. (Baltimore: Johns Hopkins University Press, 2008), offers a good sample of that manner of chronicling history.

writers, the public speech. Second, the *History*, very much like the *Elegantissima desriptio,* is not an original work as a whole. Contarini, like so many of his contemporaries, does not seem to have had the sense of plagiarism. The *History* is cobbled together from several previously published treatises, newsletters, and short tracts and pamphlets. While not all of them can be identified with certainty, those making up the bulk of the *History* are clear. The account of the siege of Nicosia, for example, is directly borrowed from Francesco Altomira's *Narratione della guerra di Nicosia,* published in Bologna in 1571. Altomira himself cites as his source the work of Giovanni Sozomeno, a native of the island and eyewitness of the siege.[12] For the siege of Famagusta, Contarini incorporated verbatim the detailed report of Count Nestor Martinengo, one of the commanders of the besieged Venetian forces, published and available in Venice in 1571.[13] Also rendered verbatim are two speeches of Ascanio della Cornia, the commander of the coalition's infantry, published in 1571 in Florence in various formats.[14]

---

12. Francesco Altomira, *Narratione della guerra di Nicosia, fatta nel Regno di Cipro da' Turchi nel' anno MDLXX, al illustre Sig. Conte Pompeo Trissino* (Bologna: Biagio Bignami, 1571); Giovanni Sozomeno, *Narratione della guerra di Nicosia fatta nel regno di Cipro da' Turchi l'anno 1570* (Bologna: Biagio Bignami, 1571). The account of Sozomeno, along with the accounts of other eyewitnesses, is translated into English by Claude Delaval Cobham, *Excerpta Cypria* (Cambridge: Cambridge University Press, 1908, repr., New York: Kraus, 1969), 80–148.

13. For the original appearance of the report as part of the *avvisi*, or newsletters on the war, see Tulio Bulgarelli, *Gli avvisi a stampa in Roma nel Cinquecento: Bibliografia-Antologia* (Rome: Istituto di Studi Romani Editore, 1967), 68, no. 109. Martinengo's account is also translated in Claude Delaval Cobham, *Travels in the Island of Cyprus,* 2nd ed. (Cambridge: Cambridge University Press, 1909, repr., London: Zeno, 1971). Martinengo's report was translated into English by William Malim and published in London in 1572.

14. Ascanio della Cornia publicized his position at the League's war council at Messina by publishing, on August 24, the day after the council, a manifest addressed to Don Juan; he did the same after the second war council. The manifests were circulated immediately, separately or together, as *avvisi* on

Meticulous information on the movements of the Venetian naval forces in their attempt to provide relief for Cyprus and the journey of the allied armada was available on an almost daily basis in Venice through copious *avvisi*, early modern newsletters. Many published descriptions and depictions of the battle order at Lepanto, lists of casualties, and lists of the division of the spoils of war were available in the months after Lepanto as well. Contarini most certainly used more than one of those, as his lists of the battle order, for example, filled lacunae that some of them had, while having omissions of his own.[15] Tracking down his precise sources here is difficult. Difficult too is the identification of the source of one of his major original contributions, the discussion at the Ottoman war council before the Battle of Lepanto. Ranking Ottoman officers who took part in the council were captured and questioned in Venice. Their accounts are not consistent, and which of the circulating versions Contarini used cannot be easily ascertained.[16]

---

the League's considerations. Both are published by Maria Gabrielli Donati Guerrieri, *Lo stato di Castiglione del Lago e i della Corgna* (Castiglione del Lago: Grafica, 1972), 208–9.

15. Compare one of the widely distributed lists, Giovanni Francesco Camocio, *L'ordine delle galere et le insegne loro, con il Fano, Nomi, & Cognomi delli Magnifici & generrosi patroni di esse, che si ritrovano nella armata della santissima Lega, al tempo della vittoriosa & miracolosa impresa ottenuta, & fata con lo aiuto Divino contra la orgogliosa & superba armata Turchescha* (Venice: Giovanni Francesco Camocio, 1571).

16. The conflicting accounts are first succinctly discussed by Jurien de la Gravière, *La Guerre de Chypre et la Bataille de Lepante*, 2 vols. (Paris: Plon, 1888), 2:102–8. The principal difference between the Western and Ottoman accounts (the latter as preserved in the later work of the Ottoman historian Hadji Kalfa) is the position of Uluj Ali. Western sources, most notably the immediate report of the Venetian Girolamo Diedo, stress that at the war council Uluj Ali advocated for immediate action, while Hadji Kalfa writes that Uluj Ali was in the camp counseling against giving battle. Contarini adopts the Venetian version. De la Gravière's explanation of the contradiction makes sense: Uluj Ali knew that it was unlikely that any of the commanders at the war council would live to tell the story, so once he arrived in

This however, does not make the *History* merely a handy compendium of already known facts, worthy of telling as they may have been. Rather, it is a "chronohistory," a carefully compiled factual narrative governed by a distinct philosophical agenda. The *History* is not just an account of a concrete military confrontation. It offers keen insights into the operation of the historical forces that determined the outcome of war between two competing powers with differing worldviews.

To begin with, Contarini did not mechanically conjoin the borrowed segments of his account. He went through them carefully, altering the voice of his sources to fit the overall aim of the *History*, condensing their information, and rendering them in a concise, seamless narration. More importantly, he excised any and every factual reference to, and suppressed or succinctly explained away, authorial commentaries that showed a particular bias, favoring or criticizing a particular protagonist of either camp to the detriment of the party's overall unity. Submerging diverging voices in his narrative, both adversaries subscribe to coherent and directly opposite political philosophies. The viability of the latter's organizing principles decided, ultimately, the outcome of the war—and would, in time, determine the result of any future confrontation. Finally, even though the parties stood for radically different world views and represented separate worlds in their own right, they were both parts of a unified universe. The conceptual organization of the latter gave a clear advantage to only one of them and predetermined its ultimate victory over the other. Contarini thus provided his readers with a fresh compendium of facts about the Christian success, which he knew they would eagerly devour as antidote to the anxiety caused by the seemingly endless string of Ottoman victories. More importantly, he offered them a thoughtful reflection that explained the war and the triumph at Lepanto as a symptomatic event on a larger trajectory

---

Constantinople after the disaster he insisted he had advised *against* engaging the Christian armada. For Diedo, who cites as his sources Mehmet Bey and Kara Ali, both captured at Lepanto, see Salvatore Mazzarella, ed., *Onorato Caetani, Girolamo Diedo, La battaglia di Lepanto, 1571* (Palermo: Sellerio, 1995), 177-224.

that rationalized the inevitability of Western prevalence in terms of human agency. Therein, perhaps, lies the appeal of the *History* to the its reading public for as long as it was confronted by the Ottomans. This theme also helps heighten its interest for the modern student of history.

INDEED, IN CONTARINI'S MEDITERRANEAN UNIVERSE, providential action, and the causalities of just war and holy war afforded to the Holy League, form a thin layer of ideology over the empirical facts. The divine hand shows up in crucial moments on the side of the Christians even when they suffer setbacks, but its interventions are universal in scope and leave most causality to human agents. A specific course of action was fully in the hands of the European allies, guided by a set of conceptual premises, which their opponents lacked. Chief among these is historicism. The Christian camp was steeped in historical time. For Contarini, the Western allies operated on an awareness of the progress of history and the evolution of context. In his rendering of the deliberations of the Ottoman war council on the eve of Lepanto, Contarini asserts that cooperating with the flow of time and its ever-shifting contexts matters most in formulating policies and achieving success in action. Time awareness is indispensable for conducting proper observation. Reconnaissance facts need to be put in the context of time to produce credible intelligence on the basis of which proper decisions can be taken. Deliberating against the background of historical inertia, dismissing changes produced by the evolution of time, results in faulty conclusions. The success of action depends on the degree to which the perceptions upon which it is built are rational, and awareness of the flow of time is a critical component of rationality. There is no direct causal connection between observed facts and adequate perception. The relation between the former and the latter is mediated by awareness of the impact of time and the contexts it creates. Ignoring the impact of time creates misleading perceptions; actions undertaken on them are detrimental.

Curiously, Contarini's concept of the western Christians primarily as "beings in time," emerged from what he considered the Christians' curse, their inherent diversity. Time and again, this diversity had led to disunity that undermined the Christian war effort. That, however, was a thing of the past. A new condition had set in, and to reflect it faithfully, Contarini combed diligently through his sources and subtly edited them, eliminating indications of discord, internal strife, and assignations of blame among the allies. Inherent diversity notwithstanding, the Holy League was a unified power, a miracle indeed, as Contarini stressed, brought about by Christ's personal intervention on behalf of the faithful. Disunity cancelled, difference-engendering diversity became a positive force. It provided the League with the best blend the western powers were able to muster in terms of brawn and brains, the complementary skills of the rank-and-file in action, and the varied experiences of the commanders in deliberation. Furthermore, acutely cognizant of difference — national, cultural, and above all political — the western allies were conceptually sensitized to recognize difference wrought by time. By contrast, the Ottoman autocratic system of governance overruled the inherent diversity of their forces and homogenized politics to the extent that the very notion of difference became non-operational. The imperative of total obedience to the autocratic state muted dissenting voices among the commanding officers. They disregarded indications that their current Christian opponent was a force of a different kind from the ones they had easily prevailed upon before. Heeding dictatorial authority, they let themselves be persuaded by advocates of historical inertia, eschewed proper rationality, obeyed orders divorced from the realities of time and context, and suffered the consequences.

Cognizance of time-defined context and collective decision-making, duly accounting for diverse viewpoints, are thus crucial in a conflict, but prevailing upon one's opponents takes more than crushing them in a particular encounter. Ultimately, the victory belongs to those who are firmly in charge of their destiny, who control the course of action themselves, and deny agency to external forces. Contarini was aware that the Christian-Ottoman confrontation was a long-term engagement, a drawn-out clash not to be resolved in a single conflict. It was also clear to him, the League's advantages notwithstanding, that the adversaries were, for all practical purposes, evenly matched. The battle order at Lepanto, which he offered to his readers, testifies to that. Victory therefore, could be a toss, the result of pure luck and the good fortune of one of the parties in the ever-shifting conditions of Mediterranean naval warfare. But luck and fortune are capricious forces outside humans' purview. In an evenly matched competition, luck could bring success in war.

Preserving successful gains however — and therefore obtaining victory — was another matter altogether. It had nothing to do with luck. It depended entirely on a specific human propensity, prudence, rational action attuned to specific context. Through prudence, humans are able to take charge of any situation and to neuter the impact of whimsical forces outside their control. Against this background, in Contarini's political philosophy the string of Ottoman successes, even the most recent conquest of Cyprus, meant little in the final analysis. They were the product neither of providential support — God was with the Christians — nor of superior human faculties rooted in proper rationality. The Ottomans' failure to pursue their advantage after Cyprus and the crushing defeat after the chance they took at Lepanto against better advice proved that they acted on luck, surrendering their ultimate destiny to the whims of fortune, which they could not control. Western Christians, for their part, managed to turn the tables on their adversary precisely because they prudently took charge of affairs themselves. Within such a juxtaposition, Lepanto clearly demonstrated who would prevail in the long term.

Far from being a mere chronicle of bygone days, therefore, the *History* offers its readers, early modern and modern, a fascinating conceptualization of war and its outcomes. War is the clash of human actors otherwise quite alike, but with identities construed purposefully around opposing world views and political philosophies. Extra-human forces do play a role, but those who account for change, embrace diversity, and prioritize human agency emerge victorious. Having synthesized the Western advantage for his audience, Contarini used both the defeat of Cyprus and the triumph at Lepanto to paint an optimistic picture of Western ascendancy. Readers would turn to the story of Lepanto because it gave hope to the embattled Christian West, crushed so many times by the irresistible Ottomans. But no less important, perhaps, was the interpretative framework into which Contarini put it in the *History*, for it guaranteed that the triumph was not a fortunate incident but a signpost on the road to the ultimate victory of the Christian forces.

FOR A GOOD STRETCH of the early modern period, the *History* enjoyed significant popularity. First published in early 1572, the volume went through two more printings later that year, one in Venice and one in Milan. The following year, 1573, two translations, one in Latin and one in German, appeared in Basel. The Latin version was translated into German one more time in 1599 and published in Dresden. A new edition in the original Italian was printed again in Venice in 1645, in the wake of another Ottoman-Venetian war. It was widely used as an informational treasure-trove by a roster of later writers. Some, like the noted historian Francesco Sansovino, incorporated large sections of it verbatim, as he did in his *Universal History of the Turks*.[17] Other authors drew on it more selectively, but it remained as undisputable authority on the subject throughout the seventeenth century.[18]

THIS TRANSLATION IS MADE from the *History*'s first edition of 1572. Pages from the *Elegantissima descriptio* are reproduced from the copy in Rome, Biblioteca Alessandrina, Rari, 215/4. Contarini wrote in standard sixteenth-century Italian, occasionally slipping

---

17. Francesco Sansovino, *Historia universale dell'origine, et imperio de' Turchi: Raccolta, & in diversi luogi di nuovo ampliata, da M. Francesco Sansovino* (Venice: Altobello Salicato, 1582).

18. Contarini was copied, for example, verbatim by Andrea Corner, *Storia universal dell'isola e regno di Candia, del clarissimo Sig. Andrea Corner q. Giacomo, N.H. Mss di ser Vettor Molin fu Avogador di Comun l'anno MDCCLXX*, in Venice, Biblioteca Nazionale Marciana, BNV MVII 1566, ff. 1-187r.

in the Venetian idiom, mostly in technical terms and some proper names. His prose is heavy, with long, often convoluted sentences, but relatively easy to follow. I have tried to stay close to his style whenever possible and follow him verbatim, only rarely resorting to truncating or dividing sentences to convey his meaning in readable English. Contarini's narrative was continuous, but this translation divides it into several chapters to make navigating the text easier. Some of his longer paragraphs have also been divided into shorter ones for ease of reading. Transliteration of proper names and place names is always a problem, as there is no accepted universal standard, and Contarini himself often mangled Greek, Turkish, and Arab proper names. I have tried to be at least consistent in rendering them in a recognizable form, as close as possible to their original phonetic spelling. To ease the flow of reading, the text uses Roman characters for commonly used terms like *fusta* or *provveditore*. These are explained in footnotes and in the Glossary.

# GIOVANNI PIETRO CONTARINI
# HISTORY OF THE EVENTS

*that occurred from the beginning of the war brought against the Venetians by Selim the Ottoman to the day of the great and victorious battle against the Turks, described truthfully and in detail by the Venetian*

*Messer Giovanni Pietro Contarini*
*With Privilege*
*Venice, Francesco Rampazzetto, 1572*

# PREFACE

TO THE MOST ILLUSTRIOUS AND REVEREND MONSIGNOR GIOVANNI
GRIMANI,[1] PATRIARCH OF AQUILEIA

It is the nature of rumor, your most illustrious Grace, to blow things out of proportion in the ears of men and exaggerate their consequences. Nevertheless, there is no doubt that no account of the naval battle that took place in 1571 between the mighty fleets of the Christians and the Turks at the rocks of Curzolari can overestimate its importance. Given everything that truly happened there, it will be counted forever as the greatest and most famous battle that has ever been known. Among all the naval wars of different times none has been as massive and as memorable; none can be compared to the present event. It cannot be denied that there had been others that were marvelous and great and carried out to the end to great effect. Such was the defeat inflicted on Attalus, the king of Pergamum, by Phillip, the king of Macedon and father of Alexander the Great, at the isle of Chios;[2] the victory of Themistocles, captain-general of the Greeks over Xerxes, the king of the Persians, at Salamis;[3] the naval encounters between the Corinthians and the Athenians at Lepanto;[4] between the same Athenians and the Peloponnesians at Constantinople;[5]

---

1. For Giovanni Grimani (1506–93), Patriarch of Aquileia (1546–50 and 1585–93), see Gino Benzoni and Luca Bortolotti, "Grimani, Giovanni," DBI 59 (2002), online at: http://www.treccani.it/enciclopedia/giovanni-grimani (Dizionario-Biografico).

2. Polybius offers an extensive account. See *The Histories of Polybius*, Evelyn S. Shuckburgh, ed. and trans. (Cambridge: Cambridge University Press, 2012), 2:173–78.

3. On the battle of Salamis, see Herodotus, *The Histories*, Robin Waterfield, trans. (Oxford: Oxford University Press, 1998), book 8:66–99.

4. The battle of Naupactus in 429 BCE; Thucydides, *History of the Peloponnesian War* (Oxford: Oxford University Press, 1960), book 2:85sq; and Donald Kagan, *The Peloponnesian War* (New York: Penguin Books, 2004).

5. Byzantion's revolt is also narrated in Xenophon and Plutarch; see the discussion of Luis Losada, *The Fifth Column in the Peloponnesian War* (Leiden: Brill, 1972), 77–78.

between the Lacedemonians and the Athenians while they were at war in the Hellespont;[6] mighty Rome's memorable conflict with the Carthaginians at the isles of Egadi, now called Favignano. These two had fought continuously for a period of twenty-four years and had clashed two times, the first time with more than five hundred galleys on each side, the second with no less than seven hundred, and the Romans were defeated and smashed to pieces and lost their entire fleet. Finally, there is the defeat of Cleopatra, the queen of Egypt, and Marc Antony the Roman, inflicted on them by Caesar Augustus with massive fire, as Cassius Dio narrates, which happened at Preveza, not far from Curzolari.[7] But it can well be stated that the present one is much more consequential than all of them, for the following reasons: all Christendom depended on it, the art of waging naval war was brought to perfection and diversified with instruments of war that earlier times did not know, the large number of new naval machines, the infinite numbers of combatants led by so many excellent princes, the marvelous success of the encounter, and the awe with which future generations will always contemplate it.

This holy victory is more of a powerful and miraculous mystery of Christ in favor of His Christians than a feat of human prowess, even though the valor of so many illustrious men will be hallowed for eternity. As such a massive destruction of the Turks, the enemies of His name, would not have otherwise been carried out with such a minimal, if any, harm to the fleet of the faithful, I could not and should not describe to the world this holy event but in the name of your most excellent Grace, His Patriarch and Vicar in such a large province.

There the valor stirred by overflowing Christian piety was guided by insights derived from many sciences to support the naval forces,

---

6. The reference is to the battle of Aegospotami in 405 BCE, in which a Spartan navy under the command of Lysander destroyed an Athenian fleet and won the Peloponnesian War for the Spartans. Narrated by Xenophon and Diodorus Siculis, the battle and its aftermath are discussed in detail by Kagan, *Peloponnesian War,* 471–77.

7. Dio Cassius, *Roman History,* books 46–50, Earnest Cary, trans. (Cambridge, MA: Harvard University Press, 1917), 50:15–35.

and there the extreme dearth in the land of that year provided so many men to offer a splendid example for all times of how the servants of God should conduct themselves. Consider the hereditary virtue of the illustrious house of Grimani. The great gallantry of the most renowned Sir Pietro Grimani lives and gets perpetuated in the memory of men for so many years. He was procurator of San Marco, almost the highest office in this holy republic, who was great-great-grandfather of your most high Reverence. [So too lives on] the goodness of heart and the integrity of the most renowned Sir Giovanni, another procurator of San Marco, his father and your great-grandparent; of the most serene Prince Antonio Grimani, grandfather of your most illustrious Grace, who combined the splendor of the house of Grimani with the radiance of exceptional devotion; of the most renowned Sir Geronimo, yours and the country's father, most prudent senator, who served in so many offices before happily passing away as councilor of Venice; of the illustrious and most reverend Cardinal Domenico Grimani, brother of your father. Among so many other pious works, which still shine in this city, he built the rich and marvelous library in San Antonio and provided another high venue for the cultivated study of Antiquity. Later, your most illustrious Grace made [that library] so precious at inestimable cost and with much artifice. [So too lives on the memory of] the most renowned and most eloquent Sir Victor, brother of your most illustrious Grace, who was deservedly made procurator of San Marco; of the most renowned Sir Marino, your second brother. He was elected procurator of San Marco in 1522, later made patriarch of Aquileia by Pope Clement VII, and then, due to his great valor, appointed captain-general of the fleet against the Turks. [So too] his most illustrious Grace Cardinal Marco Grimani, the third brother of your most illustrious Grace, who now competes with the emperors of Antiquity by sheathing in marble — at great cost from the ground up — the entire façade and the interior of the edifice of the chapel of the church of San Francesco. He also had a palace constructed with such excellent and rich artifice that anyone kindly admitted within it is stupefied by the marvelous marbles and statues, both ancient and modern, the most precious paintings and rich ornaments in every nook and corner, and the portraits of this most devout and righteous family, as well as of the most illustrious lord who holds sway over us, admirer and patron of all kinds of virtuosi not only in the liberal but in all other arts.

By his munificence now everyone can get acquainted with the marvels of this most glorious and holy victory over the Turks. I plan to narrate it beginning with an explanation of the origins and causes of this war, with all due diligence and without sparing any effort to portray all particular details so that the world can understand how marvelous are the workings of our Lord. I studiously inquired about the thoughts of many princes in the planning and carrying out of such a great enterprise, and I would have been in great difficulty were it not for the reports of some Christians who had been slave rowers on the galleys of the enemy and were liberated by the victory. They informed me of minute details, about which later others wrote to me, concerning the voyage of the Turkish fleet and the damages, depredations, burnings, and destructions visited on the Christians. [I was also aided by] the information revealed by two captured Turkish secretaries about the deliberations of the two pashas who, in fulfilling the will of their lord, took the decision to go out and fight the battle but who now, by the immense power of our Lord, receive punishment for the many injuries they had inflicted.

Thus, besides [acknowledging] the many good deeds that your most illustrious Grace has done in the world, I will discharge the obligation to publish and announce to the world the great prudence and bravery of the many princes, nobles, and soldiers who fought in that most just war. In this way those who have never been in the Levant may behold the astounding success of this war as if they were present, and the more learned spirits who will write after me can have in minute detail my argument and subject-matter to better demonstrate the keenness of their intelligence. As for myself, I am satisfied to present to your most illustrious Grace the most simple and cordial affection of my service, which I would like to offer forever, kissing your hands.

*Humble servant of your most illustrious Grace,*
*Giovanni Pietro Contarini*

# HISTORY OF THE EVENTS

## CAUSES OF THE CONFLICT

*History of the events which occurred from the beginning of the war waged on the Venetians by Selim the Ottoman to the day of the great and victorious battle against the Turks*

CHANGE OF RULERS, because of death or for any other reason, causes many disturbances and calamities in cities, provinces, and realms. The greater the power and stature of the ruler who passes away, the greater the commotion. Sultan Suleiman, emperor of the Turks and ruler of the empire, bearer of great power, died in the year 1567 at the siege of Szigetvar, an important fortress in Hungary, after having reigned for forty-two years.[8] Selim the Ottoman inherited the empire in the same year.[9] He was the last one of the four sons that Suleiman had sired. Persuaded by his wife Roxolana, his father had Mustafa and Bayezid put to death on suspicion of rebellion several years earlier. The third son, Çihangir the Hunchback, was so devastated by his father's cruelty to his two brothers, that he died of his own volition. On inheriting the large empire, Selim assumed with it the reputation and grandeur of his father. The latter, even though his law made him an enemy of the Christians, was nevertheless feared, revered, and loved by everyone for his valor and prudence. Selim, however, was altogether ignorant of the skill and dexterity with which his savvy father had for so many years ruled considerately and had acquired the name of the greatest prince of his time. On the third year of his reign, for no good reason and without any regard for having pledged his faith, he opened war on the Venetian republic.

It is my duty to put to scrutiny all that happened so that it is better understood, and to account for the war's cause and origins, so that it can be clearly seen and comprehended by everyone how unjust it was on the part of Selim to wage it. Let me say, then, that in 1569, the third year of Selim's reign, he conceived of the idea, as

---

8. Suleiman the Magnificent (1520–66) died on September 7, 1566 at the siege of Szigetvar.

9. Selim II "the Sot" (1566–74), a succinct biography in Gábor Ágoston and Bruce Masters, *Encyclopedia of the Ottoman Empire* (New York: Facts on File, 2009), 513–14.

is the custom of Muslim princes, to have constructed, with great pomp and grandeur and in perpetuation of his memory, a madrasa or a hostel with a mosque and schools for the edification of boys in their laws. Around its precinct there were to be many round lodgings covered with lead to serve as residences of their priests and teachers, and of travelers and pilgrims, regardless of their nation and religion, who would want to avail themselves of the opportunity to stay there, with their servants and horses, three full days for free. Alongside those, there were to be other similar residences, designated for the poor people of the city, who were to receive one silver coin per day for as long as they lodged there, besides the bread allocated for their sustenance. According to ancient custom, princes fund such madrasas with assets taken from alien rulers with the sword rather than seeking to support them with other kinds of resources.

Now there are in Constantinople three such hospices with their mosques, schools, and residences, as I described them. The first and most famous was built by Sultan Mehmet II, who conquered Constantinople; the second was erected by his son Bayezid; and the third by Sultan Suleiman, the father of Selim. In the latter complex there is a mosque, a superb edifice built of the finest stone and adorned by four beautiful minarets or *campanili*. After the sultan's death it was supported by revenues raised from Szigetvar, which was conquered through the skill and shrewdness of the first vizier Mehmet Pasha. A sagacious man, he kept secret the death of his master and urged the soldiers to attack, parading the body in his litter in full view of the army and the fortress, making everyone believe that the Great Lord was inside. But these revenues were not nearly enough to cover the great expenses incurred by the hospice and the mosque, for these surpassed eighty thousand *sultanini* per year.[10]

Yet Selim, as I mentioned, wanted to have his own religious complex and ordered it built in Adrianopolis, a city a three-day journey overland from Constantinople. He commissioned it with six minarets or *campanili*, considering himself, perhaps, more exalted

---

10. Ottoman gold coins, also sequins, nominally 3 grams of .800 pure gold or .0772 Troy ounces gold content.

than his father or any of his other ancestors. The works had already been started on the site, when there was a pronouncement by his *mufti*, considered a prophet according to their belief,[11] that before the mosque of the complex was completed Selim had to accomplish a valorous endeavor in emulation of his predecessors, who always had before their mind's eye the extension and augmentation of the always victorious Ottoman Empire. He would then be able to endow the mosque with the proceeds, because according to the law he was not allowed to use other revenues of the empire and the treasury. Discussing in private, as is their custom, the advice of that prophet of theirs, the idea was brought up to undertake the conquest of Cyprus at a propitious time. Perceiving that his lord was so inclined [the *mufti*] purposefully directed the discussion toward that realm, stating that the proceeds from the large island would suffice to endow his mosque and support that of his father as well. [He added that] the merchants among his subjects who navigated the seas to Syria and Egypt would be safe from the depredations of Christian corsairs who constantly crisscrossed these waters, because they would find shelter on the island. [He also added] that it would be much easier for his holy men to go on pilgrimage to Mecca.[12] Selim listened to all this

---

11. A Muslim legal scholar; here most likely the Grand Mufti or sheikh-al-Islam, the chief legal authority in the Ottoman empire and, respectively, the principal legal advisor of the sultan on religion-related matters. See Madeline Zilfi, "The Ottoman ulema," in Suraiya Faroqhi, ed., *The Cambridge History of Turkey* 3. *The Later Ottoman Empire, 1603–1839* (Cambridge: Cambridge University Press, 2006), 213, and for details Richard Repp, *The Müfti of Istanbul: A Study in the Development of the Ottoman Learned Hierarchy* (London: Ithaca Press, 1986). The sheikh at the time was Abu Saud el-Amadi, and his *fatwa* is detailed by Kâtib Çelebi, see Eftihios Gavriel, "The Expedition for the Conquest of Cyprus in the Work of Kâtib Çelebi," in *Ottoman Cyprus: A Collection of Studies on History and Culture*, Michalis Michael, Matthias Kappler, and Eftihios Gavriel, ed. (Wiesbaden: Harrassowitz Verlag, 2009), 25-36, at 32-33.

12. Claims that Venice protected Christian corsairs and pirates in the waters around Cyprus were a staple of Ottoman diplomacy throughout the 1500s, even though regularly, and with the treaty of 1567, specifically, Venice took the obligation to suppress predatory sailing in the eastern Mediterranean and

attentively and was much pleased by it, for he had it already in his head to do it. He praised him for bringing it up and left the place having made up his mind.[13]

Not a long time afterwards some Levantine Jews informed Giovanni Michele,[14] a converted Jew in Constantinople, that on September 13 of the same year 1569, the Arsenal of Venice had caught fire by an explosion of gunpowder and other munitions and had burned to the ground, and that in the city and its territories there was a great dearth of foodstuff, and that nothing could be found but

---

faithfully delivered on the promise. See the discussion of Vera Constantini, "In Search of Lost Prosperity: Aspects and Phases of Cyprus's Integration into the Ottoman Empire," in Michael et al., *Ottoman Cyprus*, 49–61, at 52.

13. For the most recent succinct discussion of Selim's decision to go to war, see Niccolò Capponi, *Victory of the West: The Great Christian-Muslim Clash at the Battle of Lepanto* (New York: Da Capo Press, 2007), 119–52.

14. Giovanni Michele and Joseph Nasi were the Latinized aliases of the marano Joan Miches, a trusted counselor of Selim II on matters of the Archipelago and the eastern Mediterranean. He was made duke of Naxos by Selim. There is a considerable scholarly tradition on this fascinating individual. See Eliakim Carmoly, *Don Joseph Nassy, Duc de Naxos* (Frankfurt am Main: George Hess, 1868); M.A. Levy, *Don Joseph Nasi, Herzog von Naxos: Seine Familie, und zwei jüdische Diplomaten seiner Zeit* (Breslaw: Scheletter'sche Buchhandlung, 1859); Joseph Reznik, *Le Duc Joseph de Naxos: Contribution a l'histoire juive du XVIs siècle* (Paris: Librairie Lipschutz, 1936); Paul Gruenbaum-Ballin, *Joseph Naci, duc de Naxos* (Paris: Mouton, 1968); Constance Rose, "New Information on the life of Joseph Nasi, Duke of Naxos: The Venetian Phase," *The Jewish Quarterly Review* 60 (1969–70): 330–44; and the popular work of Avishai Stockhamer, *Don Joseph Nasi: A Marrano's Rise to Power* (New York: Mesorah, 1991). Nasi may have been promised Cyprus, but he also harbored bitter hostility toward Venice; and his attitude may have hardened by the Signoria's failure to bribe him appropriately at the conclusion of peace with Selim II in 1567. See also Benjamin Ravid, "Money, Love, and Power Politics in Sixteenth-Century Venice: The Perpetual Banishment and Subsequent Pardon of Joseph Nasi," in *Italia Judaica: Atti del I Convegno internazionale, Bari 18–22 maggio 1981* (Rome: Ministero per i Beni Culturali e Ambientali, Pubblicazioni degli Archivi di Stato, 1983), 159–81.

bread made of millet.[15] Giovanni Michele, who was intimate with the sultan and quite beholden to him, approached him with the news. Upon finding out that Selim's desire had always been to attack the kingdom of Cyprus, he gladly advised him that now was the time to embark on the enterprise. Such news multiplying by the day, it was not difficult for Selim to decide to put into effect what he had already resolved to do, namely, to attack and conquer the said kingdom.

Therefore, brushing aside the faith that he had pledged to the Venetians,[16] caring little for the treaty that he had signed shortly before that with his own hand, and breaking the oath that he had given there to the Republic, he sent for Mehmet Vizier, his first pasha, to hear his position.[17] The pashas have great authority in the governance of the

---

15. For the failure of the harvest and the dearth of foodstuff in 1569–73 in northern Italy, including Venice and the Veneto, see Guido Alfani, *Calamities and the Economy in Renaissance Italy: The Grand Tour of the Horsemen of the Apocalypse* (New York: Palgrave Macmillan, 2010), part 3, "Famine," and Appendix I. The fire at the Arsenal, an event that reverberated throughout Europe and the Levant, is detailed by the Venetian antiquarian historians Paolo Paruta, *Degl' istorici delle cose veneziane i qualli hanno scritto per pubblico decreto, tomo terzo che comprende gli otto primi libri della prima parte dell'istorie veneziane volgarmente scritte da Paolo Paruta* (Venice: Lovisa, 1718), 22–23; and Andrea Morosini, *Degl' istorici delle cose veneziane i qualli hanno scritto per pubblico decreto, tomo sesto che comprende i sei secondi libri dell'istorie latinamente scritte dal Senatore Andrea Morosini* (Venice: Lovisa, 1719), 248–49. For the calamities that afflicted Venice in the period, including the plague of 1570, which killed an estimated 100,000 people and crippled the navy, see Paolo Preto, "Le Grandi Paure di Venezia nel secondo '500: Le paure naturali (peste, carestie, incendi, terremoti)," in *Crisi e rinnovamenti nell'autunno del Rinascimento a Venezia*, Vittore Branca and Carlo Ossola, ed. (Florence: L.S. Olschki, 1991), 177–92.

16. As customary, at the accession of Selim II, Venice and the Ottomans had renewed their peace with a treaty of June 24, 1567. See Kenneth Setton, *The Papacy and the Levant (1204–1571)* 4. *The Sixteenth Century* (Philadelphia: American Philosophical Society, 1984), 923.

17. Sokollu Mehmet Pasha (1506–79), grand vizier under Suleiman the Magnificent, Selim II, and Murad III, at the time leader of the "peace party" at

empire, according to the institutions and the ancient customs of the Ottomans, and their advice is highly esteemed by the sultans. After acquainting Mehmet in detail with his intentions, he invited him to freely reflect on the plan. Mehmet, a perceptive man, understood why his lord and father-in-law called him.

After figuring out what was on his mind, and being apprehensive of the grave implications of opening war on the Venetians, he spoke in the following way, "Most high Lord, there is no doubt that the kingdom of Cyprus, if obtained through honorable means, would be a perfect acquisition and a great addition to the empire and your reputation. I do not see however, how it can be acquired without a war with the Venetians, who are its overlords. Consider, without succumbing to emotion, whether you have a just cause to do that. You are joined to them with a treaty and you have no justification to molest them, apart from knowing that right now they are in no position to defend this kingdom because of the fire in their Arsenal. But you cannot really do it because of that: to move against them now for that reason alone does not befit the greatness of your name, nor would it be right, most just Lord, when you are under a treaty of friendship with someone to hurt them, while they could have, but did not want, to hurt you for they adhere to the conditions of the treaty. Do you not know that they were close friends of your father's, the glorious emperor of felicitous memory, and that he always kept inviolable faith with them and treasured their friendship?

---

the Ottoman court. For the peace treaty between the Ottomans and Venice, see Setton, *Papacy and the Levant,* 4:923 sq. Lala Mustafa and Piyale Pasha were his bitter enemies, and the personal rivalry may have been a major factor in their pro-war orientation, while the future naval chief, Müezzinzade Ali Pasha, became convinced that Cyprus was ripe for the taking after a reconnoitering trip to the island in 1568. See the somewhat outdated but detailed discussion of Hill, *A History of Cyprus,* 3:880–82. According to several contemporaries, the discussion took place during a hunting trip. See Giacomo Diedo, *Storia della repubblica di Venezia dalla sua fondazione sino l'anno MDCCXLVII* (Venice: Andrea Poletti, 1751), 2:227–28, English translation in Claude Delaval Cobham, *Excerpta Cypria: Materials for a History of Cyprus* (Cambridge: Cambridge University Press, 1908, reprint, Kraus: New York, 1969), 87–89.

At the time of his death he expressly charged me to act in a way that would preserve their friendship, because they had always and in all circumstances kept their faith with us, and we have always done it too. And now you, who a short time ago have made a treaty of friendship with them and signed the stipulations of the peace, without being justly provoked, want to open war on them and violate the faith you have pledged? This should never be done. This is how I truly feel, inspired to serve you most faithfully as it pleases you, and this is what I have to say. However, I reserve the matter to the most prudent judgement of your Sublimity, because you are my lord, and it befits you to command as it befits me to obey."[18]

Selim, however, failed to acknowledge how loyally he was being advised with these words by the man who just a short time before had quietly engineered his succession to the empire of his father. It had been Mehmet who had informed Selim about the illness and death of his father at Szigetvar and kept it secret until he (who at the time was in Mingrelia) was able to reach Constantinople and take over the empire and made the army that was in Hungary acknowledge him as their lord. Enraged, Selim rebuked him with harsh words and called him a Christian, which is an insult among them. Seeing that his lord was angry with him, Mehmet bowed his head and asked for forgiveness. Then Selim asked Mustafa Pasha, the commander of his land troops, and Piyale Pasha, his admiral, for advice and counsel. They affirmed his resolve and persuaded him to embark on the conquest of Cyprus, considering that due to the fire the Venetians were in no position to defend that kingdom. Intelligence from Constantinople provided no details on the arguments and reflections that they exchanged during the following deliberation, but from what happened next the conjecture can be made that they had decided on the conquest of that kingdom.

---

18. The speech is most likely fully fictitious, even though it may have truthfully reflected Mehmet's sentiments. Here and elsewhere, speeches are Contarini's favorite device to offer his comments to the otherwise plain chronicling of events and an excellent window into his philosophy of history.

Making up his mind on Mustafa's and Piyale's advice to embark upon this undertaking, Selim therefore commanded Mehmet Vizier, in whose purview it was, to do everything that was necessary to put the navy in battle order as quickly as possible. Obeying the order, the latter inspected the Arsenal in Constantinople and gave instructions that the skilled workers be provided with everything they needed to build up their navy's capabilities to the maximum. Mehmet also had biscuits and other supplies for the fleet stockpiled at several places in the Archipelago and elsewhere, and at the same time made provisions for the infantry and the cavalry.

## PREPARATIONS

THE WORD SPREAD that Constantinople was arming, and although the target was unknown rumor had it that it was Cyprus. Confirmations kept streaming in from everywhere. In Venice, where they are obliged by their laws and permitted by their constitution to arm whenever the Turks do so, the government similarly called to arms. Preparations began in the usual manner, readying galleys, sailing ships, and other vessels according to what was needed, and sending warnings where necessary. The rectors of Candia[19] were notified to prepare the galleys of the kingdom, as they were obliged to do. Thirty-one galleys were at sea at the time, on their ordinary assignments in the Gulf[20] and elsewhere, namely: the lantern galley[21] of Giacomo Celsi,

---

19. The Venetian government of the island of Crete.

20. The Adriatic Sea.

21. Here and elsewhere, Contarini uses the technical term *fanò* (which is directly translated as "lantern galley," that is, a ship that carried three large stern lamps as opposed to the usual one), to indicate commanders' galleys, with the meaning of "flagships," because squad, squadron, and fleet commanders signaled and indicated position in a galley unit with their cluster of lanterns. On the other hand, a "lantern galley" was not necessarily better armed than an ordinary galley, and its commander may have commanded only a single ship, in which case the designation and right to more lanterns indicated the status of the commander, but "lantern galleys" served as tactical focal points in a galley formation aligned for battle. See John Francis Guilmartin, Jr., *Gunpowder and Galleys: Changing Technology and Mediterranean Warfare at Sea*

provveditore of the fleet,[22] the lantern galley of Marco Quirini, captain of the Gulf, the lantern galley of Marc'Antonio Foscarini, commander of the slave rowers' vessels, and those of Marin Dandolo, Giovanni Battista Contarini, Caterino Malipiero, Giovanni Bembo of Cyprus, Marino Contarini, Antonio Pasqualigo, Francesco Bon, Nicolò Lippamano, Filippo Leone, Angelo Suriano, Vincenzo Maria di Prioli, Pietro Badoer, Giovanni Battista Benedetti of Cyprus, Girolamo Tron, Alessandro Contarini, Teodoro Balbi, Marc'Antonio Pisani, Nicolò Donado, Francesco Tron, Lodovico Cicuta of Veglia,[23] Colane Drasco of Cres, Pietro Bertolazzi of Zadar, Christofalo Cippico of Trogir, Pietro Michetto of Šibenik, Girolamo Griffante of Kotor, Giovanni de Dominis of Rab, Giovanni Balci of Lošinj, and Giovanni Battista del Tacco.

Shortly thereafter news came to Venice that on January 13, [1570] the sultan had ordered two Venetian sailing ships, the *Bonalda* and the *Balba*, to be seized, that the armament continued at full speed, and that the sultan himself frequently visited the Arsenal and the Tapana, which is the place where they cast their cannon. The news confirmed what the Venetians suspected from the beginning: it was clear that war had been declared on Venice. They were now certain, seeing how Venice was being hemmed in from everywhere and access to her was being closed. Consequently, promptly and most diligently they applied themselves to gathering all possible provisions. Missives were sent out to the captain of the Gulf, Marco Quirini, to sail for Candia and speed up the procurement of the galleys from the island. His Holiness Pope Pius V, the Catholic King Philip of Spain, and other Christian princes were informed of the massive preparations that Selim, the emperor of the Turks, had put in motion to harm

---

*in the Sixteenth Century* (Cambridge: Cambridge University Press, 1974), 72, 243–44; and Capponi, *Victory of the West,* 262–63.

22. The printed edition uses *proveditor*, but since this is a Venetian technical term for superintendent with specific functions and carries respective connotations, I prefer the spelling of the Venetian vernacular, *provveditore*.

23. The modern-day Croatian island of Krk in the Adriatic Sea; the following names of islands and towns are entered with their modern names.

the Venetians. On February 11, Selim dispatched an envoy to Venice, the chaush Kubad, to demand the island of Cyprus and buttress the claim with threats and bravura based on the large forces that were being readied on land and sea. Meanwhile, having received the order of the Senate, on March 16 Marco Quirini left Lesina escorted by two galleys. On the next day, in the sea off Ragusa, he met up with the galley of Angelo Suriano, which conducted Kubad, accompanied by Alvise Buonrizzo, the secretary of the bailo in Constantinople, Marco Antonio Barbarigo, and the bailo's son, Alvise Barbaro.

On March 27, the day after the Resurrection of our Lord, in the church of San Marco, with great solemnity and pomp, that most excellent knight and procurator of San Marco, Girolamo Zane, received the standard of captain-general of the sea. After mass, in a procession headed by the most serene Prince Pietro Loredan and the Senate, he was conducted to his galley. He sailed for Zadar on the last day of the month. At that time, forty-two armed galleys had already left Venice, namely: *La Capitana,* lantern of Girolamo Zane, captain-general, the lantern of Santo Tron, commander of the slave rowers' vessels in the place of Marc'Antonio Foscarini, the lantern of Antonio da Canal, provveditore of the fleet, and those under the captainship of Stefano Venier, David Bembo, Gabriel da Canal, Pietro Emmo, Marc'Antonio Lando, Girolamo Contarini, Marco Cicogna, Pietro Salomon, Ferigo Nani, Pietro Zanne, Benedetto Soranzo, Battista Foscarini, Andrea Bragadin, Alvise Emmo, Agostin Venier, Giorgio Pisani, Pietro Dolfin, Mattio Calergi, Polo Nani, Bartolomeo Celsi, Pietro Pisani, Marc'Antonio Quirini, Giulio Bragadin, Francesco Tron, Pietro Cuiran, Girolamo Gritti, Priamo da Lezze, Bernardo Sagredo, Bernardo Giustinian, Georgio Cornaro, Antonio Michiel, Sebastian Tiepolo, Antonio di Cavalli, Michiel Barbarigo, Nicolò Suriano, Carlo Quirini, Onfre Giustinian, Francesco Vendramin, and Girolamo Dolfin.

During the last days of March, Murat Reis left Constantinople with twenty-five armed galleys and sailed for Rhodes to prevent relief for Cyprus, the sultan having received detailed information about the war effort underway in Venice and the strengthening of the island's strongholds.

# HISTORY OF THE EVENTS

In the beginning of April, Kubad, the envoy of the Turk, arrived in Venice. Even before his arrival rumors circulated in the city that he was sent to demand Cyprus.[24] Accordingly, the Senate had already considered carefully the issue and concluded that it was more fitting the dignity and greatness of the republic to defend themselves against the Turk in open war rather than let themselves be consumed one piece at a time and then subjugated by the Ottoman forces, leaving the matter in the hands of God, the righteous Lord and defender of the Christians, and hoping for divine and human aid in the unjust war threatened by the common enemy. The Senate announced that laudable and well-founded decision to chaush Kubad and dismissed him at once.

On April 13, Commander Girolamo Zane reached Zadar. On the following day he was received by the bishop of the place and accompanied in procession by Hector Tron, count of Zadar, Captain Andrea Barbarigo, and other captains, lords, noblemen, and soldiers stationed in the fortress, as well as by many captains and other officers of the galleys. They entered the cathedral church, where solemn mass was celebrated in honor of our Savior. A little more than a month had passed since Bernardo Malipiero, provveditore of the horses in Dalmatia and a valorous nobleman, had frequently sallied forth from Zadar on horseback, accompanied by a large company, to prevent the Turks from raiding and damaging the district and capturing and killing many people. In the end, too confident in his great courage, he rode out without shoulder armor, considering it an impediment, and during a skirmish was wounded by a spear thrust in the part that was not protected. He was brought back to the city where he expired from the injury, to the great consternation of all who knew him, for he was a man of great promise, liked by everyone, and only twenty-nine years old. On March 14, Fabio Canale, a brave nobleman too, was elected to replace him. Earlier in the month Francesco Barbaro had been elected general provveditore of Dalmatia, but he passed away before being able to take office; he was replaced by Giovanni da Lezze, knight and procurator of San Marco. Marco Quirini arrived at

---

24. According to a letter of the Senate, *chaush* (state messenger) Kubad arrived on March 25, 1570. See Setton, *Papacy and the Levant*, 4:953.

Candia on April 3 and, finding that the galleys of that kingdom were in excellent condition, diligently undertook their armament, aiming at having them sail out before the Turkish fleet arrived in those seas.

On April 17, Piyale Pasha sailed out of Constantinople with eighty galleys and thirty galiots; seventeen armed galleys put out to sea from Venice, namely those of Vincenzo da Canal, Giovanni Contarini, Alvise Lando, Giacomo di Priuli, Andrea Tron, Simon Guoro, Girolamo da Canal, Bernardo Giustiniani, Alvise Pasqualigo, Francesco Contarini, Girolamo Salamone, Giovanni Mocenigo, Tomà Michiel, Marco da Molin, Marc'Antonio Foscarini, Pietro Trevisan, and Donado Tiepolo.

Kubad left Venice on May 5 and returned to Constantinople with the decision of the Senate. Selim was shocked, for he had expected that the kingdom he demanded would be conceded. Finding out that the answer had been exactly the opposite, he flew into anger and immediately dispatched twelve chaushes to Pera to arrest the bailo and his entourage. Vincenzo degli Alessandri, who had stayed there to learn the language, managed to get away just before they arrived and brought to Venice detailed information about the formidable preparations that the Turk was making both on land and sea.

On the fifteenth day of the month the armada was ready in Constantinople. On May 16, Ali Pasha sailed out with thirty-six galleys, twelve fuste, the two Venetian sailing ships that were seized earlier, four Turkish ships, the galleon of the vizier Mehmet Pasha, eight maone, forty horse transports, and several caramuscialini loaded with artillery, munitions, and other provisions, under the charge of Mustafa Pasha, the commander of the land forces.[25] Piyale, who had

---

25. Just as the *fusta* was a galley subclass of small, light, fast, and shallow-threading vessel under a lateen sail, the *maona* was what the Venetians called a "large galley" or a galleass, a large and heavy oared vessel, galley-type, normally heavily armed, and also used as a transport, as was the *caramuscialin*. The latter name likely derives from Karamursal, a small port on the Gulf of Nicomedia, where such ships were built. See Hill, *Cyprus*, 4:895 n.2. The Venetian galleasses at Lepanto, called *maone* by the Ottomans, carried between 23 and 40 guns. See Capponi, *Victory for the West*, 190–93. For short

left earlier, devastated Tinos on his way, an island in the Archipelago held by the Venetians, but only at the loss of many men of his fleet.

In the middle of this massive war effort passed away Pietro Loredan, doge of Venice. On May 11, a new doge was elected, Alvise Mocenigo,[26] and on the next day, with general celebration and acclamation by all the people, he entered office. On the fifteenth of the same month Sebastiano Venier, who used to be procurator-general of the island of Corfu, was elected procurator of San Marco in the place of Doge Mocenigo.

King Philip of Spain, learning about the Turks' massive preparations, which threatened not only Venetian territories but places subject to him as well, ordered fighting men to be assembled with all deliberate speed in the ports of Naples, Sardinia, Corsica, La Goleta, and elsewhere. A similar order went out on behalf of the Pontiff Pius V for his territories. In addition, the pope offered to arm at his own expense twelve galleys to aid the Venetians; and many other lords and noblemen offered to assist them in their righteous defense. Here they are listed, along with what they offered: Patriarch Grimani, 1,000 ducats; Patriarch Barbaro, 1,000 ducats;[27] the knight Honofrio Maggi of Brescia, 2,000 ducats;

---

and accessible surveys of Ottoman naval hardware, see Gábor Ágoston, *Guns for the Sultan: Military Power and the Weapons Industry in the Ottoman Empire* (Cambridge: Cambridge University Press, 2005); Palmira Brummett, *Ottoman Seapower and Levantine Diplomacy in the Age of Discovery* (Albany: State University of New York Press, 1994); Svat Soucek, "Certain Types of Ships in Ottoman-Turkish Terminology," *Turcica* 7 (1975): 233–49; and Henry Kahare, Renée Kahare, and Andreas Tietze, *The Lingua Franca in the Levant: Turkish Nautical Terms of Italian and Greek Origin* (Urbana-Champaign: University of Illinois Press, 1958, reprint Istanbul: ABC Kitabevi, 1988). For the variety of Mediterranean ships and nautical equipment in the period, the best resource remains the monumental work of Auguste Jal, *Glossaire nautique: Répertoire polyglotte de termes de marine anciens et modernes* (Paris: Firmin Didot, 1848), 219-20 for *caramuscialin*, and 181 for *caiques*, for example.

26. On principle, Contarini uses the Latinized forms of titles and proper names rather than their Venetian form, employing *"principe"* for "doge" and often using *"Luigi"* for "Alvise." I have preferred to use the Venetian forms.

27. Daniele I Barbaro, patriarch of Aquileia 1550–74.

Pandolfo Attavanti of Florence, 1,000 ducats; the bishop of Cividale, 600 tallers; Monsignor Valier, 1,000 scudi;[28] the bishop of Vicenza, 1,000 scudi;[29] Abbot Giuliano, 1,000 ducats; the patriarch of Venice, 1,000 ducats;[30] the bishop of Torcello, 1,000 ducats;[31] Monsignor Pesaro, 1,000 ducats;[32] the archbishop of Cyprus, 2,000 ducats; the community of Bergamo, 10,000 ducats; the community of Padua, 9,000 ducats; the community of Vicenza, 12,000 ducats; Benedetto Civran, 200 ducats; Ottaviano Grimani, from the taxes, 2,000 ducats.

Infantrymen were offered to the Venetian Signoria, as follows: Andrea Morosini sent one of his sons with the fleet, with 20 soldiers at his own expenses; the count of Carpass, 25;[33] the community of Brescia, for six months, 1,000; the clan of Porcelaga, for six months, 200 soldiers; the community of Verona, for six months a year, 500; the community of Treviso for six months, at 1,200 ducats per month, 400 soldiers; Count Lucrezio Gambara, 25 soldiers; Count Nicolò Gambara, 25 soldiers; Count Marc'Antonio Martinengo, 30 soldiers; noblemen of Padua with one soldier, 200; the knight Pietro Lipoman, 30 soldiers; Ferrante Averaldo, with his three sons, 4; Benedetto Civran, for the duration of the war, 4; Domitian Moschetti of Rome, 20 soldiers; Sergio Pola, 12; Milanese noblemen, 4.

In addition, the following sums were offered for hiring fighting men: Sforza Pallavicino, 5,000 [ducats]; Paolo Orsini, 4,000; Girolamo Martinengo, 1,000; Alvise Martinengo, 1,000; Cesare Carafa, 1,000; Count Hippolito Porto, for light cavalry or infantrymen, 1,000; Brunoro Zampesco, 3,000; Count Fabio Pepoli, 2,000; Passotto Fantuzzi, 1,000; Colonel Spolverino, 1,000; Palavicino Rangone, 3,000; Camillo Fantuzzi, 2,000; Roberto Malatesta, 1,000; the spouse

---

28. Agostino Valier 1531–1606, cardinal and bishop of Verona 1565–1606.

29. Matteo Priuli, bishop of Vicenza 1565–79.

30. Giovanni Trevisan, patriarch of Venice 1560–90.

31. Giovanni Delfino, bishop of Torcello 1563–79.

32. Giulio Simonetti, cardinal of Pesaro 1560 (or 1561)–1576.

33. The county of Carpass was one of the twelve baronies of Cyprus, held in hereditary possession by members of the Giustiniani clan.

of Sir Astor Baglioni, 2,000; Alessandro Zambeccari, 1,000; Alfonso Vitelli, for 200 light cavalry and infantrymen, 4,000; Count Hercole de Contrarii, 2,000; Count Pietro Avogadro Ferazzo, 4,000; Count Nicolò Gambara, 2,000; the son of the duke of Atri, 2,000;[34] Giulio Rangone, 1,000; Camillo Bonacelli, 1,000; Malvezzo Fauri, 1,000; the count of Montebello, 2,000; Count Alvise Avogadro, 2,000; Count Francesco Martinengo, for 150 light cavalry or infantrymen, 1,000; Hercole Saulo, 1,000; Count Ottavio Tiene, 1,000; Renuccio Ottone, 1,000; Cesare della Penna, 1,000; Galeazzo da Vepi, 1,000; Honorio Cioti, 1,000.

In sum, the Venetians received 46,800 ducats in cash and 1,578 paid-for soldiers, or in total 58,200 men, and every day more fighting men, mercenaries, and other persons offered to serve their Signoria.

In the said month of May twenty-two galleys and two galleasses left the port of Venice, with galley captains Zaccaria Barbaro, Nicolò Donato, Marco Donato, Giacomo Morosini, Alvise Bembo, Francesco Dolfin, Agostin Sanudo, Francesco Gritti, Vicenzo Quirini, Zuan Balbi, Andrea Tiepolo, Girolamo Tiepolo, Zaccaria Valier, Giovanni Battista Quirini, Gabriel Emmo, Francesco Badoer, Pietro Francesco Malipiero, Andrea Donado, Francesco Cornaro, Girolamo da Pesaro, Sforza Palavicino, and Lorenzo Barbarigo, the lantern galley *La Capitana* of Francesco Duodo, captain of the galleasses, and the galleass of Giacomo da Mosto. Four old hulks were ordered to Corfu, two to Zara, and two to Kotor, to be armed there.[35]

On May 28, Piyale, having rigged and supplied the fleet with provisions at Negroponte, set off from there to sail for Rhodes. On

---

34. The ranking head of the Aquaviva family of Abruzzo, which in the early fifteenth century obtained the title of dukes of Atri.

35. Contarini uses "arsile," also "arsilo" or "arsilio," Venezian "arsil." See Salvatore Battaglia, *Grande dizionario della lingua italiana* I (Turin: Unione tipografico-editrice torinese, 1961), 704; Giulio Bertoni, *Dizionario di marina medievale e moderno* (Rome: Reale Academia d'Italia, 1937), 46. See also Jal, *Glossaire nautique,* 184–85.

his way he joined with Ali and Mustafa and the rest of the armada, and all together arrived at Rhodes on June 1.[36]

In the same time Sebastian Venier,[37] procurator of San Marco and provveditore-general of the island of Corfu, found himself in the company of Giacomo Celsi, the provveditore of the fleet, with ten galleys (those of Giovanni Bembo, Giovanni Battista Contarini, Alessandro Contarini, Pietro Badoer, Nicolò Lippomani, Vincenzo Maria di Priuli, Caterino Malipiero, Piero Michetto of Šibenik, and Colane Drasco of Cres). Accompanied by Manolis Mormori of Nauplion in Romania,[38] a courageous and prudent local man, he decided to take the opportunity to attack Sopot, a Turkish stronghold in Albania, not far from Corfu, and furnished the galleys with what was necessary for that. On June 7, he set sail from Corfu, disembarked the men, and fought with the Turks without respite for three days, forcing them to abandon the site. Not being able to defend it, they stole into the night, and the place remained in the hands of the Christians. After provisioning it, he left it under the guard of the above-mentioned Manolis Mormori.

The Turkish pashas, after spending three days at Rhodes, on June 4 departed with the entire armada, sailing in the direction of Fineka, a place in Anatolia a short distance from Cyprus, to pick up the sipahi cavalry, the Janissaries, and the munitions they were to take to Cyprus.

Meanwhile Girolamo Zane, the captain-general of the Venetian fleet, realized that he would not be able to remain in Zadar with the armada and with so many men, and decided to leave and sail for

---

36. Rhodes was taken over by the Ottomans in January 1523 after a long siege. See Kelly DeVries and Robert D. Smith, *Besieged Rhodes: A New History* (Stroud: The History Press, 2012).

37. On Venier and Lepanto the principal study is still Pompeo Molmenti, *Sebastiano Venier e la battaglia di Lepanto* (Florence: Barbèra, 1899).

38. Modern Nafplio on the Peloponnesus peninsula in Greece. Manolis (Emanuele) Mormori belonged to a family of Venetianized Greeks, several generations of whom served Venice as ranking military officers in the sixteenth and seventeenth centuries.

Corfu. He hoped to be able to provision there, because the city had already suffered quite a lot. The Turks continued their depredations, despoiling the city's hinterland, seizing animals and cutting down and carrying away fodder, destroying and burning everything. It had become difficult to go out of the city without being molested by their incessant raids and constant ambushes. Many times horsemen sallied from the city, along with sizable companies of infantry, to protect the district, but there was little hope that victuals would be forthcoming from any part. Provisions were sent from Venice, Puglia, and the Marches, which brought considerable relief to Zadar and its territory. There was no lack of bread, biscuit, and other foodstuff, but that was not sufficient to support the fleet with its large number of servicemen. Inadequate nourishment and so many men in close quarters were bound to cause infectious diseases; indeed, the latter grew more serious and multiplied by the day, swept through the entire fleet, and brought many a man to a bitter end.[39] For that reason, on June 12, Zane set off with seventy galleys, and on June 23 arrived in Corfu.

For his part, Marco Quirini tried several times to sail from Canea with all the galleys duly appointed but was held back by northerly winds, against which he could not row because the galleys' rowers were newly recruited and had not yet acquired the necessary skills. And yet, it was imperative that they all sailed together, because the Turkish fleet was reported to have been in the Archipelago. Finally, on June 28, he set off for Corfu with twenty-one galleys, which had been armed in the kingdom,[40] namely those of Giovanni Francesco Zancaruol, Nicolò Avonal, Andrea Calergi, Polo Polani, and Pietro Barbarigo from Retimno, Alessandro Vizzamano, Giovanni Michel Vizzamano, Antonio Zancaruol, Francesco da Molin, Giacomo Calergi, Filippo Polani, and Vincenzo Zancaruol from Canea, and Girolamo Zorzi, Francesco Bon, Pietro Barbarigo, Antonio Bon,

---

39. It was likely some sort of skin disease. See Hill, *History of Cyprus*, 4:910 n. 4 and Luciano Serrano, *Correspondencia diplomatica entre Espana y la Santa Sede durante el pontificado de S. Pio V* (Rome: Junta, 1914), 3:447.

40. The Regno di Candia, or Venetian Crete.

Francesco Cornaro, Francesco Mudazzo, Nicolò Fradello, Giorgio Barbarigo, and Giovanni Dandolo, all from Candia.

On his way, Quirini had the opportunity to attack the fortress of the port of Quaglie, on the promontory of Maina in the Morea, which he gladly undertook, as it did not divert him from his destination.[41] He decided this had to be done because the harbor was very convenient for sailing ships and other vessels that navigated in those waters, but its fortress denied access to Christians. He arrived there during the night of June 29 and to avoid detection had the galleys retreat behind a nearby outcrop. Early the next morning Quirini sent [men out] to reconnoiter the place and placed a good number of them armed with arquebuses on a hill directly opposite the fortress of Maina. He ordered them to take aim at the enemy who were to appear on the ramparts to man the artillery battery as the galleys entered the port. This they did. The Turks in the fortress felt secure under the protection of their thirty-six pieces of artillery, many of them large, and prepared to defend themselves, but after a few shots two were neutralized. The arquebusiers, who had mounted the hill, shot so valorously at the Turkish defenders that they were not able to appear on the ramparts because of the deadly fire. Unable to protect themselves from the hail of bullets, the Turks retreated to a strongly fortified tower. Seeing that the ramparts had been abandoned, Quirini passed with the galleys under the fortress, disembarked many men with ladders and other siege instruments, and began the assault. After a token resistance they climbed the walls and took control of the fortress but found the place abandoned and figured that the Turks had holed themselves up in the tower after those on the hill had chased them away from the ramparts. They turned the fortress artillery on the tower preparing to shoot, and set its gates on fire at several points. The Turks despaired of being able to hold onto the tower and, without waiting for the artillery to open fire, surrendered into slavery on the condition that

---

41. Modern Porto Kagio on the eastern side of the peninsula, on a bay of the Laconian Gulf north of Cape Matapan. The Ottoman fortress there controlled coastal sailing between the Ionian and Aegean Seas and threatened Venetian access to Cyprus. The attack on Porto delle Quaglie was the opening shot of the war on the Venetian side.

their lives would be spared; the promise was faithfully adhered to. The fortress, however, was dismantled with mines, so that the Turks could not man it again. Loaded with much booty and the slaves, they set off for Corfu.

Piyale, who spent twenty-eight days at Fineka, took on board a large number of Janissaries sent by the sultan from Constantinople and on June 27 departed for Cyprus with one hundred and sixty galleys, one galleon, sixty galiots and fuste, eight maone, six sailing ships, three palandarie, forty horse transports, thirty caramuscialini, and forty frigates.

Throughout June in Venice they prepared their fleet, as well as the galleon *Fausto* (named after the man who built her), for whose commander was elected Girolamo Contarini, and the seven fuste and twelve arsili, which were to be armed by His Holiness. In total, during the month of June the Venetians completed and prepared one hundred and twenty-seven light galleys (including those of Candia), thirty-one of which had already been armed, eleven large galleys, the galleon already mentioned, fourteen sailing ships, apart from other sailing craft, large and small sent to garrison different places, and continued the work on more galleys, fuste, brigantine, and longboats, consigning them to several companies.

The remaining light and large galleys put out to sea: the large galley of Vincenzo Quirini, the large galley of Antonio Bragadin, the large galley of Lorenzo Bernardo, the large galley of Andrea da Pesaro, the large galley of Marco Michiel, the large galley of Zaccaria Solomon, the large galley of Marc'Antonio Morosini, and the large galley of Ambrogio Bragadin under commander Nicolò da Mosto. Eleven arsili were sent to Ancona. Almoro Tiepolo set off as captain of the fuste, Geronimo Contarini sailed in a large galley, and so did the fuste of Marco Vetturi and Giustiniano Giustiniani. This was a veritable demonstration of the might of the Venetians: in time of unheard-of dearth, after the devastating fire in their Arsenal, and much else, they built and armed with all that could be desired such a large and well-appointed fleet, and continued work in the shipyards of the Arsenal on another fifty galleys, four large galleys, and twelve fuste, not to mention the rebuilding of other craft destroyed by the blaze.[42]

## THE BATTLE FOR CYPRUS

ON JULY 1, PIYALE ARRIVED with the armada at Limasol in Cyprus, disembarked immediately, and took many slaves; on the same day Quirini reached Corfu with the booty from Maina. On the next day Piyale sailed to Salines[43] with all the galleys and other vessels. On July 3, quite pleased to encounter no resistance, he disembarked easily the entire infantry, the horses, the artillery, and all other war materiel. Those in charge of the place had decided that it was better to allow the enemy to disembark without offering opposition because the small number of horsemen they had would not be able to prevent it anyway as the circumference of the island was seven hundred miles, and the ride from Salines to Nicosia thirty miles, and they could have only done it if it were four or six miles. Consequently, the cavalry of stratioti that was stationed at Salines under Count Roccas retreated to Nicosia. Mustafa, who had been appointed supreme commander of the expedition, remained at Salines to conduct some repairs. He sent Piyale with one hundred galleys, twenty horse transports, and twelve maone to the Gulf of Aiazzo[44] to collect more horses, sipahis, and Janissaries; at the same time, he dispatched Ali with the remainder of the fleet to the Gulf of Satalia to pick up the men of that land,

---

42. Indeed, as it became clear that the war was inevitable, Venice revved up the production of warships, and between 1569 and 1570 the number of galleys in service jumped from 45 to 140. See Luciano Pezzolo, "The Rise and Decline of a Great Power: Venice 1250–1650," *Working Papers of the Department of Economic, Ca' Foscari University of Venice* 27 (2006): 1–31; and, for a detailed account of the economic side of the Venetian military capabilities in the period, his *L'oro dello stato: Società, finanza, e fisco nella Reppublica veneta del secondo '500* (Venice: Il Cardo, 1990).

43. One of the eleven districts into which Cyprus was divided under Venetian rule; it has a convenient bay that offered excellent anchorage for the invading Ottoman force.

44. Modern Yumurtalık on the Cilician shore; ancient Aegeae, Laiazzo of the Venetians, or Ayas in the local vernacular.

## HISTORY OF THE EVENTS

being unwilling to leave the place before all the infantry and cavalry designated for the expedition had massed together.

When the Catholic king[45] found out that the Turkish armada and expeditionary force had been sent to Cyprus, he ordered his own fleet of fifty galleys, under the command of Giovanni Andrea Doria, prince of Melfi, to set sail for Messina and provide assistance to the Venetians in anything they might need, even though the League had not yet been fully constituted, due to intrigues and delays, as usually happens when things depend on the will of more than one person.

After the entire Venetian fleet had assembled at Corfu, Commander Zane was advised by Sebastian Venier, provveditore general of the island, that for a number of important reasons they had to attack Malgaritini, and made up his mind to do it.[46] On July 3, fifty galleys set sail, carrying five thousand men and five large pieces of artillery, under the command of Sforza Pallavicino. During the following night, he disembarked the men and the cannon and, taking along an engineer and some colonels, undertook to reconnoiter the place and the site of the fortress. It appeared that the endeavor would not be as easy as it was presented to him. The artillery could not be brought to place from where it could batter the stronghold, as the fortress was built on a hill's summit, and without artillery nothing useful could be done. They estimated that fifty soldiers would suffice to defend the fortress. Considering it likely that they would also get relief, he burned the residential quarters outside the walls, devastated the countryside, and on July 7, having loaded the men, secured the artillery pieces in place, and put back on board whatever else had been carried ashore for the expedition, they sailed back.

---

45. Philip II of Spain (1556–98).

46. Malgaritini was located about 8 miles on the mainland opposite the southern extremity of Corfu, and figures in the 1573 map of Simone Pinargenti, *Isole che son da Venezia* (Venice: Simone Pinargenti, 1573) and in one of the maps of Giovanni Francesco Camocio. See also Hill, *Cyprus*, 912 n. 2.

On the twenty-third of the same month the entire Christian armada departed from Corfu and set sail for the island of Candia,[47] as it was decided that it was better to recruit men and slave rowers there, that it provided generally a better springboard for aiding the island of Cyprus, and that during the voyage it would be possible to quickly acquire both fighting men and rowers by picking them up from all the nearby islands to replenish the crews, which had been cut in half due to the disasters suffered earlier.

On July 22, Piyale and Ali, who had sailed out with their fleets, the first to the Gulf of Aiazzo, the second to the Gulf of Satalia, returned to Salines with the reinforcements. After immediately disembarking them, on July 23 Mustafa set out from Salines with the entire army and marched toward Nicosia. It is said that there were four thousand cavalry, six thousand Janissaries, and four thousand sipahis, plus many irregulars, whose numbers cannot be estimated. The troops marched at ease, seeing how easily they had become masters of the countryside, and on July 25 the infantry encamped before Nicosia. The next day the cavalry arrived as well, except five hundred horsemen, who had been sent from Salines to besiege the city of Famagusta. As the entire army united before Nicosia, they pitched their pavilions in the surrounding countryside and on the hills of Mandia, where the pavilion of Mustafa was set up and where they dug deep pits from which mighty streams of water gushed out. A large part of the army, and especially the cavalry, camped in the direction of St. Clement, where the water source of the citadel originated; there were also camps at Galanga and Callassa, two villages about five miles away from Nicosia, to avail themselves of the water springs that were found there.

Nicolò Dandolo, the lieutenant of Cyprus,[48] was in Nicosia, as were the count of Carpass, lord coadjutor of the Signoria,[49] the

---

47. The author means the island of Crete. The official name of Venetian Crete was Regno di Candia.

48. The title of the Venetian civil governor of Nicosia.

49. Eugenio Sinclitico, count of Roccas and coadjutor of Venice, appointed commander of the cavalry and supreme military commander after Astorre Baglione left for Famagusta to support the local forces.

counselors Pietro Pisani and Marc'Antonio di Priuli, the chamberlains Zuane Longo and Antonio Pasqualigo, the grand chancellor Pietro Albini, as well as Giovanni Battista Colomba, the knight Maggi, an engineer,[50] five hundred stratioti cavalry, five hundred supply and feudatory horsemen with a number of men picked from the local militias, Colonel Palazzo, commander of the Italian infantry, with one thousand and three hundred footmen, Captain Piovene of Vicenza, Alberto Scotto, Giovanni Falier, Captain Pocopani, and other nobles and soldiers from Italy and the island [of Cyprus].

The armada of Admiral Zane reached Modon on August 2. Marco Quirini, captain of the Gulf, who had gathered a good number of men from the nearby islands, sailed out to join up with him. Together, on August 4 they arrived at Porto Picorna on the island of Candia and then at Souda,[51] from where Zane sent out to many places of the Archipelago to recruit more people. Meanwhile he expected the arrival of the fleets of His Holiness and Spain, which, according to reliable information received, were fully prepared for war. On August 7, Marco Quirini sailed for Rhodes to catch informants and came back on August 24 with the news that the Turkish fleet was already in Cyprus.

## NICOSIA

ONCE MUSTAFA SET CAMP before Nicosia, the first thing the Turks did after joining up their forces and pitching tents was to ride on horseback around the fortress to provoke skirmishes, but the coadjutor did not want to let anyone go out of the city except on one occasion, during which Cortese, one of the stratioti captains, was

---

50. The engineer was most likely not the knight Geronimo Maggi (or Maggio), but Magrino, who was killed during the siege. According to Angelo Gatto, the knight Maggi left Nicosia and went to Famagusta, and was taken prisoner after the fall of the city. Imprisoned in Constantinople, he tried to escape, and was caught and strangled on March 27, 1573. See Hill, *Cyprus*, 954 n. 2.

51. A small island off the northwest coast of Crete.

killed.⁵² The Turks figured that those inside were not going to venture out of the city to skirmish with them and began to build forts. The first one was on the hillock of Santa Maria, a hundred and thirty feet from the bastion Podocataro.⁵³ It was erected very quickly and with little opposition, for even though those inside tried to obstruct the building, firing from the rampart walls of Podocataro and Carafa⁵⁴ with eighty-pound pieces, the works continued through the night when no opposition was offered. From that fort they fired on the houses and the open spaces behind the curtain, but few people were harmed. The second fort was constructed at St. George di Magnana, from which they also battered the houses and forced the defenders to take cover, but the destruction of houses did not help them much. The third was on the mound called Margheritti, between the bastions of Costanza and Podocataro, and the fourth halfway up the hills of Tomandia. From these forts they could inflict no real damage on the walls but began to dig trenches closer and closer to the ditch and the outskirts of the old city. From there they pushed the trenches to the four bastions of Podocataro, Costanza, Davila, and Tripoli, against which they erected four formidable earthworks, eighty feet from the ditch. From these places they fired briskly with sixty-pounders for four days nonstop, from dusk till dawn, except for a four-hour respite at midday to allow the cannon to cool down because of the excessive heat.

Meanwhile Commander Zane, who was in Candia with the armada, continued to prepare the galleys with due diligence, and kept sending out galleys and frigates to scout the whereabouts of the enemy fleet, even as news came from all places that the latter was already in Cyprus. Shortly thereafter Francesco Tron arrived from Cyprus with his galley and reported in detail on the enemy fleet

---

52. Andrea Cortese, an Albanian officer of the *stratioti*, led his company to meet the advancing Ottoman troops as they closed on Nicosia, charged alone a group of Turkish horse and died a valiant death; Diedo, Cobham, *Excerpta*, 92.

53. The south-facing of the eleven bastions fortifying the walls of Nicosia.

54. Another of the bastions, next to Podocataro.

## HISTORY OF THE EVENTS

and the condition of Nicosia. During the same month, the fuste of Lorenzo Cocco, Francesco Trevisan, and Tomà Morosini, and the galleys of Lorenzo Giustinian, Lorenzo Pisani, and Commander Paolo da Molin put to sea from Venice.

Giovanni Andrea Doria sailed out from Messina with the galleys of His Catholic Majesty. At Otranto he met up with the duke of Paliano and commander of His Holiness, Marc'Antonio Colonna.[55] Knowing the intentions and fervent desire of His Holiness and the king of Spain to aid the Venetians— notwithstanding the information that the Venetian armada was still in Candia and ill-prepared for war— they decided to join up with them and set sail for the island with every vessel they had available.

Seeing that the artillery did not deliver as expected because the cannonballs were absorbed by the defenses without causing damage to the walls and fell there in vain, Mustafa began to tunnel toward Nicosia with hoe and shovel, digging up deep trenches. Those inside did not fail to immediately respond with artillery fire, with which they did great damage to the Turks, surprising them and blowing up some of their cannon. Nonetheless, they pressed all the way to the counterscarp and dug alongside it a deep fosse, piling up the dug-up earth toward the city. On top they placed an infinite number of arquebusiers, who shot day and night at those who appeared on the walls. The enemy trenches and forts were protected all around by long fosses and sizable dugouts. Large numbers of troops could keep guard there, and neither artillery fire could harm them not could cavalry and infantry attack them except at considerable disadvantage. After that, they began cutting out deep fosses up to the fosse of the city, throwing up the earth to the banks to protect them from attack and damage.

Furthermore, they prepared formidable embankments with earth and bundles of faggots that their cavalry fetched from far away. With these embankments they blocked up the side walls so that they could

---

55. A good work on Colonna's role in the Holy League remains Alberto Guglielmotti, *Marcantonio Colonna alla battaglia di Lepanto* (Florence: Felice le Monnier, 1862).

not be harmed from there and then began to demolish the flanks and the faces of the bastions. Those inside saw themselves hard pressed and, fearing what was to come, at noon on August 15 a group of militiamen, citizens, and Italians sallied forth in a powerful sortie, timing it so because the Turks were always vigilant and armed in the morning but by midday they sought shade to rest and doze off. A thousand infantry marched out under Captain Piovene of Vicenza and the lieutenant of the lord coadjutor. Even though he was a cavalryman, on this day he decided to fight on foot and together with Count Alberto Scotto and other captains led the infantry and other valorous Italian soldiers so well that they reached the entrenchments of the enemy and took over two of their forts, abandoned by the Turks who thought that the assailants were a large party. The rumor spread all the way to the pavilions where it caused such a great confusion that many took to their heels. But the Turkish cavalry joined the battle before our horsemen (who, according to their orders, were supposed to aid and support the footmen), sallied forth from the city, and our men were forced to beat a hasty retreat, during which Captain Piovene and Alberto Scotto lost their lives, and the lieutenant of Captain Pocopani and several other Italians and Greeks— about one hundred men altogether— were taken prisoner. The remainder got back in the city through the same gate, bringing with them Turkish arquebuses, scimitars, turbans, and other spoils taken from the enemy.

From that point on no other sorties were made, as that was deemed too dangerous. Meeting no opposition, the enemy kept up with their attacks. On the advice of Colonel di Fano, work began on a retreat wall between the two bastions of Podocataro and Costanza. The colonel wished to encircle the approaches to the bastions; it was done for Davila and Tripoli in the same manner under the command of Giovanni Sozomeno, constructing a simple obstacle to deny the enemy room to maneuver. It was now impossible to prevent the enemy from erecting a convenient, sloped ramp to attack one, two, or all four bastions at the same time. Those inside valiantly repulsed them, with casualties on both sides, and the damage caused by fires and the depletion of water sources forced and compelled them to write in cypher to Famagusta to request infantry reinforcements. The response was late to arrive. Suspecting that the messengers have been caught (indeed they were, and the Turks displayed them), [the defenders became] anxious that if no aid was in sight they would have to surrender. They therefore dispatched one of their prudent commanders, Captain Giovanni Battista Colomba, who went out at great risk for his life and came back without any aid. They wrote to the mountain commanders to the same effect, but the messengers were similarly intercepted.

Admiral Piyale, who was at Salines with the fleet, set off toward Rhodes with one hundred galleys. To scout the whereabouts of the Christian fleet, around August 20 he sent five galiots in the direction of the island of Candia. The latter landed some men and seized five of the islanders, from whom they found out that only the Venetian fleet was there, in poor condition due to the pestilence they had suffered, and expecting the Spanish armada, without which they would not leave the island. With that news Piyale immediately turned back to Salines in Cyprus, arrived by the end of August, and reported in detail on everything he had learned about our fleet.

At the same time, news came to Candia that a fleet had appeared off Cape Gramvousa on the northern side of the island. The commander concluded that it must have been the Spanish armada (as it actually was), and sent the captain of the Gulf, Marco Quirini, with six more galleys to reconnoiter what kind of fleet it was. Quirini set sail on August 30 and found out that it was indeed the Spanish fleet, with the fleet of His Holiness. Quirini met them with great display of joy and delight. On the next day they sailed together to Souda,[56] where the commander resided. As the armada reached about a mile from the port, the Venetians saluted them with salvos from the arquebusiers, which lasted for a good half hour. Meanwhile the commander ordered the oars lowered in the water and went out to meet the two commanders, His Holiness' Marc'Antonio Colonna and the Catholic King's Giovanni Andrea Doria, the salvos

---

56. An islet in Souda Bay on the northwest coast of Crete.

still going on nonstop. When the two fleets closed to the distance of an arquebus shot from each other, their cannon fired with such thunderous sounds that nothing could be heard or seen because of the veil of smoke. The salutes exchanged, the Venetian galleys sailed between the galleys of His Holiness and those of the king and conducted them into the port.

The next morning, September 1, the commanders and other high persons convened a war council. They considered the force they had and the progress of the enemy and concluded that they must give battle, being secure in the knowledge that the blessed Lord would grant them victory against the enemy, which would mean the delivery of the island of Cyprus and certain death for all those who were besieging Nicosia. Having made up their minds, they decided to attack the enemy fleet. On September 6, Quirini, the captain of the Gulf, and another galley were sent to reconnoiter. On September 8, after some of the galleys were rigged and all took on victuals, the entire armada set off and on the next day arrived in Candia. From there, they sent out Alvise Bembo, Anzolo Soriano, and Vincenzo Maria di Priuli to catch informants from the enemy.

In Cyprus, Mustafa was doing everything he could to capture the city of Nicosia, but the vigorous defense cost him so many men every day that he lost hope that advance was possible with the forces he had and decided to reinforce his troops as much as possible. He therefore dispatched two chaushes to Salines, one to Piyale and the other to Ali to request and demand that they send him a hundred men of theirs from every galley, because without them it would be impossible to accomplish the endeavor, while a good number of men was all that was needed to overcome the Christian defenses, given that the ramp made the access [to the city walls] easy and comfortable. The two pashas were concerned not to be surprised by the Christian fleets and discussed the matter with their counselors. Various opinions were broached, and in the end it was decided that it would be impossible for the two fleets, the Venetian and the Spanish, to coordinate action even if they came together, because it would be difficult for their commanders to be of one mind, a conclusion borne out by the diligent consideration of the history of their recent league against the Turks. Thus reassured, they supplied him a hundred men per galley. On the night of Saturday, September 8, each galley landed her men, and under the command of Ali they sped off for Nicosia. Ali arrived there at the twenty-second hour[57] on the same Saturday[58] with nearly twenty thousand men and was received by Mustafa with great honors and much rejoicing.

The same night, at dawn on Sunday, September 9, all four bastions were assaulted at once by a great number of men. Caraman Pasha was at Podocataro with the troops from Caramania;[59] at Costanza was Muzaffer Pasha;[60] at the other two bastions, Davila and Tripoli, were Mustafa Pasha and Ali Pasha with the men from the fleet. Now all these, at the same time, in a great surge and with massive effort, threw themselves in the battle. Those inside defended themselves with their usual valor. They did not allow themselves to be knocked off the parapet, resisted the assault, and repulsed the enemy. Both sides sustained casualties, more from the Turks, but it was not yet known that enemy reinforcements had arrived from the galleys. The fight went on for a long while, until (from what kind of unknown inadvertence) a large number of Turks poured in through the bastion of Podocataro and took control of the open space and the retreat wall. In the course of the attack many nobles and soldiers who valiantly stood their ground were instantly cut to pieces as some

---

57. Contarini uses the early modern Venetian hour system, which divided the day into twenty-four hours beginning with the sunset. As the latter varied depending on the season, the hour of the day would fall on a different hour of the modern standardized system. In high summer, the twenty-second hour would correspond to about seven o'clock modern time. For an orientation in the early modern time-keeping systems, see Gerhard Dohr van Rossum, *History of the Hour: Clocks and Modern Temporal Orders* (Chicago: University of Chicago Press, 1996).

58. That is, in the late afternoon or early evening of September 8, the Venetian day having begun at sunset the previous day.

59. Most likely Hasan Pasha, *beylerbey* of Caramania.

60. Muzaffer Pasha was ex-*beylerbey* of Shehrizur and *beylerbey* of Marash, and after the conquest remained as the first governor of Nicosia.

of the countryside militiamen, chased down from the walls by the cannonade, took to their heels.

Hearing the great uproar and shouts, the coadjutor with his brothers and Colonel Palazzo, together with other noblemen, ran to the rescue of the bastion, but it was already too late. Even so, they pushed the enemy back vigorously and forcefully, but the numbers of the Turks were so vast that they killed them along with all the noblemen who had joined them. The other bastions held on until the Turks entered and penetrated the city, encircled them from the flanks, and poured in through the entrances of the fortifications. Now began a pitiful and horrible spectacle, a most cruel slaughtering of the poor defenders, soldiers and nobles, who fought back courageously. Scattered around, they did not know which corner to turn to escape with their lives. A few managed to save themselves by cutting through the ranks of the enemy: they broke through the entrances of the bastions and dispersed into the city's narrow alleys, where they continued the battle together with some of the citizens.

Fighting went on in all of the city's neighborhoods and squares, without any order and command. The carnage continued until six o'clock, when Mustafa Pasha entered the city. Those who resisted were killed, those who surrendered were enslaved. Beholding the slaying and the many men still with weapons in hand in the square of the palace (where the bishop of Pathos, who attempted to join them, was killed) and in many other places, he ordered his men to cease fighting and exhorted the Christians to surrender, promising to save their lives. Many desisted, but others preferred to avenge themselves on the enemy and die gallantry with arms in hand than to fall prey to such a great tyrant. In the end, twenty-five to thirty from the nobles had remained alive, and not many of the commoners: they were all enslaved. The miserable sacking of the unhappy city of Nicosia completed, Ali took his leave from Mustafa and departed with the men recruited from the fleet. Once the men were back on board, the entire armada sailed for the Gardens, about three miles distant from Famagusta.

## FAMAGUSTA

BEFORE DEPARTING FROM NICOSIA, Mustafa installed a garrison of four thousand footmen and a thousand cavalry under the command of Muzaffer Pasha; then he left with the army for Famagusta. Once there, he began putting up shows for the defenders. To induce those in the fortress to surrender, he marched many of the slaves before them; to spread terror in the city, he had the heads of the killed mounted on spears and paraded before the fortifications. But all this was in vain. As all the soldiers in Famagusta stood staunch and unwavering, he encamped at the village of Potamo, at a distance of three miles from the fortress, preparing for siege. Inside were Marc'Antonio Bragadin, captain; Lorenzo Tiepolo, captain of Paphos; Astorre Baglioni; and Gian Antonio Quirini, treasurer of the army, with many other valiant captains and soldiers, all tough, battle-hardened men, who now prepared determinedly to defend themselves.

The pashas convened a war council, at which they concluded that before they made any decision, they should send to Candia to catch informants and immediately dispatched Caia Chelebi with six galiots.

The Christian commanders meanwhile had prepared munitions, solders, and rowers, and on September 13 put out to sea from Candia to intercept the enemy. On September 16, they arrived at Sitia.[61] The same day Quirini returned with verified information that the Turkish armada was in Cyprus and that Nicosia still held out; which encouraged our forces to press on with their voyage. As Sitia was the last port eastwards, the commanders undertook to personally inspect the galleys. Commander Zane disarmed three galleys there, besides the two that were already disarmed in Candia, to better outfit the other galleys.

The head count yielded the following results. On the twelve galleys of His Holiness there were 1,100 fighting men, under captains Giorgio Capizuco, commanding officer,[62] Flaminio Zambeccari,

---

61. A port on the northeastern coast of Crete, a major Venetian naval base.

62. Contarini uses *maestro di campo,* normally a regiment commander under a colonel in charge of all infantry regiments.

Giovanni Vicenzo Valignano, Camillo Penelo, Fabio di Massimi, Cornelio di Monte de l'Ormo, Vido Tromba, Santo Corfo, Filippo Angelo di San Severino, and Dario Osmo.

On board the fleet of his Catholic Majesty there were 3,500 infantrymen, under captains Marco Pignatello, commanding officer; Giovanni Calesano, sergeant-major; Francesco di San Giovanni, marquis of Torre Magra; Alfonso Papacoda; Lucio Pignatello; Ottavio di Capua; and Prospero di Ruggiero.

With the Venetian fleet there were 8,561 infantrymen under captains Sforza Palavicini, general of the land troops, 3,000 men; Count Cesare Bentivoglio, lieutenant-major, 302 men; Lazaro Fiaterra, commanding officer, 292 men; Giacomo Malaspina, 206 men; Camillo Malaspina, 204 men; Ettore Palavicino, 200 men; Francesco Carissimi, 200 men; Antonio di Rossi, 150 men; Cesare Bachini, 200 men; Paolo dalla Lata, 201 men; Andrea Cameti, 192 men; Camillo Barattier, 204 men; Guerrier Celan, 194 men; Vicenzo da Monte, 250 men; Giovanni Maria Baldinazzo, 200 men; and Livio Eroto and Lodovico Turco, sergeant-majors; Paolo Orsini, colonel, with 1,500 infantry; under Geronimo Zamboti, 200 men; Antonio da Caglie, 150 men; Baron Barone, 209 men; Federico Barila, 206 men; Stefano Pasquini, 150 men; Curzio Simoneta, 214 men; Alfonso Archangelo, 200 men; Ortensio Bienzini, 205 men; Hercole Pio, colonel of 1,000 infantry, with his company of 400 men; the rest under Alessandro Cereteli, 200 men; Francesco Persio, 176 men; Sigismondo Pazinardo, 200 men; Alessandro Zambeccari, colonel, with 1,000 infantry, with his company of 253 men; the rest under Paolo Zambeccari, 250 men; Antonio dal Vin, 250 men; Antonio Herculiano, 250 men; Pietro Paolo Mignanello, colonel of 500 infantry; under Roberto Congoli, 250 men; Giovanni Maria Rocca, 153 men; Agostino da Fabiano, 150 men; Ottaviano Dami, colonel of 500 infantry, with his company of 300 men and 200 under Bonifacio Adami; Antonio Martinengo, colonel of 400 infantrymen; under Imperiale, 200 men; and Giovanni Orlando, 200 men; Count Antonio da Thiene, captain of 300 men; Roberto Santoni, captain of 300 men; Carlo Ducco, colonel of 1,000 infantrymen, with his company of 200 men; the rest under Marco Provaio, 200 men; Camillo Brunello, 200 men; Ortensio Palazzo, 200 men; and Ludovico Ugone, 200 men.

The community of Verona sent Ugolino da Seffa, colonel of 500 infantrymen, with his company of 300 men; and Federico della Riva, 200 men. The community of Salò sent [the following] gentlemen and mercenaries: Count Scipione Porcelaga, 200 men; Count Marc'Antonio Martinengo, 60 men; Cesare Carafa, 14 men; Sergio da Pola, 12 men; Antonio Morosini, 10 men, Giacomo Mocenigo, 10 men; Bruto da Dulcigno, knight, 10 men; Ludovico Santa Croce, 8 men; Orazio Gonzaga, 6 men; Giovanni Maria Riminaldi, knight, 6 men; Benetto Ciurano, 4 men; Count Bonifacio Bevilacqua, 4 men; Count Bonifacio da Padua, 4 men; Rambaldo Avogadro, 4 men; Antenore Malfatto, 4 men; Count Ludovico da Padua, 3 men; Hercole Taffone, 3 men; Cesare Grotto, 3 men; Vido da Lonà, 3 men; the knight of Monte Santo, 2 men.

One hundred noblemen of Padua, each with an infantryman, altogether 200 men.

The following are lords and noblemen who went with Marc'Antonio Colonna, admiral of His Holiness: Honorato Gaetano di Sermonetta, Marquis di Lucito, Marquis Malaspina, Giacomo Frangipani, Prospero di Castello, Giulio Gabrielli, Camillo Accoramboni, Francesco Dinati, Biagio Capizuco, Angiolo Mazatosto, Celsi da Napoli, Piero Benzati, Ottaviano Gioachini, Ottaviano Albarino, Hieronomo Martelli, Tiberio Boccapodoca, Vincenzo di Capis, Giovanni Bartolomeo Boccabella, Fulvio Stalla, Lelio di Massimi with his two brothers, Fabrizio Villano, auditor general.

Lords and noblemen in the Venetian fleet, altogether 14: Andrea Barbarigo, Christoforo Barbarigo, Vettor Soranzo, the knight dall' Nero of Florence, Rosano Bureter, Giacomo Barise of Bergamo, Josef Bagnato of Bergamo, Canona of Bergamo, Galeazzo of Bergamo, Ludovico d'Ada, Camillo of Bergamo, Hieronimo Vicomercato of Crema, Onorio Barbetta of Crema, Count Annibale Provaio.

Soldiers recruited in the army from the strongholds of Corfu: Captain Marco Calabrese with 20 men, Captain Tomaso Fermo with 150 men, Captain Lucio of Napoli with 150 men.

From Canea: Alvise Martinengo, governor general of the city, with 10 men; Captain Antonio da Colalto with 300 men; Captain Alvise Naldo with 50 men.

From Candia: Moretto Calabrese, governor of the city, with 150 men; Captain Piero Conte with 200 men; Captain Baldistera Boschetto with 200 men; Captain Fabio Naldo with 200 men; Captain Alessandro Travel with 200 men.

All this to the effect that besides the regular detachments, in the fleet of His Holiness there were 1,100 infantrymen and 23 nobles, in the fleet of His Majesty, 3,500 infantrymen, and in the Venetian fleet, 8,561 infantrymen, 585 mercenaries, 14 noblemen, 1,600 infantrymen sent by the communities of Brescia, Verona, and Salò, and 1,632 infantrymen recruited from the strongholds.

In the meantime, Caia Chelebi, who was sent by the pashas who were in Cyprus to spy on the progress of our armada and catch informants, arrived with his galiots at the island of Candia. There, on September 15, he seized a boat that was traveling from Cape Salomon to Sitia with a crew of five Christians, sailors from a ship that was at anchor in that port. They informed him about the rendezvous of the fleets and that the latter were preparing to sail for Cyprus, and he immediately turned back to report the news.

Having loaded water and supplied with enough victuals to feed its men, on September 17, at five o'clock at night, the entire Christian armada set sail from Sitia, organized in the following order:

Quirini led the vanguard with the following twelve galleys: Quirini's flagship, and those of Marin Dandolo, Filippo Leon, Giovanni Battista Benedetti, Piero Badoer, Alessandro Contarini, Antonio Pasqualigo, Geronimo Tron, Caterino Malipiero, Colane Drasco of Cres, Marino Contarini, and Giovanni Battista Contarini.

# HISTORY OF THE EVENTS

Marc'Antonio Colonna, duke of Paliano and admiral of His Holiness, led a squadron of twelve galleys: Colonna's flagship, captained by Francesco Brutto Hierosomilitano; and those of Pompeo Colonna, duke of Gazaruolo and governor, captained by Andrea di Somma; Prospero Colonna, governor, captained by Giovanni Mattio Palavicini, Mattio Frangipani, Domenico di Massimi, Horatio Orsini, Fabio Santa Croce, Alessandro Ferretti, Girolamo Minotto, Alvise Zorzi, Alfonso Malaguzzi, knight of Jerusalem, and Francesco Baglione.

The squadron of Giovanni Andrea Doria, prince of Melfi, captain general of His Catholic Majesty: the said admiral's flagship, his *Padrona*, and *Temperanza*, *Donzella*, *Marchesa*, *Donna*, *Perla*, *Fortuna*, *Aquila*, *Monarca*, *and Vittoria*; Ambroggio di Negro's flagship and his *Padrona*, and *Bastardella*, and *La Nova*; Giorgio di Grimaldi's *Padrona*; the flagship of Don Álvaro da Bazán, marquis of Santa Croce and general of Naples, his *Padrona*, and *Marchesa*, *Ventura*, *Fortuna*, *Bazana*, *Leona*, and *Costanza*; the flagship of Alonzo da Bazán, and his *San Giovanni*, *San Filippo*, and *Vittoria*; Bernardino da Velasco's flagship and his *San Giosefo*, *Santa Caterina*, and *Santo Bartolomeo*; the flagship of Stefano de Marin, and his *Padrona*; the flagship of Bodinello; the flagship of Sicily; *Padrona*, *Vigilanza*, *Cardona*, *Sicilia*, *San Giovanni*; the flagship of [Davide] Imperiali and his *Padrona*; the flagship of Nicolò Doria, and his *Padrona*.

Squadron of Girolamo Zane, knight and procurator of San Marco, admiral of the Venetians: the admiral's flagship, and those of Bernardo Sagredo, Agostin Sanudo, Zorzi Pisani, Giacomo di Priuli, Nadal Donaldo, Zorzi Corner, Bernardo Giustiniani, Mattio Calergi, Vicenzo Quirini, Stefano Venier, Alvise Bembo, Tomà Michiel, Andrea Tiepolo, Gabriel da Canal, Francesco Corner, Nicolò Suriano, Onfre Giustiniani, Michiel Barbarigo, Marc'Antonio Foscarini, Marco da Molin, Zuan Cigogna, Marc'Antonio Lando, Piero Zanne, Lorenzo Venier, in place of Priamo da Lezze, who went to Venice, Nicolò Lippomano, Zuan Bembo, Zuan de Dominis d'Arbe, Marian Bizanti of Kotor; Alvise Cippico of Trogir.

Squadron of Sforza Palavicini, captain general of the land troops: his flagship, under Piero Emmo; and those of Francesco Badoer, Lorenzo Barbarigo, Piero Francesco Malipiero, David Bembo, Andrea Donado, Francesco Gritti, Nicolò Donado, Zuan Mocenigo, Marco Donado, Zuan Contarini, Alvise Pasqualigo, Ferigo Nani, Zuan Battista Quirini, Andrea Barbarigo, Alvise Lando, Zaccaria Barbaro, Alvise Emmo, Marc'Antonio Pisani, Francesco Bon, Nicolò Avonal and Andrea Calergi of Retimno, Pietro Bertolazzi of Zadar, Giovanni Battista del Tacco, and one from Capo d'Istria.

Squadron of Giacomo Celsi, provveditore of the Venetian fleet: his flagship, Lorenzo Celsi in the place of Bartolomeo, Antonio Bon of Candia, Giacomo Morosini, Alessandro Vizzamano of Canea, Antonio Michiel, Francesco Corner of Candia, Carlo Quirini, Polo Polani of Retimno, Francesco Contarini, Francesco Muazzo of Candia, Geronimo Gritti, Piero Barbarigo of Retimno, Geronimo Tiepolo, Nicolò Fradello of Candia, Donà Tiepolo, Zorzi Barbarigo of Candia, Antonio di Cavalli, Zuan Dandolo of Candia, Francesco Zen in place of Giacomo Salomon.

Squadron of Antonio da Canal, provveditore of the Venetian fleet: his flagship, Piero Trevisan, Zuan Balbi, Piero Pisani, Polo Nani, Simon Guoro, Vecenzo da Canal, Andrea Tron, Geronimo da Canal, Geronimo of Pesaro, Zuan Michiel Vizzamano of Canea, Francesco da Molin of Canea, Giacomo Calergi of Canea, Filippo Polani of Canea, Vicenzo Zancaruol of Canea, Geronimo Zorzi of Candia, Francesco Bon of Candia, Piero Gradenigo of Candia.

Rearguard of Santo Tron, commander of the slave rowers: his flagship, Zaccaria Valier, Agostin Venier, Francesco Tron, Antonio di Priuli in place of Benedetto Soranzo, Bertuzzi Contarini in place of Piero Dolfin, Carlo Contarini in place of Francesco Vendramin, Nicolò da Mosto, Andrea Minotto in place of Gabriel Emmo, Nicolò Malipiero in place of Battista Foscarini, Alvise Balbi in place of Francesco Dolfin, Marc'Antonio Quirini, Todaro Balbi, Zuan Balci, Lodovico Cicuta, Piero Michiel, physician, of Šibenik.

Squadron of large galleys in charge of Francesco Duodo, captain: his flagship, Marc'Antonio Morosini, Giacomo Guoro, Lorenzo Bernardo, Marco Michiel, Giacomo da Mosto, Antonio Bragadin, Vicenzo Quirini, Andrea da Pesaro, Ambrogio Bragadin, Zaccaria Salomon, Geronimo Contarini, captain of the galleon of Fausto Nani.

Galleoncini under the command of Piero Tron: his flagship, and the ships *Cypriotta, Cornara, Barbara, Giustiniana, Quirina, Mauntia, Dolfina, Bona, Trincavella,* and the galleoncini *Zapino, Mugri, Cornaro,* and *Lodovici.*

Quirini's vanguard sailed 20 to 25 miles ahead, followed by the rest of the armada, arranged in squadrons as described above.

On September 23, Caia Chelebi arrived in Cyprus and handed over to the pashas the slaves he had seized in Candia. The pashas immediately got together to discuss between themselves what was to be done. Piyale was anxious not to have the fleet destroyed, considering that the Christian armadas have united, that they planned to deploy a good number of vessels, and that the Venetian fleet had so easily replenished the manpower it had lost. But Mustafa and Ali were of the contrary opinion: they asserted that it would be an indignity for their Lord if they were to avoid giving battle, and advised him to sail out. With that decision, Piyale disembarked all slaves and men he could not use and put all the galleys and artillery of the Turkish people in excellent order; then, with all the oared vessels he took off for Limasol, leaving at the Gardens of Famagusta only the maonas, the palandarie, the caramuscialini, and other boats. As they were setting off, they sighted twelve sails; believing them to be the Christian armada, they were startled and confused and aligned themselves in battle order. As it turned out, these were the caramuscialini, which were bringing reinforcements from Anatolia, so they assumed a wing formation and lay waiting not far away from the island.

The Christian armada, which sailed at some distance behind its vanguard toward Rhodes, massed the sailing ships and the large galleys together at the island of Karpathos and, enjoying a fair tailwind, entered the channel of Rhodes. Around the twenty-second of the month [of September] Quirini's vanguard sighted two galleys. Quirini went out to intercept them and found out that they were Luigi Bembo's three galleys. The latter informed him of the fall of Nicosia on the eighteenth of the said month; he had learned about it from some Christian subjects of the Turks, which he had seized in two caiques.[63] Quirini turned back to the armada and reported the news to the admirals, who took it with much consternation. The entire fleet spent the night at a port called Kastellorizo and Fineka, at a distance of about two hundred miles from Cyprus.[64]

The next day the admirals and other lords convened a war council to discuss whether they had to continue their voyage, given that Nicosia had fallen. Some noted that the victorious enemy could now put on board the galleys many more men than they would have normally been able to. Others, familiar with these seas, feared tempestuous weather, it being already autumn, and as they were to sail through the Gulf of Satalia, exposed to powerful storms, did not know where would they find shelter. Such and many other concerns were taken into account. As a result, it was decided that the best thing was to turn back. Thus, at seven o'clock at night on [September] 22, they set sail. While underway, at six o'clock during the day of September 23, a big storm broke out, with a heavy rain, and the galleys barely saved themselves in the port of Piga, between Rhodes and Karpathos. From that place Admiral Zane took care to send a frigate to Famagusta to give them hope that they would soon be rescued and inform them in detail of what was known and done to this moment. On [September] 26 the entire armada sailed into the port of Tristamo on the island of Karpathos.[65]

---

63. A sailing vessel of the Eastern Mediterranean with a sprit mainsail, square topsail, and two or more jibs or other sails.

64. A small island (official Greek name Megisti) off the southern coast of Anatolia, opposite the modern-day town of Kaş, 170 miles northwest from Cyprus.

65. An ample harbor on the northwestern tip of the island.

# HISTORY OF THE EVENTS

As winter was around the corner and there was nothing more to be accomplish this year, Andrea Doria took his leave, and by the end of September the entire Spanish fleet departed. On the same day, the Venetians and His Holiness' [fleet] set sail as well. They had not covered more than twenty five miles when a new storm from the north hit them between Spinalonga and Sitia. Two of the galleys of His Holiness capsized, and the armada was forced to remain at the coast until October 4. As soon as the wind abated, the admiral continued the voyage, leaving Quirini behind to recover the artillery pieces and other war materiel from the two wrecked galleys. On arrival in Sitia, the admiral ordered some galleys to Souda, while others were to go with him to Candia. He entered the port with the latter on October 5, and the rest continued the voyage to Souda. On October 6, another powerful storm front descended from the north. In Candia, some of the galleys that were at anchor outside of the port were beached, but those that sailed for Souda fared much worse, as many of them were pinned against the shore during their voyage. The armada as a whole escaped, save eleven galleys that were wrecked on that island of Candia, namely those of Pietro Zane, Geronimo Gritti, Carlo Quirini, Simon Guoro, Nicolò Donado, Alvise Lando, Lodovico Cicutta of Veglia, Geronimo Grisanto of Kotor and, of His Holiness' squadron, Geronimo Minotto, Alessandro Feretti, and Domenico di Massimi, but some of these were salvaged.

After the admiral arrived in Candia he convened a council with Marc'Antonio Colonna, Sforza Palavicini, and the governors of the place; also present was Sebastian Venier, who had been elected provveditore general of Cyprus and was en route from Corfu to his province. They discussed how to expedite aid to Famagusta, which was besieged by the enemy, and appointed several captains of the island of Candia on the relieve force, while leaving enough in place. After issuing the requisite orders, the admiral dispatched Caterino Malipiero to Venice to advise them of the decision, enjoined Giovanni Battista Contarini to accompany him to Corfu, and on October 16 departed from Candia. On October 22 he entered Souda, from which he sent Pietro Emmo with two galleys to catch informants and, shortly thereafter, Vincenzo Maria Priuli and Angelo Suriano as well to gather more information about the enemy.

The pashas in Cyprus realized that the Christian armada was not going to arrive, and were confirmed in the belief that as it was composed by the forces of more than one prince and was not acting under one command, and as the usual animosities that always existed in the endeavors of the Christians were thus exacerbated, it would not have been able to inflict harm on the Turkish [fleet] to begin with. Considering also that their fleet was of no use on the island, they decided to allow it to depart and take winter quarters in the Archipelago or in Constantinople. Having so resolved, they turned to loading the slaves and the large amount of cargo, and on October 6 the fleet set sail.

Two days before that a memorable event occurred in full view of the city of Famagusta. They say that the galleon of the first vizier Mustafa Pasha, a galiot, and a caramuscialin were being loaded with male and female slaves, the flower of the youth of the city of Nicosia, along with a large amount of precious booty destined to be presented to the Great Lord[66] and scheduled to depart with the fleet. The boatswain of the galleon was having some powder kegs transferred over at the request of Mustafa. At that point, an enslaved noblewoman, who loved death better that life in slavery, courageously threw fire in the gunpowder. Others say that it was because of the negligence of the boatswain. However that may be, it was a horrendous spectacle to see the bodies of these unfortunate souls who were blown up fly in the air. The blaze consumed the galiot and the caramuscialin at once. Only the captain and three slaves of the galiot got away, everyone else was literally burned to death and killed.

The armada departed from Cyprus, leaving only seven galleys behind at the Gardens to prevent any aid to Famagusta, and sailed directly to Kastellorizo, opposite of Setecai in Caramania.[67] There they were informed that the Christian armada had visited those seas,

---

66. The Ottoman sultan.

67. Most likely the modern town of Kaş.

but for unknown reason or because of lack of agreement between them it had turned back and left. From Kastellorizo the Turkish fleet travelled to Rhodes, where they got the same news, plus that the Spanish and the Venetian squadrons had separated. Piyale sent five galiots from there to Caocolonne to catch informants while the [Turkish] armada continued toward Stampalia.[68] From the latter place he dispatched twelve other galiots with the same task of monitoring the Christian fleet at the island of Candia, thinking to shadow it once he knew its precise whereabouts.

Pietro Emmo, who had been sent to reconnoiter the Turkish fleet, returned to Cyprus to report that he had found it at Stampalia. In the same time, news came from Sitia that twelve Turkish galiots have appeared off the island of Candia and then left without disembarking a single man. Immediately after having the news, Quirini, who was still at Candia, set out with all the galleys he had toward the admiral to join up with his forces, fearing that the enemy fleet — being so close — might approach and endanger him. While the entire Christian armada was at Souda, on October 26, there arrived Fra Pietro Giustiniani, commander of the fleet of [the Order of] Saint John of Malta, with two other galleys. He had sailed out to join Colonna with five galleys of the Order, but on the way they had been attacked by eighteen Turkish galleys and two of his galleys had been captured; he and the other two managed to get away.

On November 7, all Christian galleys left Souda together and repaired to Canea, a more secure and convenient port. There arrived Angelo Suriano, who reported that on the fourth day of the same month Vincenzo Maria Priuli, who had been with him in the Archipelago, had been cut to pieces by five Turkish galiots at Paros, everyone fighting bravely and going down only after inflicting great damage to the Turks.

The enemy fleet departed from Stampalia and arrived at Longos,[69] where it took provisions, and continued its voyage through the

---

68. The westernmost island of the Dodecanese Archipelago, Astypalaia in Greek.

69. The smallest of the ports of Paros, on the northeastern side of the island.

Archipelago. For a number of reasons it was decided not to go to Candia, mostly because the island and its ports were exposed to the northerlies, and thus were unsafe on account of the winter season. It was God's will, because when the enemy got news that the Venetian galleys had been dispersed by the storms that had battered them, Piyale was already in the Archipelago with the armada. There the five galiots, and the galley captured from Priuli joined him and reported to the pasha the tremendous courage of Priuli. He had attacked all five of them with a single galley and fought so bravely that two of the galiots were taken. The third was about to be lost before, exhausted from the fighting and weakened by the loss of a great number of his soldiers taken out by the incessant arquebus fire, he was finally killed together with all of his men.

On November 7, Admiral Zane left Canea with the entire fleet, wishing to relieve the island, leaving Quirini behind to provide aid to Famagusta according to the orders he and Palavicini had given him, with the galleys of the kingdom [of Crete] reinforced by a few others. Shortly thereafter the galley of Nicolò Donado arrived from Famagusta with Bishop Ragazzoni on board. He reported in detail on the fall of Nicosia and the condition of Famagusta and was immediately dispatched to Admiral Zane in Corfu.

Piyale directed the armada to the port of Soassera,[70] and as the harbor was not convenient enough he put the slaves to work to enlarge the anchorage, planning to spend the winter there, but then thought better of it and decided to winter in Constantinople. He left a naval guard squadron in the Archipelago to protect and patrol it and to prevent aid to Famagusta, and repaired with the rest of the armada to winter quarters in Constantinople.

On November 17, Admiral Zane arrived at Corfu where he disarmed the galleys that were in poor condition. Marc'Antonio Colonna did the same. In the meantime, Nicolò Donado arrived from Famagusta with the news that he had already reported in Candia, and Admiral Zane sent him to Venice. On November 27,

---

70. Most likely "Calogiero," as it is in Paruta, *Storia della guerra di Cipro* (1827). See also Hill, *Cyprus*, 939.

Marc'Antonio Colonna took his leave from Admiral Zane and with three galleys set sail for the port of Kassiopi on the northern side of the island. After being held back there by contrary winds for a little less than a month, he set off. But at the entrance to the Gulf of Kotor a furious storm broke out, with heavy rain, thunder, and lightning. A thunderbolt struck the mast of Colonna's galley and burned it to ashes, but the men got away unscathed; yet the same storm pushed Francesco Tron ['s galley], which had taken Colonna on board, to the shore and it was wrecked.

In Constantinople preparations were under way for an even greater war effort in the following year, planning not only the invasion and conquest of the island of Cyprus, but of other islands as well, and hoping that their forces would become masters of those islands and of Dalmatia too, and from there they would go on to subjugate all of Christendom. But Pope Pius V, the guardian of the religion of Christ and universal Father of all Christians, was aware of the grave danger to Christianity. He therefore put everything he had behind the effort to conclude the Holy League and union between him, the Catholic king of Spain, and the Venetian Senate, to oppose and obviate in a timely fashion the designs of so powerful a tyrant. The pope hoped to bring into agreement the two other parties and resolve their differences, never ceasing, through letters and emissaries, to implore them to conclude the above-mentioned union. While His Holiness occupied himself with bringing this most important endeavor to completion, the Venetians were busy with procuring the provisions needed for the defense of the island of Cyprus.

According to the orders of Girolamo Zane, Marc'Antonio Colonna, and Sforza Palavicini, the rectors of Candia and Quirini worked diligently on the speedy dispatch of the vessels that were at Fraschia after delivering the men allocated for that fortress.[71] At the end of December, Quirini, who was in Candia with the said lords, decided that the four transports loaded with the garrison for

---

71. A Venetian fortress located on the site of the ancient Cytaeum or Paleocastro, at the Dium promontory, Crete's chief promontory on the north, called Ponta della Fraschia by the Venetians.

Famagusta would not be able to deliver them to the fortress without escort by galleys. He had concluded that there had to be [enemy] galleys left to guard the island of Cyprus and that they could easily cause trouble to the transports. He therefore offered to accompany them in person.

Quirini was appointed commander of the fleet by the lords of Candia, replacing Piero Tron, who had passed away shortly before that. Thus decided, on January 16 [1571], Quirini set sail from Candia with twelve galleys (some of them recruited from the island) and the four transports carrying the reinforcements for Famagusta. The galleys that sailed out were Quirini's flagship, and those of the commander of the slave rowers Santo Tron, Vincenzo Quirini, Todaro Balbi, Marc'Antonio Pisani, Filippo Lione, the galley of Alessandro Contarini, the galley of Girolamo Tron (without him, as he had fallen ill), Francesco Bon, Antonio Bon of Candia, Nicolò Fradello of Candia, Alessandro Vizzamano of Canea, and Francesco da Molin of Canea. Sebastian Venier, who was to act as provveditore general of the island of Cyprus, fell ill and did not sail out.

At Cape Salomon, Quirini sent back the galley of Francesco Bon, as some of his men had fallen ill. On the twenty-sixth of the same month they arrived at the island of Cyprus. The transports were already there, as they had taken a different route from that of the galleys, and had on the same night entered the harbor of Famagusta.[72] The galleys used the terrain to spend the night in hiding, planning to join the transports before daybreak, to lure the seven [enemy] galleys that were at the island (as had been espied) to take on the transports, considering them an easy target. And as it was planned, on the morning they sighted the seven galleys making directly for the transports. Not yet fully deployed however, they spotted the twelve galleys bound to intercept them, and turned right back, finding shelter on the coast.

---

72. Contarini's expression is "entrorno il Dromo di Famagusta;" *dromo* in nautical terminology is a column, obelisk, or another highly visible artificial signpost erected for sailors' orientation in daytime coastal navigation.

# HISTORY OF THE EVENTS

Quirini shadowed them the entire day but, unable to get close because of the great number of men massed in the marina to protect them, fired on them with his cannon and sent three of them to the bottom. As the night came and a storm broke out, the transports pulled closer to the fortress to avoid being caught in the open sea by the bad weather. The reinforcements were received with an outburst of great joy in Famagusta. On the next day Quirini sighted a vessel in the open sea, gave chase, and captured it. It was a maona, bound for Mustafa's camp and loaded with Turks, munitions, and provisions. It was seized without much resistance, because they thought that the galleys that closed in on them were friendlies. The day after, Quirini, wanting to engage the four remaining galleys, now in Constanza, found out that they had fled, and burned down a caramuscialin and the parts of the three galleys he had sunk that stuck out above the waterline. On the next day, another vessel was spotted on the high seas, similarly loaded with Turkish irregulars, munitions, and victuals for the army, and he pursued and seized her.

In Famagusta, the transports were unloaded while the galleys continued to crisscross the high seas. They also destroyed some fortifications erected on the rocks of Gambella not far from the fortress of Famagusta and a mole constructed by the Turks at Constanza to protect the galleys they kept there. After busying himself with these matters for twenty-two days, Quirini took his leave from the lords of Famagusta, assuring them that they would be helped out. He first had the four transports conducted out of the port, together with three other sailing ships that had been sequestered there, and after towing them to a convenient spot where they were able to set sail, on February 16 he departed and on the twenty-first of the same month arrived at Candia.[73]

---

73. From this point on Contarini transcribes verbatim the account of count Nestor Martinengo on the siege of Famagusta and follows him until the fall of the city. The excerpt of Martinengo's account, being his report to the doge of Venice, was published several times in 1572. See what appears be the editio princeps, Nestore Martinengo, *Relatione di tutto il successo di Famagosta; dove s'intende ... tutte le scaramuccie, batterie, mine, & assaltidato ad essa fortezza. Et ancora i nomi de i Capitani, & e numero delle Genti morte... et medesimamente*

There he found that Sebastian Venier had received missives from the Senate, giving notice that on December 20 he had been elected admiral of the fleet in place of Girolamo Zane, that on the sixteenth of the said month Quirini had been elected provveditore of the said fleet, that on the twenty-first, the commander of the transports, Piero Tron, had similarly been elected provveditore of the fleet, the Senate being yet unaware that he had passed away at Candia. On January 1, Marco Grimani had been elected duke of Candia, on February 10, the captain of the Gulf Santo Tron, commander of the slave rowers, and on [February] 18 Vettor Bragadin, duke of Candia in place of Marco Grimani. In the same month of February, Agostino Barbarigo, who had been elected provveditore general of the armada, sailed out from Venice, while on the thirteenth [of the month] Sforza Palavicini disarmed his galley, as he was in no condition to sail due to indisposition caused by gout.

In Constantinople, the news of the reinforcements to Famagusta and the seizure of the caramuscialini, the sailing ships, and the galleys caused much displeasure to the sultan. He immediately ordered the decapitation of the bey of Chios and tore down the standard of the bey of Rhodes for allowing the said reinforcements to arrive at Famagusta.[74] He also sent a chaush to the bey of Negroponte, charging him, on the pain of impalement, to gather together all the naval garrisons in the Archipelago and sail with them to Chios, there to expect further orders. Ali Pasha was ordered to sail out of Constantinople straightaway with forty galleys, with instructions to collect the naval garrisons and sail with them to Cyprus, while the rest of the available galleys were speedily being rearmed.

---

*di quelli, che sono restati prigioni* (Venice: Giorgio Angelieri, 1572). Contarini must have had easy access to it. The relevant part of the report is translated by Claude Cobham, *Travels in the Island of Cyprus. Translated from the Italian of Giovanni Mariti by Claude Delaval Cobham with contemporary accounts of the sieges of Nicosia and Famagusta* (Cambridge: Cambridge University Press, 1909, reprint, London: Zeno, 1971). The translation is also available online at https://archive.org/stream/travelsinislando0omaririch/travelsinislando-0omaririch_djvu.txt.

74. That is, degraded the bey of Rhodes from his first-flag rank.

# HISTORY OF THE EVENTS

On receiving the news of his election as captain-general of the fleet in place of Girolamo Zane, Sebastian Venier resolved to return to Corfu to take over the command of the armada. He issued orders to rearm all of the galleys of the kingdom [of Crete], which had been disarmed, and on March 17, 1571 set out on board the galley of Santo Tron, the commander of the slave rowers, accompanied by Marco Quirini and seven other galleys. While traversing the sea between Zante and Castel Tornese,[75] Quirini seized an enemy fusta with all of the men on board.[76] [Venier] arrived at Corfu on April 1 and found there the provveditore of the armada, Agostino Barbarigo, who had already taken over from Zane, and now solemnly handed over the command to Venier. In Venice, on March 18, Zaccaria Salomon was elected provveditore of the fleet in place of Santo Tron, who had passed away.

Ali, who had left Constantinople with forty galleys, arrived at Chios, where the bey of Negroponte joined him shortly afterwards with another forty galleys from the naval garrisons and elsewhere, and with these set sail for Cyprus in the beginning of April, providing Mustafa with a sizable reinforcement.

Around the end of April, Pertau Pasha[77] departed from Constantinople with the rest of the fleet, Piyale remaining in Constantinople at the request of his spouse, the sultan's daughter. Some thought that the sultan was not satisfied with his service,

---

75. Chlemoutsi, a crusader stronghold in the northwestern tip of the Elis area of the Peloponnese, opposite of the island of Zakynthos (Zante), occupied by the Venetians in the war of 1463–79.

76. The *fusta* (sometimes rendered "foist" in English), the galiot, and the brigantine were all subclasses or the galley, all oared vessels under lateen sails, differing only in the number of rowing benches. The galley normally had 24–26 benches along each side of the ship, the galiot, 15–24, the *fusta*, 12–15, and the brigantine, 8–11 benches.

77. Pertau Pasha was the Ottoman serasker or commander of the troops, and in naval campaigns served as commanding officer of the fighting compartments on board the galleys. He took the place of Piyale, who was demoted after neglecting to pursue the Christian fleet when it was most vulnerable, as Contarini correctly states.

implying that out of negligence he missed the opportunity to destroy the Venetian fleet the previous year, seeing that it would have been an easy thing to do if on his way back from the island of Cyprus he had sailed from Karpathos to Candia, where the said fleet had been dispersed between several ports, and blaming him that he had known of the departure of the Spanish fleet. But he got away with it because he was the sultan's son-in-law. Pertau and the fleet sailed straight to the island of Negroponte and arrived at Castel Rosso, planning to resupply there and furnish the fleet with everything they needed.

During the month of May, the galleys of Andrea Foscarini and Antonio di Cavalli sailed from Venice. Quirini left Corfu with his galleys to return to Candia to protect the island. He arrived on April 6, to find out that shortly before, two Venetian ships, sent from Venice under the command of Nicolò Donado, had arrived there with soldiers and munitions for Famagusta. The latter had not sailed immediately from the island [of Crete] to Cyprus, according to the orders he had from his superiors, but had remained there. It was all God's will, because there is absolutely no doubt that if he had not stopped with the ships at the island the relief would have certainly reached Famagusta. Yet that nobleman, as he wished to make sure the said ships arrived safely at the fortress as he had so eagerly promised the Senate, was advised to stop at the island, with the expectation that he would obtain from there information of the enemy fleet. He achieved just the opposite: there was no reliable information, and the intemperate weather kept him from proceeding. Meanwhile missives arrived that the Turkish fleet was in the Archipelago, bound to attack the island of Candia. At this news, a galley was immediately dispatched to Corfu to report to Admiral Venier the details of the new information.

Ali, who had left Constantinople before Pertau, had already in the beginning of April arrived at Cyprus with eighty galleys of the garrisons of the Archipelago, bringing along many reinforcements. He remained there until May 15, and then took his leave from Mustafa Pasha, leaving Arab Ahmad [Pasha][78] and another three

---

78. Contarini has "Rapamati." The house of Arab Ahmad Pasha is recorded

standard-bearers to protect the island with twenty-two galleys, and a number of caramuscialini, maone, and palandarie. Mustafa put the latter to work to continuously ferry over from the mainland sipachis, Janissaries, irregulars,[79] and other necessary war materiel as speedily as possible because he feared the arrival of the Christian fleet. The result was that [the number of] their men increased daily as multitudes of irregulars flocked in after word had been spread all over these lands that Famagusta, a port city much stronger than Nicosia, was also much wealthier.

In the month of April the galleys [of the commanders] listed below set sail from Venice: Giacomo Giustinian, Ferigo Renier, Piero Badoer, Pataro Buzzacarini, Marc'Antonio Santa Iuliana, Geronimo Marcello, Andrea Barbarigo, Bartolomeo Dandolo, Geronimo Contarini, Zuan Antonio Coleoni, Constantin Bollani, Giacomo Dressano, Bertuzzi Contarini, Horatio Fisogno.

On May 13, Nicolò Donado was elected commander of the convict [rowers] galleys.

In mid-May, Mustafa had fifteen pieces of artillery brought over from Nicosia. He broke camp and relocated to the western side of the Gardens. [The Turks] also threw up earthworks and dug trenches from there to a place called Precipola. On the 25th, the enemy constructed bastions to place the cannon and kept raising entrenchments for the arquebusiers, one after another, creeping up closer and closer. It was impossible to prevent them from approaching, as more than forty thousand sappers worked incessantly under the

---

in Constantinople in 1594. According to the eyewitness and prisoner of war Angelo Gatto, he was bey of Rhodes and was murdered by his own troops in 1578. See Policarpo Catizzani, *Narrazione del terribile assedio e della resa di Famagusta nell' anno 1571 da un manoscritto del Capitano Angelo Gatto da Orvieto* (Orvieto: Tosini, 1895), 88, quoted after Hill, *Cyprus*, 963 n.3.

79. Ottoman troops included, besides the regular units of the heavy cavalry of timar-holders, the *sipachis*, and the Janissary infantry, large contingents of unskilled workers, serving as sappers, and many irregulars, such as the *azabs*, militiamen from the towns, and the *akıngı*, light cavalry units, which served for a share of the booty.

cover of darkness. As the enemy's design and plan of attack unfolded, those inside took to work with great diligence to thwart it. A large guard stood duty around the clock on the section of the covered way at the entrance to the counterscarp. New flanks were added to the sorties that guarded the counterscarp. Traverses were added to the embankments, and along the entire length of the wall that was under attack a brick gangway was constructed, two feet high and wide, with embrasures for the arquebusiers who defended the counterscarp. Bragadin attended to all that in person, as did Baglione, and everything was executed in perfect order. Bread for the soldiers was made in only one place, supervised by Lorenzo Tiepolo, Captain of Paphos, who did not spare any effort in anything he undertook. Andrea Bragadin was in charge in the Castel and most diligently applied himself to the protection of the strip facing the sea, fixing up the old flanks and raising new ones to defend the area of the Arsenal.

The captain of the artillery was Cavalier Goito, and as he soon perished in a skirmish Bragadin put Nestor Martinengo in charge of his company. Three captains, with twenty men apiece recruited from the units, were put in charge of explosives. All good cannons were moved where bombardment was expected and embrasures were outfitted with cauldrons. Frequent sorties from all posts were made to harass the enemy, and they caused considerable damage. On one occasion, three hundred Famagustans sallied out with swords and shields, along with as many Italian arquebusiers. They inflicted great damage, but because the enemy trenches were set up so close, even though they were put to flight by our men and many were killed, such a multitude surged back that they killed about thirty of our men and wounded sixty. No more sorties were undertaken after that, as it was too dangerous.

Little by little, the enemy crept up with their trenches all the way to the summit of the counterscarp, and completed their forts. On May 19, they opened fire from all ten forts with seventy-four pieces of large cannon, among them four "basilisks" (as they were called) of extra-large size. The attack covered the area from the gate of Limasol to the Arsenal. The barrage began at five places: the tower of the

# HISTORY OF THE EVENTS

Arsenal was battered by five pieces from the fort on the rock in the harbor; the curtain itself of the Arsenal was fired upon from a battery of eleven pieces; the great tower of Andruzzi, with two cavaliers that were up there, from a battery of another eleven guns; the great tower of Santa Nappa was battered by the four basilisks; and the gate of Limasol, which was outfitted with a high cavalier and a ravelin facing out,[80] was shelled from the batteries with thirty-three pieces of artillery, attended in person by the commander-in-chief Mustafa. In the beginning they were not trying to breach the wall but shelled the city and our guns, which inflicted much damage. For that reason, as soon as the cannonade started, the Greeks and the soldiers inside relocated to the wall and remained there until the end. Bragadin took up residence in the tower of Andruzzi, Baglione in Santa Nappa, and Tiepolo in Campo Santo. They were present at all clashes and encouraged and castigated according to merit.

Luigi Martinengo, a valorous man, was put in charge of the artillery. He divided the positions between six captains, who were to look after the men and whatever the gunners needed. At every gate a company of Greeks was assigned to serve the batteries. Captain Francesco Bogone was in charge of the great tower and the large cavalier of the Arsenal. Captain Pietro Conte had the curtain at the cavalier de Volti and the tower of Campo Santo. Nestor Martinengo attended at the cavalier of Campo Santo, that of Andruzzi, and the curtain all the way to the tower of Santa Nappa. Count Hector Martinengo was in charge of the cavalier of Santa Nappa and the length of the curtain to the gate of Limasol. The ravelin and the curtain toward the bastion were under the command of Captain Horatio da Veletri. The high cavalier of Limasol, which was shelled more than the others, was guarded by Captain Roberto Malvezzi.

As the bombardment began, on Bragadin's orders soldiers (Greeks and Italians alike, and the gunners) were given wine, soup, cheese, and salted meat. Everything was brought up to them on the wall in very good order, so that the soldier did not spend more than two

---

80. Part of the defense architecture of the gate, projecting outwork protecting the wall.

soldi per day on bread. They were paid every thirty days under the strict supervision of Giovanni Antonio Quirini who, besides that charge, was present at all important encounters to bolster the soldiers' spirits. For ten days, the counter-offensive went on with such a fury that fifteen of [the Turks'] best guns were blown up and up to thirty thousand men were slain. They did not feel safe even in the forts and were scared out of their wits. But then our men figured that they were running low on powder, and a limit was set to fire no more than thirty guns per day, thirty shots a piece, and this only when the captains were in attendance to make sure that the shots were not wasted.

On May 29, a frigate arrived from Candia.[81] Its appearance gave a mighty boost to everyone's spirits, as it brought the hope of rescue to our men. In spite of the fierce resistance and the many casualties on both sides, the enemy gained the counterscarp. From there, to counter the five batteries, they began to throw earth in the fosse, digging it up from the foundations of the wall by the counterscarp. Those in the fortress carried all that soil and the rubble from the wall damaged by the artillery inside, everyone working day and night, until the enemy cut embrasures into the wall, from which their arquebusiers fired on the entire fosse and prevented safe access to it. The engineer Giovanni Mormori invented a portable device of conjoined planks as protection from the arquebusiers' shots, and some more material was carried off, but not much. The said Giovanni, who had rendered excellent service for all that was needed, perished there. After the enemy had dumped enough earth to fill up the fosse, they made a hole in the wall of the counterscarp and from there, pushing up more earth in front of themselves, little by little they built a traverse up to the wall, on both sides of the batteries, padding it further with sacks of wool and bough sheaves to protect themselves from flanking fire from the walls.

---

81. According to Martinengo, as Contarini renders him here. Angelo Gatto and Riccoboni give May 28, and Podocataro, June 3. See Hill, *Cyprus*, 1013 and note 5.

# HISTORY OF THE EVENTS

While our men toiled in defense of Famagusta, in Candia they continued to rearm the galleys of that kingdom and prepare for the speedy dispatch of aid. From Corfu, Admiral Venier sent to Candia the provveditore of the fleet, Antonio Canale, with fifteen galleys to convey the galleys of the island to Corfu. Finding them not yet fully armed, however, and as one of the vessels that had arrived under the command of Nicolò Donato was still being unloaded, he left Marco Quirini in Candia to supervise the rearmament of the said galleys and the loading of the sailing ships. Canale himself departed for Canea where, due to the diligence and solicitude of the rector Luca Michiel, he found all galleys already armed and in good condition.

In the month of May the galleys of Lodovico da Porto, Piero Capello, Daniel Moro, Valerio Valaresso, and Zuan Strafoldo put out to sea from Venice.

From Cyprus, Ali Pasha arrived at the island of Negroponte with fifty-five galleys, and found there Pertau Pasha with the rest of the armada. After joining forces, they set out all together from the island of Negroponte and on June 14 reached Milos. On the following morning he took off under foresails only, to avoid being spotted by the islanders in Candia, and as darkness fell in the evening, he unfurled the mainsails as well and changed course to Cape Meleca.[82] The same night of the fifteenth of the same month they entered Souda, disembarked, seized many people of the local farmsteads, and destroyed and burned what they could. The enslaved Christians informed them that there were thirty galleys in Candia and another thirty in Canea. They left Souda on the eighteenth of the month with forty galleys to devastate the coasts round about the island, but contrary winds forced them to return back to port.

[At Famagusta] on Cyprus, the Turks, who now controlled the fosse and could not be attacked except from above and only if they were careless, began to tunnel under the ravelin, under the tower of Santa Nappa and those of Andruzzi and Campo Santo, under the curtain, and under the great tower of the Arsenal. Our men were no longer able

---

82. A promontory to the northeast of Canea, possibly the ancient Drepanum, modern Cape Drepano.

to hinder them from the few flanks [of the wall] and threw wildfire grenades upon them, which caused great damage as the woolsacks and the bundled sticks caught fire. To those who ventured to destroy the sacks Bragadin gave a ducat apiece. Counter-tunnels were dug at all those sites, supervised by an engineer, the knight Maggi, who attended to all that was needed as diligently and courageously as he could, but these were not able to thwart them, except at the towers of Santa Nappa, Andruzzi, and Campo Santo, because they were empty. Several sorties in the fosse were made, by day and night, to spy out the mining tunnels and set the bough sheaves and wool on fire. With marvelous industry and dedication Baglione, who supervised all these actions, never ceased to harass the enemy with all sorts of inventions of ingenious design. He divided the companies between the batteries, and added to each site a company of Albanians; on foot or on horseback, time and again they displayed great valor.

On June 21, they set fire to the mine under the tower of the Arsenal, in charge of Giambelat Bey. The powerful explosion split the thick wall, opened a breach, and brought down more than half of it, destroying as well a section of the parapet that had been constructed to oppose the attacks. A large number of Turks immediately swarmed up the rubble and carried their standards to the top, where Captain Pietro Conte was in charge with his company, severely shaken by the explosion. But Nestor Martinengo arrived promptly with his company and they were repulsed. Reinforcements were sent up five or six times, but the enemy could not accomplish what they wanted. Baglione fought there in person, while Bragadin and Quirini stood in arms close behind, ready to encourage the troops. The castellan Andrea Bragadin displayed marvelous feats of arms with the artillery of the spur throughout the assault and mowed down a great number of enemies during this attack, which lasted five hours. A large multitude of Turks perished there. Our losses were about one hundred wounded and killed, due to an accidental explosion of our grenades which, because of improper handling, burned many of the troops. There died Count Giovanni Francesco Goro and Captain

# HISTORY OF THE EVENTS

Bernardino Ugubio, while Ercole Malatesta, Captain Pietro Conte, and other captains and officers were badly wounded by the stones.

The following night a frigate arrived from Candia. It brought news of aid, sure and certain, and spread joy and encouragement. Under the command of Captain Marco Grivellatore and the knight Maggi flanked retrenchments were constructed at all sites under attack and where noise from digging mining tunnels was heard. Barrels, crates, and sacks full of wet earth, as well as mattresses were used. The Greeks had speedily brought whatever they had available, and as there was no more canvass they brought hangings, curtains, carpets, and finally even their bed linens to make the said sacks. These were used as an excellent and quick method to rebuild the parapets, which were ruined by the furious and never-ceasing artillery fire. All that was destroyed at day was rebuilt at night, with no sleep at all. The soldiers were on the wall all the time, continuously inspected by the officers, and everyone hardly slept, except during the midday heat. There was no other time to rest, because the enemy called to arms all the time to leave no respite to our men.

On the twenty-ninth of the month [the Turks] set on fire the mine cut in the stonework of the ravelin. It shattered everything and opened a large breach. Allowed easy access, the enemy rushed madly to the top, Mustafa being present throughout [the attack]. Count Hercole Martinengo's company took the brunt of the initial assault and pushed them back, fighting in the open as the parapet was destroyed by the mine. Of our captains there were killed Sergeant-major Celio of the grenadiers and Erasmo da Fermo, and Captain Soldatello, Antonio d'Ascoli, Giovanni d'Istria. Many other ensigns and officers were wounded; about thirty soldiers died there as well. At the Arsenal, the enemy was repulsed with great losses, while only five of our men were killed. There died Captain Giacomo da Fabriano, and Count Nestor Martinengo was wounded by an arquebus shot in the left leg. The attack lasted six hours. The bishop of Limasol stood there with the Cross, encouraging the soldiers. There were also brave women who carried arms, rocks, and water to assist the soldiers.

While the Turkish armada was at Souda, on the nineteenth [of the month], four sailing ships were sent from Venice, loaded with soldiers and war materiel for the kingdom of Candia. They miraculously navigated no farther than three miles from the enemy fleet, but the enemy did not spot them due to the light morning fog that hid them from the sight of the enemy armada that was at Souda. By the will of God they passed through safely to Candia.[83] At the same time, another ship arrived in Canea as well, carrying Corsican soldiers dispatched to garrison that city.

The following day, which was June 20, Ali sent Uluj Ali with forty galleys to Rhetymno. Ali himself landed a large number of men on the island, but the rectors, who had diligently prepared its defense and the garrisons of the fortresses, especially those of Canea, offered a spirited resistance to the Turks, including those who attacked on land, and forced them to retreat with great losses. Uluj Ali with his forty galleys reached Rhetymno, a site opened to attack from all sides. Finding it abandoned, he devastated the entire place without resistance. Upon his return, the entire fleet sailed from Souda to Turlurù.[84] Passing by Canea, they suffered damage from land-based fire, and one of the shots took out the rostrum of [the galley of] the corsair Kara Ali.[85] He disembarked many Turks at Turlurù, and they burned down and sacked many farmsteads. Two days later, a sea storm drove twelve of his galleys to the shore and three of them capsized and could not be recovered. As the weather grew better, Ali prepared to leave. The two pashas had each galley fire a shot and hoist lanterns on the yardarms to announce the departure so that the men who had landed would return to the ships. The pashas waited the entire day and the following night ready to sail. Late on the next day, seeing that no more were coming, they ordered a head count of the

---

83. This repetitive sentence is typical of Contarini's style and cannot be rendered concisely without taking too much liberty with the text.

84. A Venetian fortress on the highest point of the small island of St. Theodore opposite Platanias, c. 11 km or 7 miles west of Chania/Canea.

85. "Black Ali," Contarini has "Caurali," a noted Algerian corsair who operated primarily on the Italian and Spanish coasts.

men to figure how many were missing. As is their custom, the count was conducted with beans. It was found that the galleys were short of 3,700 Turks, and they stayed to continue the devastation of the island. Knowing [however] that they were at a disadvantage, the said fleet left Turlurù and sailed for Cerigo,[86] where they landed at San Nicolò and devastated many places. From there they sailed for Zonchio or Navarino to tar.

The rectors of Candia were eager to send aid to Famagusta, and after the arrival of the five ships they wanted to send them without delay to that kingdom. They decided, therefore, that it was mandatory to dispatch them as soon as possible. By all means, sending aid to such an important kingdom was to be sped up, definitely before the Turkish fleet sailed west, as it was expected to do for sure. They also determined that the ships destined for Cyprus needed an escort of at least thirty galleys. Provveditore Quirini, who undertook to accompany the ships to Famagusta, did not have all his galleys ready and duly sent to Provveditore Canale in Canea, asking him to send over all available serviceable galleys to the extent that he could do so safely. Canale, aware of how important it was to send reinforcements to Famagusta, set out from Canea as soon as he could and sailed to Candia in person with the galleys. There, together with the lords of Candia, they decided that as the ships were not yet ready to sail, Quirini was to spy out the whereabouts of the enemy. Thus, on July 2, Quirini set sail to catch informants.

By the will of God, our lord Pope Pius V finally concluded the Holy League and confederation between himself, the Catholic king of Spain, and the Venetians, and not only for defense but for perpetual offensive as well. Its forces included: from the said Pontiff, twelve armed galleys, three thousand infantry, and 250 horse; from the Catholic king, three-sixths of all forces and expenses; from the Venetians, two sixths, as it is properly detailed in the agreement, signed on May 20 by the confederates, solemnly proclaimed at the consistory on May 25, and published in Venice on June 11, the

---

86. Greek Kythera. San Nicolò de Modari is one of the two townships on the island, built by Venice in 1567.

day of our Lady. The league concluded, his Holiness never ceased, through letters and envoys, to urge most concernedly the king and the Venetians to promptly unite and not only provide timely relief for the besieged Famagusta but attack the enemy as well.

In the month of June the galleys of Evangelista Zurla, Polo Capello, and Francesco Pesaro put out to sea from Venice.

Admiral Venier, who was in Corfu, resolved to send two galleys to Zakynthos to spy on the Turkish armada and on July 1 dispatched Zuan Loredan and Colane Drasco of Cres. On July 5, they got word to Cephalonia that the Turkish armada had sailed from Navarino to Zakynthos to devastate the island, reporting all details to his Excellency. Thereupon he sent General Francesco Tron, teamed up with the same Cresan galley, to obtain fresh information. At Cape Ducato[87] they were attacked by Kara Ali, who had sailed with ten galleys to devastate Little Cephalonia.[88] Tron was captured on return from the sea.[89] The Cresan managed to get away in the canal of Corfu. The pashas were very pleased by the seizure of Tron's galley and by the news that a good part of the Venetian fleet was at Corfu, and they decided to sail to the island to harass it. In the meantime, Admiral Venier heard about the capture of the galley and, wary of the enemy armada, decided to depart for Messina and join forces with the Spanish and papal fleets. Before setting sail, he sent the Cypriot Giovanni Battista Benedetti to Quirini and Canale in Candia, requesting that they sail as soon as possible and with as many galleys as they had for Messina, where they would find the entire fleet united together. On the eighth of the said month, after another six

---

87. Cape Ducato is located on the southern side of the island of Lefkada, now connected to the mainland by a causeway. Since 1479, with a brief interruption from 1500 to 1503, the island was an Ottoman possession.

88. I was not able to identify that location; it is possible that Contarini refers to Ithaca.

89. Contarini writes "havendo presa la volta del mare," referring to the navigational technique deployed in dependable wind wheels, first perfected by the Portuguese in the Atlantic, here apparently indicating similar conditions of sailing in the Ionian Sea.

galleasses had arrived in Corfu, Venier set out with fifty light galleys, six large galleys, and three sailing ships. At Merlere he transferred the victuals and munitions of one of them onto the galleys and sent it back to Corfu.

In Cyprus, the enemy saw what losses they had sustained at the two attacks of Famagusta and changed their approach. Their artillery began a furious bombardment everywhere. As the Christians pulled back, they went to work with the upmost speed and constructed seven new forts facing the fortress, and brought in guns from the more distant ones. When they reached the number of eighty, they went on firing them with such ferocity that on the day of July 8, including the night, five thousand shots were counted. The parapets were ruined to the point that they could be repaired only at enormous loss because our men who worked on them were continuously killed by artillery fire and by the raging tempest of the arquebuses so that few remained standing. The retreat of the ravelin was demolished to such an extent by shot and hoe that the footway behind it disappeared. This was because as they reinforced the parapets from the inside they encroached on the footway, and had to enlarge it with gangplanks. The knight Maggi constructed a mine under the ravelin so that if it were lost, the enemy would pay a huge price for gaining it.

On July 9, the third attack began on the ravelin, the tower of Santa Nappa and that of Andruzzi, on the curtain, and the tower of the Arsenal, and lasted more than six hours. They were repulsed on all four points, but the ravelin had to be given up to the enemy with heavy losses on both sides, because during the assault our men could not use their piques due to the restricted space, and as they turned to retreat at Baglione's command, they were thrown in confusion and mingled with the Turks just as our mine was set on fire. A horrendous spectacle blew up more than a thousand of the enemy and more than a hundred of our men. Captain Roberto Malvezzi was killed there, and Captain Marchetto da Fermo was severely injured. Captain David Noce, quartermaster, was killed at the assault on the Arsenal, and Nestor Martinengo was wounded by an artillery shrapnel.

The attack went on uninterruptedly for four hours. The Famagustans, women and children included, demonstrated their valor at all sites. The ravelin was so shattered by the mine that no attempt was made to retake it, given that it provided no protection. Only the old[90] flank remained standing; another mine was prepared there. The gate of Limasol faced the ravelin and was lower than it; it was kept always open as it had a heavy iron portcullis studded with spikes and closed by cutting a rope. Through it material from the ravelin was brought in. For four days the enemy did not approach it but then they entrenched themselves on the higher ground and from the higher flanks did not allow anyone to exit through the gate as they were wary of the frequent attacks launched though it by our troops.

On July 13, Quirini returned to Candia and brought the news that the Turkish armada had sailed west. On the fourteenth of the same month, Barzotto Barbaro was on the verge of delivering the reinforcements to Famagusta, but a storm shipwrecked him on the shore. It was a great disaster as now more time was needed to aid the fortress because another ship had to carry the troops. As the latter were not ready, Quirini sailed to the channel of Rhodes to reconnoiter and get news about Famagusta.

On the day of July 14, the enemy troops [at Famagusta] on Cyprus moved to attack the gate. Opening fire at all other points, they proceeded to plant their standards right in front of the gate. Baglione and Luigi Martinengo, who were in charge of the gate's defenses, raised the soldiers' spirits, and they burst out and killed and put to flight the better part of them. The mine on the flank was set on fire and killed four hundred Turks. Baglione captured an enemy standard, snatching it from the hands of an ensign. On the following day, the mine under the curtain was blown up. But, as it did not benefit them much, [the Turks] held back the prepared attack and went on to enlarge and raise higher the traverses in the fosse to make their attacks safer. After digging out all the terrain in front of the counterscarp,

---

90. Contarini uses "solo il fianco stanco," which I take to mean part of the original structure before reinforcements were added.

they pitched their pavilions there, and our soldiers could not see them. They mounted seven pieces of artillery on the counterscarp in a way that they were hidden from sight: two at the ravelin of the tower of Santa Nappa, one at that of Andruzzi, and two at each side of the battery at the curtain. They came to dig under the parapets protected by tables covered in raw hides. Those inside threw grenades at them and on occasion sallied forth from the sorties to harass them but that resulted in great losses for the Christians. Our forces patched up the parapets with wet buffalo hides stuffed with earth, rags, and water-soaked cotton, fastened all together with ropes.

The women of Famagusta were divided in companies per each quarter and supervised by an Orthodox monk.[91] They went to work every day at designated spots, carrying stones and water, which was stored by all batteries in half-barrels to put down the incendiary grenades hurled by the Turks. After failing to take the gate, [the Turks] invented a new, unheard-of device. They gathered great quantities of a wood called *teglia*, which burns easily, giving a foul odor,[92] piled it up in front of the gate, and flared up such a blaze with fascines and beams suffused with pitch, that it was altogether impossible to quench it, even though water casks where cast down from the tall cavalier and burst open over it. The said fire lasted four days and the great heat and stench forced our men to pull back. [The Turks] climbed down into the lower flanks and began to dig new mines. The gate was closed, as it was no longer possible to keep it open. In no time at all (like a marvel, one can say) [the defenders] cleared up the piazza of the ravelin and set up a gun against the gate, which those inside had walled up with rocks, earth, and other matter.

In the city, there was extreme shortage, everything lacking except hope, the courage of the commanders, and the ardor of the soldiers. There was no wine. Fresh meat, vegetables, and cheese could be had only at excessive price. The horses, asses, and cats were consumed.

---

91. Cotarini uses "Calojero" from the Greek καλόγερος.

92. Most likely a local product, with the Italianate name deriving from the Latin *teda*, for a kind of pinewood suffused with pitch, used for kindling fires and for torches.

There was nothing to eat but bread and beans. Vinegar diluted with water was drunk, but it was exhausted before long.

The digging of mines under the cavalier of the gate was heard; they worked at all points more furiously than ever. At the fosse against the battery of the curtain [the Turks] heaped up a mound of earth as tall as the wall. Before long, they reached the wall of the counterscarp at the entrance of the tower of the Arsenal, after constructing a cavalier reinforced from the outside with hawsers, and as tall as ours. Within the walls there were left 500 Italian soldiers in fighting condition and these were worn out by the long watches and the toil of fighting under the blazing sun. The larger and better part of the Greek troops were killed.

By June 20, the fortress had been reduced to a very poor condition, without defenders and deprived of foodstuff, with no hope for aid. The [citizens] had given up their lives and possessions for their deliverance and in service of the most illustrious Government [of Venice]. The city leaders therefore wrote a letter to Bragadin, beseeching him to consider surrendering on honorable terms, which would safeguard the honor of their wives and the lives of their children, who would become spoils of the enemy. Bragadin responded with words of consolation, entreating them that they were not to fear, that assistance would come, and sought to alleviate the terror that had seized everyone's heart. At their insistence, he sent a frigate to Candia to appraise them of the condition they were in.[93]

King Philip of Spain prepared his fleet and put it in charge of Don Juan of Austria, brother of His Majesty, appointed him leader, commander-in-chief, and supreme commander of the entire undertaking, and ordered him to load the Spanish infantry detailed to the fleet and embark as soon as possible with the Austrian princes Rudolf and Ernest, the sons of Emperor Maximilian [II], who were called to Germany by their father.[94] Don Juan of Austria accepted

---

93. The date of the request is uncertain, but it appears that it was in the beginning of July; the frigate was sent on July 14. See Hill, *Cyprus*, 1019–22.

94. Archduke Rudolf, the future Emperor Rudolf II (1552–1612), and

## HISTORY OF THE EVENTS

the command of the fleet consigned to him and put out to sea from Catalonia together with the said princes with forty-seven galleys. On the twenty-sixth of the month he arrived in Genoa. He was met twenty miles out, that is at Savona, by two ambassadors, and all three were received by the signoria in majesty, with all the honors and acclamations that are accorded to princes of their rank.

Admiral Venier arrived with the fleet from Corfu at Messina on July 24. He was met there by Marc'Antonio Colonna, the admiral of His Holiness, with twelve galleys armed by His Holiness and four from Malta.

On the twenty-sixth of the same month Quirini, who had not obtained any fresh news, returned to Candia. There he found an order from Admiral Venier that he was to go and join his Excellency at Corfu, though it appeared more urgent to assist Famagusta than to sail to join the admiral. Without aid the fortress was sure to fall, while the outcome of a naval battle was uncertain. They discussed this, and other issues, and it was decided that they should sail [to Famagusta]. Twenty galleys were assigned to Quirini to escort the transports, but as they were not yet ready, it was resolved that the expedition would set sail on the last day of the said month.

After devastating the settlements of Zakynthos and Cephalonia, the Turkish fleet relocated to Butrint, opposite the island of Corfu,[95] hoping to find the Venetian fleet there. From there, forty galleys were sent to Sopot,[96] where they took on sipachis to make up for those lost on the island of Candia. Around July 1, while the forty galleys were at Sopot, they spied two armed vessels, which were

---

Archduke Ernest of Austria (1553–95) were raised and educated in the court of their uncle, Philip II of Spain, and only returned to Vienna in 1571.

95. An ancient Greek and Roman city and bishopric in Epirus, currently Butrint in Albania. It became a Venetian possession in 1386, but during the war it was ruined and devastated.

96. Sopot was a settlement and fortress between Himarë and Sarandë on the Albanian coast, north of Butrint, near the modern village of Borsh in Albania. It dates back to medieval times and was re-fortified by the Ottomans in the sixteenth century.

two Venetian galleys, under the command of Michiel Barbarigo and Piero Bertolazzi from Zadar. Some Turkish galleys gave chase, the galleys fled toward Corfu, and at Port Kassiopi were met by Uluj Ali with ten galleys. Barbarigo and Bertolazzi thought that these were Venetian galleys, and boldly went ahead to meet them but then realized that they were enemy galleys. Losing hope and separated, they gave up without resistance. Uluj Ali conducted them both to Butrint, to the great pleasure of Ali.

Ali then left with the rest of the galleys for Sopot. At that place, on the twenty-second of the month, the day of the Magdalen, he seized the ships *Leze* and *Moceniga*, which had put out to sea from Venice on the eighth of the month. [The Venetian ships] defended themselves against eighteen enemy galleys and inflicted substantial damage on them, not giving quarter to the enemy. As long as they were in a favorable position they defended themselves courageously. They were taken only after a large number of galleys arrived from Sopot, alerted by the thunder of the guns.

Uluj Ali conducted the ships to Sopot, and with eighteen galleys went out on the corso in Dalmatia. At Sopot, Ali disembarked fifteen hundred men, sipachis and Janissaries, all armed with arquebuses, for an attack on Sopot. The arquebus fussilade forced the soldiers off the wall, and [the assailants] mounted it. Seeing themselves overwhelmed, the defenders of the place set fire to their munitions, and the destruction was such that five hundred Turks were burned. In the end, the [Turks] were partly killed, partly captured, but Captain Manolis Mormori was seized and enslaved.

From Sopot the [Turkish] fleet sailed to Durazzo[97] with Uluj Ali, who was furious with the Ragusans for not wanting to hand over the galley of Francesco Tron, which had managed to slip away after those in the galley cut through the chain[98] and found refuge in the said port

---

97. Modern Durrës in Albania, and an important fortress on the coast. It became Venetian possession in 1392 and was seized by the Ottomans in 1501.

98. The galley had probably been towed to port by its captors with the crew unsecured.

of Ragusa.⁹⁹ Thereafter Ali left Durazzo and, entering the Gulf with the entire fleet, appeared before Dulcigno¹⁰⁰ and forced it to surrender, as its defenders were not able to fight on two fronts, on land and sea. Up to that point they had defended themselves courageously and held their ground. But when they saw the fleet and despaired of being able to hold out on both sides, they surrendered to avoid worse, saving the liberty of all inhabitants and the lives of the soldiers. But as the pasha on the land and the one on the sea disagreed as to whom the place had surrendered, they enslaved many, not allowing them to walk away free, except for the governor-general of Dalmatia, Martinengo, with some soldiers and the rector of the place, Geronimo Venier. After that Ali took Antivari,¹⁰¹ which the rector of the place, Alessandro Donato, surrendered in a cowardly way. A storm wrecked eight Turkish galleys there. The Turks garrisoned Antivari and sailed for Budva.¹⁰² Its seaside defenses being weak, they took it on the above-mentioned conditions, the podestà being Agostin Pasqualigo.

Around the middle of July, Ali went with the fleet to Castel Nuovo,¹⁰³ were they tarred. Meanwhile, Uluj Ali and Kara Hodja went out on the corso in the Gulf with sixty galleys. They sacked the town on Lesina.¹⁰⁴ At Curzola¹⁰⁵ they did not do anything apart from

---

99. Modern Dubrovnik, then an independent city maintaining a precarious balance between Venice and the Ottomans.

100. Modern Ulcinj, on the southern coast of Montenegro, a Venetian possession between 1405 and 1571. Both Durrës and Ulcinj are on the Adriatic Sea, but Ali's short foray north along the coast crossed the line between the Ottoman-controlled and the Venetian-controlled parts of the lower Adriatic.

101. Modern Bar in Montenegro, about 25 km north of Ulcinj on the coast.

102. Another Venetian-held fortress on the modern Montenegrin coast, c. 35 km north of Bar.

103. Modern Herceg Novi at the entrance of the bay of Kotor in Montenegro, an Ottoman possession since 1482.

104. Modern Hvar, one of the larger Croatian islands, since 1409 a Venetian possession. Contarini writes that the Ottomans sacked the "Borgo," likely the city of Hvar, where the major Venetian naval installations were located.

105. Modern Korčula, the second-largest Croatian island. Vlati, modern

burning down a village called Vlati, whose cowardly male inhabitants fled, but the women defended it vigorously, held out, and repulsed the enemy.

The ships at Candia detailed to carry aid for Famagusta were not yet ready, nor could they be dispatched until August due to the intervening problems, such as Barzotto Barbaro's shipwreck and the inclement weather. But God must be praised for all the impediments that had occurred, because it was all to the benefit of the Christians. There is no doubt that if the aid had been escorted by twenty-five, or even thirty galleys to Famagusta (as had been decided) the armada of the League would not have fought without them nor would it have sought battle. Thus, everyone better be quiet, and God be praised for what He had granted us to this point.

In the month of July, Zuan Malipiero and Daniel Pasqualigo put out to sea from Venice.

At Famagusta, the enemy had completed their mines, and on July 29 they set them on fire. In the meantime, work continued on rebuilding the parapets demolished by the artillery in the usual manner under the supervision of Tiepolo. As all other stuff was exhausted, the sacks were made from kersey cloth.[106] The three mines at the cavalier did great damage, bringing down the better part of it and killing Commander Rondacchi.[107] The mine at the Arsenal destroyed the remaining part of the tower and blew up nearly an entire company of our soldiers. Only the two flanks remained standing. The enemy now endeavored to demolish these flanks and to mount the other batteries. The assault lasted from the twentieth hour until the night, and very many enemies were killed. Among many, Giacomo Strambali stood out with his valor at the assault, as did others.

---

Blato, is a land-bound settlement on the island.

106. Heavy, coarse English-made woolen cloth, a staple of the Venetian trade in the Levant.

107. The commander of the light cavalry.

On the following morning, at dawn, they attacked at all points, and the assault lasted six hours. Our losses were minimal, as the Turks fought more reservedly than before. The greatest pressure was from the seaside, the galleys firing in all attacks and bombarding all parts of the city they could reach. The attack was repulsed, but the situation was grave, and as there were no more than seven barrels of powder left in the city, the commanders decided to surrender on honorable conditions.

On August 1, in the afternoon, a truce was concluded with a representative of Mustafa, with whom it was decided that on the following morning two hostages were to be given on each side while the negotiations were underway. On Bragadin's orders, Count Hercole Martinengo and Matteo Colsi, citizen of Famagusta, went out as hostages on our side. From the enemy, the lieutenant of Mustafa and the Aga of the Janissaries came into the city. They were met at the gate by Baglione with two hundred arquebusiers, and our men were met by the enemy with great pomp, by cavalry and arquebusiers, and Mustafa's favorite son in person. Baglione negotiated the terms with the hostages who had come in. Besides saving the lives, arms, and possessions [of the defenders], he requested five pieces of artillery, three fine horses, and safe conduct to Candia in the accompaniment of galleys. The Greeks were to stay in their houses and enjoy what they had, living as Christians.

Mustafa assented to what was demanded and signed off on it. Galleys and other vessels entered the harbor forthwith and the soldiers began to embark. The better part embarked and only the commanders remained to come on board. On the morning of August 5, Bragadin sent Count Nestor Martinengo with a letter to Mustafa, letting him know that he wished to go out and hand over the keys that evening and that he had left Tiepolo in charge of the fortress. As up to this moment Turks and Christians had interacted, in deed and word, in a courteous and trustful manner, he implored him not to allow those inside to be molested while he was outside. Mustafa responded verbally to be conveyed to Bragadin that he could go out whenever he pleased, that he would gladly see him and make his acquaintance, given the great courage he had displayed, as had the other captains and soldiers, whose valor he would praise wherever he happened to be, and that [Bragadin] could rest assured that he would not allow any annoyance to those inside the city. Martinengo came back and reported accordingly.

That evening, around the twenty-first hour, Bragadin, accompanied by Baglione, Alvise Martinengo, Giovanni Antonio Quirini, the castellan Andrea Bragadin, the knight dalle Haste, Carlo Ragonasco, Francesco Stracco, Hettor of Brescia, Girolamo da Sacile, and other noblemen and fifty soldiers and commanders armed with swords, and the soldiers with arquebuses, went out and walked to Mustafa's pavilion. At first, he received them with courtesy, had them seated, and spoke with them. As they passed from one subject to another, he raised the issue that Bragadin had some slaves murdered during the truce, which was absolutely not true. He then rose angrily to his feet and ordered them tied up, disarmed as they were, for they had not been allowed to enter the pavilion with their weapons. Thus bound, they were led out one at a time to the open space in front of the pavilion and cut to pieces in his presence.

Bragadin was made to stretch out his neck two or three times, as if they were to cut off his head, which he bore showing no fear, and then they cut off his ears. As he lay on the ground, Mustafa addressed him, blaspheming against our Savior, saying, "Where is now your Christ? Why doesn't he deliver you?" but Bragadin never responded to that. Count Hercole, the hostage, who was also bound, was hidden by Mustafa's eunuch until the killing frenzy passed, and he later spared his life, taking him as a slave. The three Greeks who were in the pavilion were let go, but all the soldiers who were in the camp, and all other Christians, to the number of three hundred, were all murdered at once, never suspecting such perfidy and cruelty. Those on board the galleys were chained up and enslaved.

On the second day after the carnage, which was [August] 7, Mustafa entered the city for the first time and had Tiepolo hanged. Count Nestor, who was in the city while the others were murdered and enslaved, hid himself for five days in the houses of Greeks. After that, unable to find shelter for the penalties were too harsh, he surrendered and became slave of the sanjakbey of Birejik, with a ransom of 500 zecchini,[108] and stayed with him in the camp. On Friday, August 17, which is a holiday for them, Bragadin was paraded around the forts of the city in the presence of Mustafa. He made him carry two baskets of earth, one up and one down, each battery, and kiss the ground every time he passed before him. Then they took him to the port, put him in a basket sling, and hoisted him up onto a yardarm, spread like a stork, to display him to all slaves and Christian soldiers who were in the port. After that they took him to the piazza, stripped him naked, made him sit at the grid of the pillory, and most cruelly flayed him alive. Such were his grit and faith, that his spirits never faltered, and with a firm heart he kept reproaching them for breaking faith. Showing no sign of wavering, he commended himself to God and expired by the grace of His divine Majesty. His skin was taken, stuffed with straw, attached to the yardarm of a galiot, and paraded along the coasts of Syria.

The Turks had 200,000 men of every condition at the siege of Famagusta. Of these, 80,000 were salaried soldiers, 14,000 Janissaries, recruited from all the garrisons of Syria, Caramania, Anatolia, and from the High Porte, and 60,000 were sword-armed irregulars. During the sixty-five days of bombardment, 140,000 iron balls were fired.

The [commanding] persons in the army with Mustafa were: the pasha of Aleppo, the pasha of Anatolia, Mustafer Pasha of Nicosia (killed), the pasha of Caramania, the aga of the Janissaries, Giambelat Bey (killed), the sanjakbey of Tripoli, the beylerbey of Greece, the pasha of Sivas and Marash,[109] sanjakbey Ferhat,[110] the sanjakbey of

---

108. For the value of the Venetian gold ducat *(zecchino)* in 1571, see Jean-Claude Hocquet, "Venice," in *The Rise of the Fiscal State in Europe, 1200–1815* Ricard Bonney, ed. (Oxford: Oxford University Press, 1999), 408. Birejik (Urfa) was one of the *sanjaks* of Syria, in the *eyalet* of Aleppo, on the Euphrates.

109. Marash or Ablistan was a Syrian *sanjak* in the *eyalet* of Aleppo.

110. Contarini uses "Ferca Famburaro," mangling the proper name Ferhat and posing the title, which likely derives from *flammularius* "small banner

Aintap[111] (killed), Suleiman Bey (killed), three sanjakbeys of Arabia (one killed), Mustafa Bey, commander of the irregulars (killed), Ferhat Bey of Malatya (killed), the sanjakbey of Divriği (killed).[112]

Christian captains killed at Famagusta: Astorre Baglione, Alvise Martinengo, Frederico Baglione, the knight dall'Asta, vice-governor, David Noce, quartermaster, Mignano of Perugia, sergeant-major, Count Sigismondo of Casoldo, Count Francesco di Lobi of Cremona, Francesco Troncavilla, Aniballe Adamo of Fermo, Scipione of Città di Castello, Carlo Ragonasco of Cremona, Francesco Stracco, Roberto Malvezzo, Cesare of Adversa, Bernardino of Agubio, Francesco Bugon of Verona, Jacopo of Fabiano, Bastian of Sole Fiorentino, Ettore of Brescia, who replaced Cesare of Adversa, Flaminio of Florence, who replaced Bastian of Sole, Bartolomeo dalle Cernole, Erasmo of Fermo, who replaced dalle Cernole, Giovanni Battista of Rivarolo, Giovanni Francesco of Venice.

Captains enslaved: Count Hercole Martinengo, with Giulio Cesare Ghelso of Brescia, soldier, Count Nestor Martinengo, (escaped), Marco Crivelatore, Ercole Malatesta, Piero Conte of Mont'Albero, Oratio of Veletri, Alvise Pezano, Count Jacopo della Corbara, Giovanni of Istria, Soldatelli of Agubio, Giovanni of Ascoli, Antonio of Ascoli, Bastian of Ascoli, Salgano of Città di Castello, the marquis of Fermo, Giovanni Antonio of Piacenza, Carletto Naldo, Lorenzo Fornaretti, Bernardo of Brescia, Bernardino Coco, Simone Bagnese, who replaced David

[holder]," as last name. "Famburaro" would be direct translation of *sanjak*; the identification was proposed by Hill, *History of Cyprus*, 4:20 n. 4, and it makes sense, for even though the title *sanjakbey* is also used, Contarini's account here depends on Count Martinengo's and other sources, and the confusion of Ottoman names and titles is normal. It is possible that the person in question is the Bosnian fellow-countryman of Mustafa Pasha, Ferhat Pasha, who was *sanjakbey* of Bosnia in the 1560s and built a mosque there in 1562. Another Ferhat, Bey of Rhodes, was appointed *sanjakbey* of Famagusta after the conquest.

111. Another of the Syrian *sanjaks* of Aleppo, modern-day Gaziantep in southeastern Anatolia, Turkey, c. 100 km north of Aleppo.

112. A town in east-central Anatolia, Byzantine Tephrike, Armenian Tewrik, now in Turkey's province of Sivas.

Noce, Tiberio Ceruto, who replaced Count Sigismondo, Giuseppe of Lanciano, who replaced Francesco Troncavilla, Morgante, who replaced Annibale, the lieutenant who replaced Scipione, the ensign who replaced Roberto, Ottavio of Rimini, who replaced Francesco Bugon, Mario of Fabiano, who replaced Giacomo, Francesco of Venice, who replaced Antonio, Matteo of Capua, Giovanni Maria of Verona, Mancino, Giovanni Mormori, engineer (killed), and the knight Maggi (enslaved).

The sanjakbey of Rhodes was appointed governor of Famagusta. Mustafa left 20,000 persons on the island and 2,000 horses, as Count Nestor Martinengo, who was set free from slavery, duly writes in the report to the most serene prince of Venice.[113]

## THE HOLY LEAGUE

As DON JUAN OF AUSTRIA had to depart from Genoa on the last day of July, on the morning of the previous day Rudolf and Ernest, accompanied for a short distance, continued their journey on horseback. On August 1, Don Juan set sail on board the galley *Reale*. On [August] 5, he left Juan de Cardona and Giovanni Andrea Doria with twelve galleys to lead the men, and he continued for Naples, where on the ninth of the same month he was received with a magnificent pageant and a celebration.

Meanwhile, in Candia they sped up the dispatch of assistance to Famagusta, being unaware that it was already in the hands of the enemy. On August 13, there arrived Giovanni Battista Benedetti, with orders from Admiral Venier and express commission from the Senate to depart forthwith for Messina, where Venier had gone to join the fleets of His Holiness and King Philip. Given the new order, they were forced to abandon the unfinished preparations for assistance, and also on the thirteenth [of the month] Quirini and Canale departed for Messina with all galleys.

---

113. Here the segment borrowed from Martinengo's account ends and Contarini continues with the affairs at sea.

The Turkish armada, refurbished at Castel Nuovo, returned to Budva, which they falsely accused (as is their habit) of having put to death certain Turks. For that, they enslaved everyone, and sacked and despoiled the entire place. Thence they sailed to Valona, from where Uluj Ali and Kara Hodja returned by the middle of the month with many slaves and booty. They gloated most at having snatched from the church of the Madonna of Lesina the standard of provveditore Canale, taking that for a good omen.

From Valona, Ali sent two galiots toward the island of Sicily and Uluj Ali with five galiots toward Calabria to catch informants. He then set sail for Saseno[114] and left there the treasurer and Mehmet Bey, being unwilling to move farther from Saseno until first hearing either from Constantinople or about the Christian armada.

Loading the transports with victuals and munitions, on August 21, Don Juan of Austria sailed with them from Naples, where he had been forced to stay for several days on account of bad weather. On the twenty-fourth of the same month he arrived at Messina. The city received him with great pomp. Among the many notable installations, a superbly designed wooden bridge was constructed, complete with several well-styled arches and decked out with the finest fabrics, with flares, and other adornments, and with many emblems praising his Highness. He was met by the galleys of Marc'Antonio Colonna and Sebastian Venier, firing infinite salvos of guns and arquebuses.

Now, news came to Messina that the Turkish armada was devastating Dalmatia, and the Venetian envoys diligently entreated the high lords to speed up their intervention, reporting in detail on the progress of the enemy. For that reason, on the following day the principal commanders and other lords sat in council. Sebastian Venier argued that the galleys at Candia would be prepared shortly, while everyone else was in doubt, not so much that they would not arrive, but that they would be late. Most everyone took a stance on that issue, as it was not clear what was to be done in the absence of the commander of the fleet at Candia.

---

114. Albanian Sazan, a small island off the Albanian coast, between the entrance of the Straight of Otranto and the entrance of the bay of Vlorë.

## HISTORY OF THE EVENTS

Ascanio dalla Cornia[115] presented an argument in the following vein: "Your Highness commanded me to give you in writing my opinion on what is to be done at present with the forces that we have ready here, presupposing, on the one hand, that we have in the fleet one hundred and forty six galleys, six galleasses, twenty sailing ships, and twenty fuste, and that we expect sixty more galleys from Candia, of which we have not heard anything for many days now. On the other, [we are presupposing] that the Turkish armada numbers two hundred and fifty sail under oar, and is now in Dalmatia, where there are also land troops of the Turk in the number of forty or fifty thousand men. I would say that given all of the above, your Highness does not have sufficient forces to go out and seek an engagement with the enemy fleet, nor to attempt a diversion or any other endeavor, without placing us in clear dander of a disastrous loss, as our numbers are quite unequal to those of the Turkish fleet.

"Also, it should be noted about the latter that it is well supplied with rowers and soldiers and with the men from three galleys and three sailing ships, and many others that they had picked up, all sailors. They have replenished their crews, and if there is shortage at any time, the land troops can provide them with as many men

---

115. Ascanio dalla Cornia or Corgna, appointed quartermaster-general (commander of the infantry) of the Holy League and chief advisor to Giovanni Andrea Doria, elaborated his position in a manifest to Don Juan that was published in Messina on August 24, the day after the council. For Ascanio's life and career, see Irene Fosi Polverini, "Della Cornia, Ascanio," DBI 36 (1988), online at http://www.treccani.it/enciclopedia/ascanio-della-cornia_(Dizionario-Biografico); and Maria Gabriella Donati Guerrieri, *Lo Stato di Castiglione del Lago e i della Corgna* (Castiglione del Lago: Grafica, 1972). Guerrieri also prints the manifest, ibid., 208. The manifest, as well as della Cornia's second manifest at the war council before the battle, were also printed in Florence, most likely shortly after his death: *Due discorsi dell' ill.mo s.or marchese Ascanio della Cornia maestro di campo generale della Santissima Lega. Dati da lui al sereniss. s. don Giouanni d'Austria circa al combattere con l'armata turchesca. Con la descrittione dell' esequie fatte in Perugia nella morte del medesimo. Et una canzone in lode del detto d'incerto autore* (Florence: Antonio Padouani, 1571). Contarini must have had either the texts of the published manifests or a copy of the edition and incorporated both manifests verbatim in his text.

as they need. Therefore, if your Highness could take us to Brindisi without running the risk of encountering the Turkish fleet (which I fear could happen, according to the opinion of the lords who are experts in navigation) I would consider that very well done indeed. This will warm the hearts of the Venetians, who (I think) are now quite troubled. It is also possible, once your Highness gets positioned in that place, so close to the enemy, that God would grant you a chance to do something good. However, if that involves the risk of running into the enemy fleet, I do not see what else your Highness could do but wait for the arrival of the galleys from Candia, or certain news that they are not coming. In the latter case (God forbid!) I am of the opinion that your Highness should reinforce as many galleys as possible, so that they are capable of sailing before the enemy fleet, and send the remaining ones with the sailing ships back to Brindisi. With the reinforced galleys, which must number at least seventy or eighty, it will be possible, I think, to aid the province of Dalmatia, which is being attacked by land and sea with (it can be said) no assistance from anywhere, and cause much trouble to the enemy. Besides, you would be poised to seize any opportunity that would present itself. The world will see that your Highness does everything possible to serve God and this Holy League. I would submit, of course (as I have said) to any better decision, for which I pray to God to grant us His aid and guidance."

By the end of August, Mehmet Bey and the treasurer left Valona to inform the Turkish fleet at Saseno of the conquest of Famagusta. The news inspired everyone to new endeavors. Shortly thereafter, the two galiots returned and reported that they had chased a frigate at Croton but it managed to escape. They also reported that the Christian fleets were preparing at Messina and that they had united their forces. Upon these news, [the fleet] set sail to the east straight away.

Meanwhile at Messina they awaited the arrival of the galleys from Candia. On September 2, the two provveditori, Quirini and Canale, arrived at Messina with sixty-two galleys, to the great delight and comfort of everyone, having been so eagerly expected, because without that squadron no decision could have been taken about the actions of the fleet. The previous day the marquis of Santa Croce and Giovanni Andrea Doria had arrived as well, after having been delayed at La Spezia, with twelve galleys. Shortly thereafter, eleven sailing ships and thirty galleys came in from Naples, and not long afterwards, so did those from Palermo. All the forces of the League having united therefore, joyful and comforted, they began deliberating.

From Saseno, the enemy sailed for Butrint, where it loaded five hundred horsemen, to be used in the devastation of the island of Corfu, as it was surrounded from all sides with galleys and men. But those from the fortress send three galleys to the bottom, the land troops suffered heavy casualties, and many of them were captured; among the captured was Basio the renegade, a person of high standing with the Grand Turk. As a result, many parts of the settlement were not touched and the cavalry, having ruined whatever it could, returned to its quarters. On September 10, they departed, and the enemy armada sailed to Parga,[116] where a chaush from the Porte of the Great Lord reached them with a detailed report of the conquest of Famagusta and with express orders to pursue the momentum at sea as well, not sparing any effort, to conquer all the islands round about, and by all means find the Christian armada wherever it may be and disperse, seize, and destroy it—as if all this were in their powers to do. Upon receiving his orders, on September 16, Ali left Parga and sailed for Lepanto with the entire fleet. He wanted to resupply the armada with biscuit and other victuals and then immediately to sail out to harass the Christians, according to the orders he had received from the Great Lord.

Assailed from all sides, Christendom was thrown in terror and confusion, hearing every hour of the carnage and destruction that the cruel beast, thirsty for human blood, wrought on the faithful, of the continuing advance of the savage enemy of Christ, who deployed every method and trick to scourge and destroy the Venetian Republic. There was nothing left to us but the firm hope that the

---

116. A port town in northwestern Greece, in Epirus, Venetian possession since 1401, burnt and destroyed by the Ottomans in 1537. In 1571 the Venetians were still in the process of rebuilding the fortress.

Lord God, who alone can grant any favor, and who is aware of, and knows our needs better than we do, delivers us through His mercy, managing the conjunction of His Christian fleets, which at this point were our only help, remedy, succor, and safety.

It was now heard and confirmed from everywhere that the said fleets had come together at the city of Messina and that their forces were: in the name of Pope Pius V, twelve light galleys; in the name of the Catholic King Philip of Spain, eighty-one light galleys and twenty-two sailing ships; and for the Signoria of Venice, one hundred and eight light galleys, six galleasses, and two sailing ships. Thus, in the allied forces of the Holy League there were in total two hundred and seven light galleys, including those of the Order of Saint John of Malta, besides a good number of frigates alongside them. They carried, apart from the usual number of oarsmen, convict rowers, and officers, twenty thousand Italian, Spanish, and German infantrymen, plus a good number of mercenaries, all in good order and well provided with munitions and victuals.

The commanders, Don Juan of Austria, commander-in-chief of the League, Marc'Antonio Colonna, admiral of His Holiness, and Sebastian Venier, admiral of the Venetians, considered different positions during the deliberations. There intervened the knight commander Ascanio dalla Cornia, Andrea Doria, Agostino Barbarigo, Marco Quirini, Antonio Canale, the secretary of the Venetians, their under-secretary and (many times) the princes of Urbino and Parma, Paolo Giordano Orsini, the marquis of Santa Croce, and other lords.

After many and diverse arguments were broached, Ascanio dalla Cornia spoke thus, "My most illustrious lords, I think that there are only two or three situations in which a general ought to avoid fighting. The first is if the damage inflicted by the loss would be greater, or of greater weight, than the benefit of victory. For example, when lord Guise attacked the kingdom of Naples, it would not have been prudent of the duke of Alba to give battle, because all that the French could have lost would have been their army, while we would have lost the army and the kingdom.¹¹⁷ The second case is when it is clear that the enemy army or fleet cannot last long, or are about to fall in disarray under pressure without fighting. I will cite the example of that person of glorious memory, the emperor and father of your Highness, who in the war of Saxony[118] never wanted to confront the Protestant army in the field, seeing that their League would not last long and that their army would dissolve itself shortly without fighting. The other case in which a leader should not fight if he could avoid it is when his numbers are so inferior to the enemy's that he could have no reasonable hope for victory.

"At present, your Highness is not in any of the first two situations. For even though the loss of the Christian armada would be of great importance, as those lords who have spoken before me have prudently and amply noted, nevertheless, given that we can fight if it suits us, it can be assumed that the enemy armada, even if it emerged victorious, would be so debilitated that the Turk would not be able to restore it quickly, and anyway our princes are not that weak to not find a way to recover, at least for defense. But if victory were to be ours, it would make it possible to hope for the revolt of Greece and other major dominions, although I do not believe (as I have said on other occasions) that with the forces that our League presently has, or will have in the future, the Turk can be seriously hurt, unless their fleet is broken first. But we cannot hope to win by wearing it down,

---

117. Ascanio refers to an episode of the French-Spanish war of 1557, when under the instigation of Pope Paul IV a French army under François, duke de Guise descended upon Italy en route to Naples, but the Spanish under Fernando Alvares de Toledo, the third duke of Alba and viceroy of Naples, evaded battle until the French impetus petered out. The Spanish eventually destroyed the main French forces at the battle of San Quentin, and Alba entered Rome. See Henry Kamen, *The Duke of Alba* (New Haven: Yale University Press, 2004), 49.

118. The Schmalkaldic War of 1546–47, in which the Catholic forces of Charles V defeated the Lutherans of Elector John Frederick I of Saxony and Landgrave Philip of Hesse. The war ended with the battle of Mühlberg on April 24, 1547, with the Protestants routed and John Frederick I taken prisoner.

nor will it fall apart because of lack [of supplies]. In fact, I fear there is such a danger on our part. However, as your Excellences have forces with which you can fight hoping for victory, it seems to me that we should strive to fight by all means, and not miss the opportunity.

"That is my position. The one thing that needs to be done is to see whether our forces are up to the task, in terms of manpower, and numbers and quality of vessels. So far as the men are concerned, I will have to confirm what these lords have already said, and admit that the Spaniards are for the most part rookies with little experience, and so are the Italians. The Germans are not of much use at sea, and there are not enough arquebusiers. However, I do not think the enemy would have very good men either, not better than ours in any case, because of the losses that they suffered last year and this year in the large army in Cyprus. Then, as for the numbers and quality of the vessels in the Turkish armada, intelligence disagrees, and I cannot really say whether it is superior or inferior to ours, and as I am not a great expert in maritime affairs, I cannot decide to what extent our galleasses and sailing ships counterbalance the greater number of Turkish galiots and fuste. In this matter I submit to the lords in the army who are more experienced than I am. At any rate, it seems to me that what you should do, my lords, is to commend us in part to Fortune, as military affairs cannot be guided so cautiously that Fortune would not claim her part, and sail out straight away and get the armada as quickly as possible to Brindisi or Corfu. There, close to the enemy, we can obtain reliable intelligence about their condition, and can make an informed decision on what appears to be the best course of action. If the issue of provisions or another matter I have not considered does not preclude it, I like Corfu much better than Brindisi, as it lays nearer the course and route that the Turkish armada has to take on its return to the East.

"A warning though: if we are to put out to sea, and if we sail out firmly resolved to fight in case we intercepted the enemy during their journey, your Highness must give and issue his orders in conformance with that decision, because if we were to sail irresolute, or as it is said, if we are of two minds, and if we have to consult and make a decision on the go, we will find ourselves in great confusion and will easily lose if perchance we come across the Turkish armada. This is my opinion, and as usual I will submit to those who know better than I."

Everyone agreed, acknowledging that it was what they ought to do. They resolved to set sail and, if the occasion presented itself, boldly confront the enemy. At this, his Highness, not wishing to leave any ambivalence, issued the marching orders. The fleet was divided into four squadrons, namely right wing, left wing, center, and reserve. The right wing consisted of fifty-three galleys under the command of Giovanni Andrea Doria. This wing was to fly a green pennant on the pennon.[119] The left wing, also of fifty-three galleys, was assigned to Agostino Barbarigo. It was to display yellow banderols on the right foist. The center, consisting of sixty-one galleys, was under the command of His Highness, and was to fly a deep blue standard upon the masthead. These three squadrons of one hundred and sixty-seven galleys were to sail in sync, always leaving a three to four galley-widths space between the center and the wings, so that on occasion each squadron could maneuver by itself if need be, according to the situation. The reserve was assigned to Don Álvaro da Bazán, marquis of Santa Croce. This squadron consisted of thirty-eight galleys and was to hoist white banners on the stern. Eight of these galleys, accompanied by Juan de Cardona, were to sail in the vanguard, twenty to twenty-five miles ahead of the armada.

Two fast frigates were to sail with them and relay every piece of information as events developed. If they were to discover such a number of vessels as to conclude that it was the enemy armada, they were to return back to the fleet and report in detail on what they had seen. Then Juan de Cardona was to take his designated position on the right wing and the other eight galleys were to rejoin the reserve, four behind each wing. The six galleasses were to be positioned in front of the center and wings, at a distance of half a mile or a little farther. Two of them, namely those of Antonio and

---

119. The upper or after spar of the lateen sail yard, here the peak of the mainyard.

Ambrogio Bragadin, were to be in front of the left wing, those of Giacomo Guoro and Francesco Duodo, the leader of the galleasses, in front of the center, and those of Andrea Pesaro and Piero Pisani, in front of the right wing, at a distance of a mile or so from one another, spanning the entire armada. Because the galleasses are not as easy to row as the light galleys, his Highness ordered them towed in case they could not move under sail.

His Highness and Colonna had to take care that their squadron towed the flagship galleass of Francesco Duodo; Sebastian Venier and Monsignor di Leyni to have theirs tow that of Giacomo Guoro; Agostino Barbarigo, that of Ambroggio Bragadin; Antonio Canale, that of Antonio Bragadin; the reverend Prior of Messina, that of Andrea Pesaro; and Giovanni Andrea Doria, the galleass of Pietro Pisani. His Highness was to stay in the middle of the center, with Marc'Antonio Colonna, the admiral of His Holiness, on his right side, and Sebastian Venier, admiral of the lords of Venice, on the left side. Next to Colonna was the flagship of Genoa, captained by Ettor Spinola, with the prince of Parma on board; next to Venier, the flagship of Savoy, on which was the prince of Urbino, commanded by Monsignor di Leyni. Behind His Highness and the other two admirals was the flagship of Spain, and that of the commendador mayor of Castile.[120]

Heading the right flank of the center, which separated it from the wing, was the flagship of Malta, commanded by the prior of Messina; on the left side, separating them from the wing, was the flagship of Pietro Lomellini, captained by Paolo Giordano Orsini. On the right wing, led by Doria, up front was positioned Juan de Cardona. On the left wing, next to Agostino Barbarigo, was positioned Antonio Canale, and on the other side of the wing, Marco Quirini. In all squadrons the galleys were positioned together, without any distinction between Venetian galleys, galleys from the West, and those of His Holiness. Furthermore, His Highness ordered that all captains and commanders of galleys and other vessels conducted themselves like good Christians and made everyone else do the same, arguing

---

120. Gil Andrada, who was also a Maltese knight.

## HISTORY OF THE EVENTS

that this being such a just endeavor, the blessed Lord would not fail to support them, and that as soon as the time came, everyone was to take their battle station calmly and without confusion, according to the orders issued.

These, and other orders, were issued with common consent and approval and accepted by everyone. On Sunday, September 16, they left Messina, having sent out the ships under the command of Giovanni Davalo the previous day. The same day, the armada reached the Fossa di San Giovanni.[121] Commendador Gil Andrada, who had been sent ahead to catch informants from the enemy fleet, was already there. He reported that on the fifth of the same month he had left Otranto after receiving news that the enemy armada had sailed out of Castel Nuovo at Kotor and gone to Valona. On [September] 17, our fleet reached Castel Bianco, on the next day Cape Schilaci, and on the nineteenth, the lagoon of Croton.

There it became known that a Turkish frigate had pursued a Christian frigate, which took to flight. The men saved themselves, but the frigate fell in the hands of the Turks. On the twenty-second [of September the Christian armada] left the said lagoon after spending two days there because of inclement weather, leaving orders that the sailing ships, which were following a different route, were to sail for Corfu. On the twenty-third, the armada entered the Gulf of Taranto, and on the following day was at the port of Panormo. There it was confirmed that the enemy armada had been at the island of Corfu, where it had done much damage, and had now sailed east. Following its course, at three o'clock that night the Christian armada reached a cape on the island of Corfu, at a place called Kassiopi. On the next day, they went to the fortress, where the intelligence was verified, and to be certain, galleys were sent to different places to reconnoiter the enemy. To prevent [the men] from scattering away, his Highness immediately had an order issued mandating that, on the pain of capital punishment, no one was to leave the galleys.

---

121. Fossa di San Giovanni is a port on the Calabrese coast opposite Messina, across the straights.

Taking some artillery pieces from the [fortress'] battery and furnished with what they needed, on the twenty-ninth, the galleys from the West left and set sail for Benitses, on the same island of Corfu, there to wait for Admiral Venier and the rest of the armada, which had stopped at the town to load the galleasses with six thousand stara[122] of grain (which had been designed to be sent, whenever the occasion presented itself, as aid to Famagusta). On September 30, Venier left Corfu and joined his Highness. Together, they sailed to Leschino, a cape on the eastern coast of Corfu. From there, under a brisk sirocco, they crossed the channel over against Gomeniza on the mainland. The port is safe and capacious, and with the wind picking up and clouds gathering from all directions, his Highness stopped there to inspect the armada. That night Gil Andrada arrived on his flagship, and Giovanni Battista Contarini, who had gone all the way to Zante, reported that until September 29, the Turkish armada had been in the Gulf of Lepanto, in bad shape, and that about ten galleys, galiots, and fuste have sailed for Modon, accompanying the two sailing ships, *Moceniga* and *Constantina*, with sick men on board (that was not true, however). The news inspired everyone to pursue and find the enemy, but the bad weather persisted.

## THE FORCES OF THE HOLY LEAGUE

ON OCTOBER 1, his Highness commanded that everyone was to put their galleys in order and take their positions. The next day, after the men were mustered, four galleys were selected and disarmed, the men reinforcing the other galleys. On Wednesday, October 3, the weather improved, and the entire armada sailed from Gomeniza, in the following order:

*Vanguard*
  1 *Santa Maddalena* of Venice           Marino Contarini
  2 *Sole* of Venice                      Vincenzo Quirini

---

122. An Italian corn measure, differing according to city and territory, roughly one bushel or about 80 pounds in weight; one of the most widespread standards. The Florentine had 1 *staro* equaling 1449 cubic inches. See R.E. Zupko, *Italian Weights and Measures from the Middle Ages to the Nineteenth Century* (Philadelphia: American Philosophical Society, 1981), 278–81.

## HISTORY OF THE EVENTS

   3 (lantern) *Patrona* of Sicily[123]          ... ... ... ...
   4 (lantern) *Capitana* of Sicily          Juan de Cardona
   5 (lantern) *Capitana*          David Imperiale
   6 *San Giovanni* of Sicily          ... ... ... ...
   7 *Santa Caterina* of Venice          Marco Cicogna
   8 *La Nostra Donna* of Venice          Piero Francesco Malipiero

*Left Wing*
   1 (lantern) *Capitana* of Venice          Agostino Barbarigo, provveditore general of the Venetian fleet

   2 (lantern) *Capitana* of Venice          Antonio Canale, provveditore of the Venetian fleet

   3 *Fortuna* of Venice          Andrea Barbarigo
   4 *Saggitaria* of Naples          Martin Pirola
   5 *Le Tre Mani* of Venice          Giorgio Barbarigo
   6 *Dui Dolfini* of Candia          Francesco Zen
   7 *Il Leone & la Fenice* of Canea          Francesco Mengano
   8 *San Nicolò* of Kres          Colane Drascio
   9 *Vittoria* of Naples          Occava di Rocadi
 10 *Lomelina*          Agostin Caneval
 11 the pope's *Elengina*          the knight Fabio Valciati
 12 *Madonna* of Canea          Filippo Polani
 13 *Cavallo Marino* of Candia          Antonio di Canalli
 14 *Dui Leoni* of Candia          Nicolò Fradello
 15 *Leon* of Capo d'Istria          Dominico del Tacco
 16 *Croce* of Cephalonia          Marco Cimera[124]
 17 *Santa Virginia* of Cephalonia          Cristofalo Crissa
 18 *Leon* of Candia          Francesco Bonvecchio
 19 *Christo* of Candia          Andrea Cornaro

---

123. Contarini's *fanò* vessels. I deviate from the direct translation only in four cases and use "flagship" for the galleys of the fleet commanders — Don Juan, the allied commanders Colonna, Venier, Doria, and the Maltese — and use "lantern galley" where *fanò* indicated just that.

124. Marginal note: Ambrogio Bragadin — large galley. Contarini uses *galea grossa*, "large galley" for for the heavily armed galleass. The printer placed the information about the galleasses on the page as they were positioned according to the battle order.

| | |
|---|---|
| 20 *Angelo* of Candia | Giovanni Angelo |
| 21 *Piramide* of Candia | Francesco Bon |
| 22 *La Donna con il cavallo armato* of Candia | Antonio Eudomeniani |
| 23 *Christo Resuscitato* of Venice | Simon Guoro |
| 24 *Christo Resuscitato* of Venice | Federico Renier |
| 25 *Christo* of Corfu | Cristofolo Condocolli |
| 26 *Christo Resuscitato* of Canea | Giorgio Calergi |
| 27 *Christo* of Venice | Bartolomeo Donato |
| 28 *Christo Resuscitato* of Veglia | Lodovico Cicuta |
| 29 galley of Rhetymno | Nicolò Avonal |
| 30 *Christo* of Candia | Giorgio Corner |
| 31 *Christo Resuscitato* of Canea | Francesco Zancaruol |
| 32 *Ruodi* of Canea | Francesco Molin |
| 33 *Santa Eufemia* of Brescia | Horatio Fisogno |
| 34 Giovanni Andrea's *Marchesa* | Francesco San Fedra |
| 35 Giovanni Andrea's *Fortuna* | Giovanni Alvise Belvi |
| 36 *Bracco* of Canea | [Giovanni] Michiel Vizzamano |
| 37 *Caval Marino* of Venice | Antonio di Cavalli |
| 38 *Christo* of Canea | Daniel Calesati |
| 39 *Braccio* of Venice | Nicolò Lippomano |
| 40 *Nostra Donna* of Zante | Nicolò Mondin |
| 41 *Christo Resuscitato* of Canea | Francesco Zancaruol[125] |
| 42 *Nostra Donna* of Venice | Marc'Antonio Pisani |
| 43 *Dio Padre sopra la Trinità* of Venice | Giovanni Contarini |
| 44 *Fiamma* of Naples | Giovanni dalla Cuevas |
| 45 *San Gio* of Naples | Garzia di Vorgara |
| 46 *Invidia* of Naples | Teribio de Accaves |
| 47 *Brava* of Naples | Michiel Quesada |
| 48 *San Giacomo* of Naples | Monserat Guardiola |
| 49 *San Nicolò* of Naples | Cristofalo di Mongiva |
| 50 *Christo Resuscitato* of Venice | Giovanni Battista Quirini |
| 51 *Angelo* of Venice | Onfre Giustinian |
| 52 *Santa Dorotea* of Venice | Polo Nani |
| 53 (lantern) *Capitana* of Venice | Marco Quirini, provveditore of the Venetian fleet |

---

125. Marginal note: Ambrogio Bragadin — large galley.

# HISTORY OF THE EVENTS

*Center*

| | |
|---|---|
| 1 (lantern) Lomellini's *Capitana* | Paolo Giordano Orsini |
| 2 Lomellini's *Patrona* | Pietro Battista Lomellini |
| 3 (lantern) *Capitana Bendinella* | Bendinelli Sauli |
| 4 *Patrona* of Genoa | Pelleran |
| 5 the pope's *Toscana* | the knight Metello Caracciolo |
| 6 *Uomo Marino* of Vicenza | Giacomo Dressano |
| 7 *Nostra Donna* of Venice | Giovanni Zeno |
| 8 *San Girolamo* of Lesina | Giovanni Balzi |
| 9 *San Giovanni* of Venice | Pietro Badoer |
| 10 *San Alessandro* of Bergamo | Giovanni Antonio Colleone |
| 11 (lantern) *Capitana di Mari* | Georgio d'Asti |
| 12 *Tronco* of Venice | Geronimo da Canal |
| 13 *Mongibello* of Venice | Bertuzzi Contarini |
| 14 *Donzella* of Candia | Francesco Dandolo[126] |
| 15 Giovanni Andrea's *Temperanza* | Ciprian di Mari |
| 16 *Ventura* of Naples | Vincenzo Pascalo |
| 17 *Rocca* of Spain | Roccaful |
| 18 the pope's *Vittoria* | Baccio of Pisa |
| 19 *Piramide* of ... ... ... ... | Marc'Antonio S.Vliana |
| 20 *Christo* of Venice | Geronimo Contarini |
| 21 *San Francesco* of Spain | Christofolo Guasches |
| 22 the pope's *Pace* | Giacopo Antonio Perignano |
| 23 Giovanni Andrea's *Perla* | Zuan Battista Spinola |
| 24 *Ruota con un serpe* of Venice | Gabriel da Canal |
| 25 *Piramide* of Venice | Francesco Bon |
| 26 *Palma* of Venice | Geronimo Venier |
| 27 (lantern) *Capitana* of Gil Andrada | Bernardo Cinoguera |
| * *Granata* of Spain | Paulo Bottino |
| 28 (lantern) *Capitana* of Genoa | Ettor Spinola with the prince of Parma |
| 29 (flagship) *Capitana* of Venice | Sebastian Venier, admiral of the Venetian fleet at the stern of His Highness and Venier |
| 30 (lantern) *Patrona reale* | |
| 31 (flagship) *Reale* | Don Juan of Austria, commander-in-chief of the League |

---

126. Marginal note: Giacomo Guoto — large galley.

| | |
|---|---|
| 32 (lantern) *Capitana* of the commendador mayor, | at the stern of his Highness and Colonna |
| 33 (flagship) His Holiness' *Capitana* | Marc'Antonio Colonna, admiral of His Holiness |
| 34 (lantern) *Capitana* of Savoy | Monsignor di Leyni, with the prince of Urbino |
| 35 the pope's *Grifona* | Alessandro Negroni |
| 36 *San Theodoro* of Venice | Teodoro Balbi |
| 37 *Mendoza* of Naples | Martino de Caide |
| 38 *Monte* of Canea | Alessandro Vizzamano |
| 39 *San Giovanni Battista* of Venice | Giovanni Mocenigo |
| 40 Giovanni Andrea's *Vittoria* | Filippo Doria |
| 41 the pope's *Pisana* | Hercole Lotta |
| 42 *Figiera* of Spain | Diego Lopes de Glianos |
| 43 *Christo* of Venice | Giorgio Pisani |
| 44 *San Giovanni* of Venice | Daniel Moro |
| 45 the pope's *Fiorenza* | Thomaso de' Medici |
| 46 *San Giorgio* of Naples | Eugenio de Vergas |
| 47 (lantern) *Patrona* of Naples | Francesco de Benavides |
| 48 *Luna* of Spain | Emanuel de Aguilar |
| 49 *Passaro* of Venice | Luigi Pasqualigo |
| 50 *Leone* of Venice | Pietro Pisani |
| 51 *San Girolamo* of Venice | Gasparo Malipiero |
| 52 (lantern) Grimaldi's *Capitana* | Giorgio Grimaldi |
| 53 David Imperiale's *Patrona* | Nicolò da Luvan |
| 54 *San Christofolo* of Venice | Alessandro Contarini |
| 55 *Giudit* of Zante | Marin Sicuro[127] |
| 56 *Armelino* of Candia | Pietro Gradenigo |
| 57 *Meza Luna* of Venice | Valerio Valaresso |
| 58 Giovanni Andrea's *Doria* | Giacomo di Casal |
| 59 *Religion di San Pietro* | Santubi |
| 60 *Religion di San Giovanni* | Alvise di Tessera |
| 61 (flagship) *Capitana* of Malta | the reverend prior of Messina |

*Right Wing*

| | |
|---|---|
| 1 (lantern) *Capitana* of Sicily | Juan de Cardona in the vanguard |

---

127. Marginal note: Francesco Duodo, commander of the large galleys.

# HISTORY OF THE EVENTS

| | | |
|---|---|---|
| 2 | *Piemontesa* of Savoy | Ottaviano Moretto |
| 3 | Nicolò Doria's *Capitana* | Pandolfo Polidoro |
| 4 | *Forze* of Venice | Renier Zen |
| 5 | *Reina* of Candia | Giovanni Barbarigo |
| 6 | *Nino* of Venice | Paolo Polani |
| 7 | *Christo Resuscitato* of Venice | Benedetto Soranzo |
| 8 | *Uomo armado* of Rhetymno | Andrea Calergi |
| 9 | *Aquila* of Rhetymno | Andrea Calergi |
| 10 | *Palma* of Canea | Giacomo de Mezo |
| 11 | *Angelo* of Corfu | Stelio Carchiopulo |
| 12 | *San Giovanni* of Arbe | Giovanni di Dominis |
| 13 | *Donna* of Trogir | Luigi Cippico |
| 14 | *Nave* of Venice | Antonio Pasqualigo |
| 15 | *Nostra Donna* of Candia | Marco Forscarini[128] |
| 16 | *Christo* of Candia | Francesco Corner |
| 17 | *San Vitorio* of Crema | Evangelista Zurla |
| 18 | Grimaldi's *Patrona* | Lorenzo Trecha |
| 19 | *Patroni di Mari* | Antonio Corniglia |
| 20 | *Margarita* of Savoy | Battaglino |
| 21 | *Diana* of Genoa | Giovanni Giorgio Lasagna |
| 22 | *Cingana* of Naples | Gabriel di Medina |
| 23 | *Luna* of Naples | Giulio Rubbio |
| 24 | *Fortuna* of Naples | Diego de Medrano |
| 25 | *Speranza* of Naples | Pietro de Busto |
| 26 | Lomellini's *Furia* | Giacomo Chiappe |
| 27 | (lantern) Lomellini's *Patrona* | Georgio Greco |
| 28 | *Negrona* | Nicolò da Costa |
| 29 | Negroni's *Bastarda* | Lorenzo da Torre |
| 30 | *Fuoco* of Candia | Antonio Bon |
| 31 | *Aquila* of Candia | Girolamo Zorzi |
| 32 | *San Christoforo* of Venice | Andrea Tron |
| 33 | *Christo* of Venice | Marc'Antonio Lando |
| 34 | *Speranza* of Candia | Girolamo Cornaro |
| 35 | *Re Attila* of Padua | Pataro Buzzacarin |
| 36 | *San Giuseppe* of Venice | Nicolò Donato |
| 37 | *Gusmana* of Naples | Francesco de Osedo |
| 38 | *Determinata* of Naples | Giovanni di Carasse |

---

128. Marginal note: Andrea da Pesaro — large galley

| | | |
|---|---|---|
| 39 | *Sicilia* of Sicily | Francesco Amadei[129] |
| 40 | Nicolò Doria's *Patrona* | Giulio Centurione |
| 41 | *Aquila* of Corfu | Pietro Bua |
| 42 | *San Trifone* of Kotor | Girolamo Bisante |
| 43 | *Torre* of Vicenza | Lodovico da Porto |
| 44 | the pope's *Santa Maria* | the knight Pandolfo Strozzi |
| 45 | the pope's *San Giovanni* | the knight Angolo Bisali |
| 46 | Negroni's *Padrona* | Luigi Gamba |
| 47 | Negroni's *Capitana* | Giovanni Ambroggio Negroni |
| 48 | Giovanni Andrea's *Monarcha* | Nicolò Garibaldo |
| 49 | Giovanni Andrea's *Donzella* | Nicolò Imperiale |
| 50 | Giovanni Andrea's *Capitana* | Giovanni Andrea Doria |

*Rearguard*

| | | |
|---|---|---|
| 1 | *San Giovanni* of Sicily | ... ... ... ... |
| 2 | *Baccana* | Giovanni Pietro de Morilo |
| 3 | *Leina* of Naples | ... ... ... ... |
| 4 | *Costanza* of Naples | Pietro Delagia |
| 5 | *Marchesa* of Naples | Giovanni de Machada |
| 6 | *Santa Barbara* of Naples | Giovanni de Aschale |
| 7 | *Sant' Andrea* of Naples | ... ... ... ... |
| 8 | *Santa Catherina* of Naples | Giovanni Rufis de Valasco |
| 9 | *San Bortolomeo* of Naples | ... ... ... ... |
| 10 | *Sant' Angelo* of Naples | ... ... ... ... |
| 11 | *Terana* of Naples | Giovanni de Riva de Neillino |
| 12 | *Christo* of Venice | Marco da Molin |
| 13 | *Due Mani* of Venice | Giovanni Loredan |
| 14 | (lantern) *Capitana* of Naples | Don Álvaro da Bazán |
| 15 | *Fede* of Venice | Giovanni Battista Contarini |
| 16 | *Colonna* of Venice | Caterino Malipiero |
| 17 | *Maddalena* of Venice | Alvise Balbi |
| 18 | *Donna* of Venice | Giovanni Bembo |
| 19 | *Mondo* of Venice | Filipo Leone |
| 20 | *Speranza* of Venice | Giovanni Battista Benedetti |
| 21 | *San Pietro* of Venice | Pietro Badoer |
| 22 | *San Giorgio* of Šibenik | Christofolo Lucich |
| 23 | *San Michiel* | Georgio Cochin |
| 24 | *Sibilla* of Venice | Daniel Tron |

---

129. Marginal note: Pietro Pisano — large galley.

# HISTORY OF THE EVENTS

| | |
|---|---|
| 25 *Gru* of Spain | Luis de Heredia |
| 26 (lantern) Vasquez' *Capitana* | Vasquez de Coronado |
| 27 the pope's *Soprana* | Antonio d'Ascoli |
| 28 *Occasion* of Spain | Pedro de Roig |
| 29 the pope's *Padrona* | … … … … |
| 30 the pope's *Serena* | … … … … |

So arranged, they sailed comfortably, everyone at their place, and a captain was also assigned for every twenty galleys to maintain the established order. In this manner, they passed the rock of Paxi,[130] from which they navigated under sail until they were opposite the Gulf of Arta.[131] But as it was not possible to reach Cephalonia the same day, they lowered the sails and continued their journey through the night (as it is said) until dawn on the fourth day. Then the foremast sails were unfurled, under which, squadron after squadron, maintaining the battle order, they arrived in the Bay of Fiskardo, at the island of Cephalonia, around twenty-two o'clock. The following night, at nine o'clock, they left for the port of Petala,[132] where the rocks of Curzolari[133] begin, but the strong wind blowing from the Gulf of Lepanto forced them to retreat back to the island of Cephalonia, to the bay in the lagoon of Alexandria.

There, a frigate from Zante brought letters from Paolo Contarini, provveditore of the island, which confirmed that the enemy armada was in the Gulf of Lepanto in poor condition, and that forty vessels have left under the command of Uluj Ali and sailed for Modon. Later, letters arrived, also via Zante, sent by Marino di Cavalli, provveditore

---

130. Paxi is the smallest island group in the Ionian Sea, between Corfu and Cephalonia, consisting of the larger islands of Paxos and Antipaxos and several smaller outcrops.

131. The Ambracian Gulf, one of the largest enclosed gulfs in Greece, with the towns of Preveza, Amphilochia, and Vonitsa on its shores.

132. The largest island of the Echinades group, between Cephalonia and mainland Greece and the closest to the mainland.

133. The Venetian name of the Echinades group. The name came from a peninsula to the south of the mouth of the river Achelous on the mainland, opposite the island of the southernmost island of Oxeia.

general of the island of Candia, which reported in detail on the fall of Famagusta. Marino had learned about it from slaves who had escaped to Candia on a fusta that Mustafa Pasha had sent to their armada. As the captain got off the fusta, the slaves fled with it. Upon that news, the admirals called a new council of war at which everyone confirmed that they had to proceed with the plan and attack the enemy.

## THE OTTOMAN FORCES

WHILE THEY BUSIED THEMSELVES with talking, the enemy, for their part, did not remain idle. Arriving at Lepanto on September 27 and wary of the Christian fleet, they dispatched Mehmet Bey with sixty galleys inside the Gulf, to the place called Aspropiti,[134] to gather victuals and other provisions for the armada and, above all, to recruit fighting men and do everything possible to strengthen the armada. After doing that, Mehmet brought back to Lepanto, besides what was necessary for the fleet, ten thousand Janissaries, two thousand sipachis, and two thousand irregulars.

Meanwhile, the enemy found out that the Christian fleet had sailed from Corfu to Cephalonia. But they had no precise idea either of the numbers or of the plans of our forces, except the report of Kara Hodja, who had been sent ahead to reconnoiter. He had observed the Christian fleet and [concluded that] it numbered no more that hundred and fifty galleys and had no sailing ships (which was wrong). However, before loading the provisions, they were troubled by insecurity and did not know what decision to take, as if foreseeing their future ruin and massacre. Their admiral Ali Pasha, even though he had resolved on giving battle, nevertheless decided to call a council before embarking the men. The commanders and other chiefs expert in naval warfare got together. A long discussion ensued on what was to be done, during which everyone was given full freedom to express their opinion. To please Ali Pasha and endear themselves to him, many advised to do battle. Others, in concert with Pertau Pasha, who did not feel the least bit inclined to do so, advised the opposite.

---

134. Ottoman Aspra Spitia, Greek Anticyrrha, or Antikyra, on the bay of Antikyra, on the north coast of the Gulf of Corinth.

## HISTORY OF THE EVENTS

Then Hassan Pasha, the son of Barbarossa, the former beylerbey of Algiers, obtained permission to speak and, with hands on his chest as is their custom, began speaking thus, "Most powerful lords, loved and highly favored by His Majesty, our invincible Lord, the spirit and shadow of God, may he live for all ages of the ages (in these, and other matters, these idolaters and enemies of the true Son of God fall in such bestiality with their pronouncements). Desiring to fulfill his will and exalt his glory, we should not be in such confusion and ambiguity, if the issue is whether to go out and find and destroy the enemy fleet. Apart from the most prudent arguments of those who know much better than me, made earlier in the discussion in their presence, this can be said without any doubt, of the most valorous and capable slaves[135] of His Most High Excellency [the Sultan].

"I state and confirm that these people, [the Christians,] are the same, and have allied in the same manner, as those who had been for thirty years defeated and enslaved by my brave father, Hayreddin Barbarossa. He triumphed over these pusillanimous nations, on these same seas and places, without unsheathing a sword, with much inferior number of vessels than those of the enemy. Many of them took to flight as soon as they saw the rostra of our galleys, startled and horrified by the daring shouts and determination of our soldiers, and fled terrified just by our name. These people have neither love nor affection for one another, nor do they obey any one authority that alone can motivate the army, as they belong to different nations, customs, and natures, one dissimilar to the other. The galleys of several princes have now allied just for the show of numbers, not for fighting, and would not voluntarily expose themselves to any danger.

---

135. Contarini's term here, while serving his juxtaposition of collective Christian decision-making to authoritarian Ottoman command, conveys quite correctly the status of the high Ottoman officialdom, as they were all technically slaves of the Sultan, according to the Ottoman "kul" or slave system of staffing of leadership positions. See, for a succinct recent discussion of this phenomenon, which was stereotypical of the Western perception of the Ottomans of the time, Michael Meeker, *A Nation of Empire: The Ottoman Legacy of Turkish Modernity* (Berkeley: University of California Press, 2001), 111, 144–45.

Above all, they are blasphemers of the name of God, luxuriating in precious vestments, bearing exquisite weapons, and chock-full of money and munitions.

"They are not like us. We do not know what blasphemy is, we revere and love one another. We are united and respectful toward one another, we bear arms solely for the purpose of fighting, and we are joined together for one end only: to serve and obey our only Lord, who has always been, and always will be victorious. All of us are dedicated to serve: promptly obey the valorous ardor of your hearts, you who, besides so many other dignities and favors, are now elevated to the extreme heights of representing his imperial Majesty. You can be reassured that — given our large force of courageous soldiers and well-provided fleet — we can go ahead and win a certain and indubitable victory!

"Moreover, we have two hundred and eighty perfect vessels, among which two hundred galleys and fifty galiots, fully armed. And, most prudent lords, for the greater terror of the enemy and for the encouragement of our soldiers, we should add to this formidable force by issuing orders to distribute [among the galleys] the recently recruited fourteen thousand fighters who are here in the harbor. [Also, distribute] the men from the East, who are on board the twenty small fuste, among our galleys and galiots, to augment the forces of this powerful armada. If we were to do all this, we would surely defeat them, no matter how good their fighters are. Furthermore, our adversaries do not have more than one hundred and fifty galleys, as our brave and perceptive Kara Hodja here has estimated, and of the kind and quality I have already described.

"Well then, victorious lords, if this information suits your prudence and intelligence, you will undoubtedly find them in the harbor of Alexandria, where you will catch them idle and offering no resistance, as they are more used to luxuries than to the hardships of war. They have scattered on the beaches and coasts, and when they see us, the better part will beach their vessels and seek to save themselves by flight, and will doubtlessly fall in our hands. Therefore, given the superior number of our galleys, the advantages of our weaponry, and the courage of our soldiers, the entire fleet agrees that you, my lord high counselors, must not let this opportunity slip away, against people so inferior to us in terms of numbers, spirit, vessels, and military experience. Above all, you will thus execute the order of his Majesty — may he live for eternity and all ages — and will immortalize your names with our eternal glory. Similarly, your courage will conform with the vows and promises you made in the hands of our Great Lord, when, among so many honors, he bestowed upon you the supreme dignity of commanding such a powerful armada as if he were leading it himself."

With the same arguments Uluj Ali, captain-general of Barbary, emphasized the great advantage of the Turkish forces over the Christian fleet and reminded them, with stern and forceful words, of the wrath of the Great Lord. After him Caia Beg, sanjakbey of Smyrna, spoke in a similar vein.[136] They were honor-bound, and there was no excuse whatsoever for not going out to find and engage the disarrayed and much inferior fleet of these same Christians, whom the soldiers of the Great Lord of the Ottomans had vanquished in all the past years and had scattered, captured, and bound them in chains like lowly women, regardless of their much larger numbers and vessels.

However, [Mehmet] Şuluç, governor of Alexandria, and Kara Bine, sanjakbey of Syria, soldiers and captains who had grown old fighting on the high seas, as well as many others, held the contrary opinion. Among all others, Mehmet Bey, sanjakbey of Negroponte, the son of Salih Reis Pasha, formerly governor-general of Barbary, a man of great experience in naval battles, seized the opportunity and, intending to counter the fervent advocacy of Hassan Pasha, spoke in the following manner:

"Most prudent lords, the point of Hassan Pasha's speech is truly valorous, as befits a courageous soldier obedient to our indomitable Lord and King of Kings, the sharp sword in the mighty hand of God, may he live for eternity and all ages! All this being so, however, with your permission and with all due respect, my lords pashas

---

136. Possibly the same man as Caia Chelebi, squadron commander of 20 galleys during the battle. See below the Ottoman battle order.

who govern this empire under the hand of his Sublimity, I will not refrain from stating that there are reasons to think that our enemies have not crossed over such a distance and come here without proper information and specific intelligence about the numbers and condition of our fleet. Therefore, it is reasonable and we should acknowledge and take it for certain that, as they have already arrived here, their forces are either superior or at least equal to ours, since they know perfectly well that the remainder of the kingdoms and provinces that they still hold are protected solely by the bastion of the fleet that they have, and they can only count on that force to preserve the aforementioned places with it, as they plan to do. Hence it is hardly thinkable that the enemy fleet has arrived to face manifest destruction, which would have been the case had they come in the manner presented to you, supreme councilors, and as the brave Kara Hodja here asserts, in such small numbers.

"On the contrary, besides the supposition that their numbers must be much larger, it stands to reason that a fleet that had departed from Sicily in search of its enemy in these seas and in this time of the year would not have come if not with the intention to do battle, and with a well-founded hope of winning, being well organized, strengthened, and well-armed with what is necessary for the endeavor. In fact, if we interpret properly the communications and intelligence we have received, including what captives of those same Christians say, we could not but conclude that they have come with the firm intention to fight rather than to simply put up a show and flee. Because, if their intention had been to turn their backs rather than face us, they would have never advanced so far in these seas of ours, only to bolt away afterwards and to suffer, besides their other recent losses, complete destruction. We conclude therefore, that the enemy fleet is coming strong and determined to do battle.

"Furthermore, we believe that they are coming to find us feeling neither anxious nor challenged. The present situation and conditions cannot be compared to what happened at Preveza many years ago.[137]

---

137. At the battle of Preveza on September 28, 1538, Hayreddin Barbarossa destroyed an allied Christian naval force double his numbers and asserted the

# HISTORY OF THE EVENTS

The current league of Christian princes allied against us is a different one from that of thirty years ago. This Christian league is a different kind of war machinery and thinking, and the wills of its commanders are aligned. It is not to be compared to the previous one. In that other one, there were many leaders and no single mind, which was the cause of their disorder and defeat. This one is headed by Juan of Austria, son of Emperor Charles V and brother of King Philip of Spain, heartened by the reputation and prudent successes of his father and motivated by the supreme dignity bestowed upon him by his brother with the consent of all the other confederates, revered, as we understand, by everyone in the fleet, and loved by the other commanders. He had resolved to fight having, perhaps, a leg up on us, even more so than the Venetians, whom we had so badly hurt. They cannot but fervently seek to avenge themselves for all the blood of theirs we have shed, the blood of men whose courage we cannot deny, at the price of terrible losses on our part. Besides, we ought to remember that in the past year, even before the formation of this League, we found out what a fervent desire they had for fighting us. We do conclude, therefore, that they will fight, and they will fight even more fiercely for the greater glory of their nation. As they fight before the eyes of one another, and according to their old habit, everyone will be stimulated by the zeal not to be viewed as inferior to another, something that I have always considered the greatest possible advantage an army could have.

"Furthermore, to the extent we were able to gain access to information, we have learned that he [Juan of Austria] is a daring youth who neither fears danger nor cares for riches but burns with an ardent desire to have the shouts proclaiming his valor reach all the way to Spain and his brother. What better occasion than this can he wish for, being among people who, each because of their specific interest, are so inflamed to fight? The Venetians hope to recover, with one stroke, everything we have taken away from them so far. Apart from the glory of such a glamorous victory if it falls to him, he would enjoy

---

Ottoman supremacy on the high seas in the Mediterranean. For the effects of the battle, see the pithy recent evaluation of Alan Jamieson, *Lords of the Sea: A History of the Barbary Corsairs* (London: Reaction Books, 2012), 44-45.

a large portion of what would be acquired, believing, without doubt, that after the destruction of our fleet he would lord it over the entire sea and the East with it. As for the contrary [opinion], that he would desert and flee (as it was argued here): how could he expect to face his brother after that? Where could the Venetians, who know these seas so well, expect to hide and find a safe place to save themselves? It is to be believed, then, that they had thought through quite well the situation in which they are now, and in which the question is about the safety and existence of their cities and kingdoms. They are allied, therefore, to fight, and to fight all together, unlike what they did at Preveza.

"As for ourselves, we are now in this gulf, in a strong position, controlling two excellent fortresses, comfortable in terms of munitions and abundantly provisioned, with as many men as we need. Furthermore, supreme lords, before you entered this place with the armada, you triumphed over the enemy, hurt them, and wreaked havoc upon them, devastating a part of the island of Candia, burned and despoiled Kythira, Zante, and Cephalonia, ravaged Corfu, and recovered Sopot. You penetrated the Gulf of Venice and conquered Ulcinj and Bar, important cities of the enemy, and many other places and fortresses, and burned down Budva. Now, basking in so much triumph and glory, cannot we be content for the moment, given that at the same time our men in Cyprus have captured Famagusta, and conquered the entire kingdom? Surely, I say, and will always say, it takes no less courage and prudence to know how to preserve what had been acquired than to go out, with raw force and ingenuity, to acquire it in the first place. The latter is always uncertain, and Fortune plays a large part in it, while the former is the result of human action and can be attributed to the savvy leader who knew what was to be done. Our Great Lord will always praise you, if along with your triumphs of conquering cities and kingdoms and burning down settlements and provinces, and presenting him with so many slaves, booty, and treasures, you safeguard his fleet, and do not expose it to a possible, nay certain, danger of losing it. It was very difficult and it took us many years to put together a force of such size, while the enemy easily doubled their armada in a short time, and one better fitted out in terms of firearms, soldiers, and vessels.

"To me therefore, if you, supreme counselors, agree that the Great Lord's intention and the furthering of his powerful empire matter, you should not tempt Fortune but remain quietly in this secure place, with the armada in good order, and monitor the actions of the enemy. In a short time you will find out their plans, given that, as we have learned, they are to arrive before these isles from Zante or Cephalonia either today or tomorrow. In this manner, my lords, you will always have the advantage, which is very important in warfare, especially in naval wars, as I am sure you, who are savvier than I, know better, of taking decisions based on intelligence. Moreover, it can be taken for granted that they cannot stay long in this area, as in these seas they cannot be easily supplied with the victuals they need, and if they want to stay nonetheless, it will not be in a place as safe as ours. They are, therefore, constrained to two options: either advance, or turn back right away. If they decide to proceed and find us, I cannot fancy a way they would enter here, if not at great risk for themselves, while we will have the advantage of inflicting great damage on them with the armaments of these fortresses, and of fighting under the latter's protection.

"The moment we sight them, we will know the condition, numbers, and forces of the enemy, without anyone guessing and presenting one thing for another, and if it is to our advantage, we can turn around and fight. If, however, we find out that the situation is the opposite, as I think it is, we can always safely stay here without endangering the fleet and the empire, preserving the dignity and the reputation of our emperor. If they decide to linger longer along these shores, however, that would not do because of the weather, which will soon make them regret it, besides all the inconveniences, shortages, and other difficulties that will make them turn back before long. And if they persist obstinately in staying around (which will not hurt us at all) they will be in danger from the storms, which by this time normally disturb all these seas, and it would be impossible for them to find save haven and stay together. Then, if circumstances allow, and we find them dispersed, we could pursue and attack them. On our part, we should not fail to seek, most diligently and vigorously and in any possible and trusted way, to find out and confirm the condition and numbers of their fleet, the plans of enemy, and by all means catch two, or three, or more informants from that armada of theirs, so that you, supreme counselors, can make informed and well-founded decisions, which will be of the greatest benefit to, and most fitting the reputation of our Great Lord, because no one would hardly ever praise us if we take the armada from under the protection of these fortresses for no good reason, and lose our advantage by trusting to the vagaries of Fortune.

"There is no doubt that the enemy seeks, with every kind of subterfuge, to lure us out of the gulf and distance us from the fortresses. We, however, must be even more alert, and wisely disregard for the moment what they plan to orchestrate, pressed on by the adverse season of the year. If you so resolve and command, supreme lords, you will amply display the highest grade of courage and prudence and will be eternally remembered not only for your glorious deeds in the acquisition of such a kingdom, cities, and fortresses, and striking the enemy in the heart, but even more so for being most sagacious now in the preservation of this most happy Ottoman Empire. We remain your slaves though, ready to serve and obey any decisions you would take, and we are all resolved to die at your command, whatever that may be."

The wise speech of Mehmet Bey pleased Pertau Pasha, and the sanjakbeys [Mehmet] Sirocco[138] and Kara Bine approved of it. But because the order of Sultan Selim, which was read by the commission of Uluj Ali, the captain-general of Barbary, was against it, because the impatient Ali Pasha and many others pressed for battle and sought to bend the decision their way and, above all, because it was the will of the divine Majesty to initiate the destruction of these people, in the end they resolved unanimously to go out and seek the Christian armada and engage it in battle. They believed that they would find the Christian fleet in port and deserted, and would

---

138. Mehmet Şuluç.

capture it without unsheathing a sword, persuaded, as they said, that this would net them the islands of Zante and Cephalonia, allow them to put under siege the fortresses of Corfu and the kingdom of Candia throughout the winter and, with one part of their armada reinforced with the captured [Christian vessels], penetrate the channel of Kotor. From there, as soon as the weather permitted, encountering no resistance, they were to become masters of the said places and deprive the Venetians of the rest of their maritime dominions. Thus advancing, they were to penetrate Italy and little by little conquer all of Christendom. Having so resolved, they distributed the fourteen thousand fighting men, shackled the Christian slaves who were of no other use but rowing in iron manacles, mustered the troops, and set sail, arranging the armada in four squadrons, as follows.

*Right Wing*

| | | |
|---|---|---|
| 1 | (flagship) *Capitana* of the governor of Alexandria[139] | Mehmet Sirocco |
| 2 | galley of Alexandria | Kara Kubad |
| 3 | galley of the same | Bagli Saraf |
| 4 | galley of the same | Giafer Chiagia |
| 5 | galley of the same | Osman Chelebi |
| 6 | galley of the same | Pervis Reis |
| 7 | galley of the same | Buyuk Kasapoglu |
| 8 | galley of the same | Osman Occan |
| 9 | galley of the same | Dervish Aga |
| 10 | galley of the same | Bayazid Siman |
| 11 | galley of the same | Osman Ali |
| 12 | galley of the same | Deli Aga |
| 13 | galley of the same | Dardagan Bardambeli |
| 14 | galley of the same | Casli Caia |
| 15 | galley of the same | Yusuf Aga |
| 16 | galley of the same | Yusuf Magar |
| 17 | galley of the same | Calafat Cheder |
| 18 | galley of the same | Mustafa Genovel |
| 19 | galley of the same | Dermigi Peri |
| 20 | galley of the same | Mat Assan |

---

139. Here and in what follows, Contarini uses *Capitana* and *Real* not as proper ship names but to identify squadron and fleet flagships.

| | |
|---|---|
| 21 galley of the same | Cheder Aga |
| 22 galley of Constantinople | Suleiman Bey |
| 23 galley of the same | Ibrahim |
| 24 galley of the same | Shaban |
| 25 galley of the same | Caia Chelebi |
| 26 galley of the same | Cheder Siman |
| 27 (lantern) *Capitana* | of the son of Kara Mustafa |
| 28 galley of Constantinople | Iaran Shaban |
| 29 galley of the same | Davit Yusuf |
| 30 galley of the same | Solac Reis |
| 31 galley of the same | Arnaut Ferhad |
| 32 galley of Tripoli in Syria | Yuzel Memi |
| 33 galley of the same | Shender Selim |
| 34 galley of the same | Lumagh Yusuf |
| 35 galley of the same | Bardach Chelebi |
| 36 galley of the same | Baghdad Assan |
| 37 galley of the same | Gyuzel Allib |
| 38 galley of the same | Brusali Piri |
| 39 galley of the same | Rodlu Ali |
| 40 (lantern) *Capitana* of Constantinople | Aga Pasha |
| 41 galley of Anatolia | Sinan Mustafa |
| 42 galley of the same | Giegior Ali |
| 43 galley of the same | Murat Reis |
| 43 galley of the same[140] | Calipei Memi |
| 44 galley of the same | Marul Mustafa |
| 45 galley of the same | Heder Lumett |
| 46 galley of the same | Sinan Dervish |
| 47 galley of the same | Memin Durmis [Dervish?] |
| 48 galley of the same | Algagia Sinan |
| 49 galley of the same | Agadi Rustan |
| 50 galley of the same | Chiugeve Mustafa |
| 51 galley of the same | Yusuf Chelebi |
| 52 galley of the same | Tafer Mustafa |
| 53 galleon Capitana | Ali Genovese, corsair |
| 54 galiot of the same | Megil Reis |
| 55 *Capitana* of Negroponte | Mehmet Bey |

---

140. The list repeats number 43.

## HISTORY OF THE EVENTS

*Center*

| | |
|---|---|
| 1 governor of Rhodes | Assam Bey |
| 2 guardia of Rhodes | Deli Chiafer |
| 3 galley of the same | Occi Reis |
| 4 galley of the same | Prostunagli Ogli |
| 5 galley of the same | Calafat Ogli |
| 6 galley of the same | Gazi Reis |
| 7 *Capitana* of Constantinople | Dromus Reis |
| 8 guardia of Rhodes | Herbetci |
| 9 galley of the same | Karadja Reis |
| 10 galley of the same | Orchan Reis |
| 11 galley of the same | Deli Piri |
| 12 galley of the same | Giafer Aga |
| 13 galley of Constantinople | Bachla Reis |
| 14 galley of the same | Coz Ali |
| 15 galley of the same | Colach Reis |
| 16 galley of the same | Uluj Rais |
| 17 *Capitana* of the son of Barbarossa | Hassan Pasha |
| 18 galley of Naples in Romania[141] | Saraf Reis |
| 19 galley of the same | Alma Reis |
| 20 galley of the same | Gurucli Ogli |
| 21 galley of the same | Arnaut Chelebi |
| 22 galley of the same | Magar Ali |
| 23 governor of the *gabella*[142] | Giafer Chelebi |
| 24 galley of Naples in Romania | Deli Chelebi |
| 25 galley of the same | Deli Assan |
| 26 galley of the same | Kara Peri Aga |
| 27 galley of the same | Sinan Reis |
| 28 galley of the same | Kara Mustafa |
| 29 galley of Naples | Sali Arnuar |
| 30 (lantern) governor of Naples in Romania | Preuil Aga |
| 31 galley of Mytilene[143] | Baluhji Ogli |

---

141. Nafplio, a seaport town in the Peloponnese, Greece, on the north end of the Gulf of Argolis.

142. *Gabella* has different meanings in sixteenth-century Italian; here, most likely, it stands for "customs."

143. Mytilini is the chief town of the island of Lesbos, owned by the Genoese

| | |
|---|---|
| 32 galley of the same | Bazarci Mustafa |
| 33 galley of the same | Sinan Bali |
| 34 galley of the same | Agdadi Reis |
| 35 galley of Constantinople | two sons of Ali [Pasha] |
| 36 (lantern) *Capitana* of Constantinople | Osman Reis |
| 37 galley of Mytilene | Deli Yusuf |
| 38 galley of the same | Ferath Bhali |
| 39 galley of the same | Caia Chelebi |
| 40 galley of the same | Bagdar Reis |
| 41 galley of the same[144] | Haluaghi Mustafa |
| 42 (lantern) the galiots' *Capitana* | Giaur Ali, corsair |
| 43 (lantern) galley of Valona | Kara Hodja |
| 44 (lantern) Governor of Mytilene | Mahmut Saider Bey |
| 45 (flagship) *Real* of the Turks | Ali Pasha, admiral of the fleet |
| 46 (lantern) *Capitana* | Pertau Pasha, commander of the land troops |
| 47 (lantern) *Capitana* of the Treasurer | Mustafa Esdei |
| 48 (lantern) *Capitana* of Janissaries | Mamur Reis |
| 49 galley of Constantinople | Alcicogli |
| 50 galley of the same | Kara Deli |
| 51 galley of the same | Brus Ali |
| 52 galley of the same | Salach Fachir |
| 53 galley of the same | Ferhat Karadja |
| 54 (lantern) *Capitana* of Constantinople | Tramontana Reis |
| 55 galley of Constantinople | Suleiman Chelebi |
| 56 galley of the same | Deli Ibrahim |
| 57 galley of the same | Murat Chorosan |
| 58 galley of the same | Demir Bali |
| 59 galley of the same | Cabi Heit |
| 60 (lantern) *Capitana* of the scribe of the Arsenal | Murat Trasil |
| 61 galley of Constantinople | Peruis Sinan |
| 62 galley of the same | Dardagan Bali |
| 63 galley of the same | Giafer Caran |
| 64 galley of the same | Dervish Sach |
| 65 galley of the same | Curbali |

---

in the late Middle Ages and conquered by the Ottomans in 1462.

144. The edition reads "44."

# HISTORY OF THE EVENTS

66 governor of Tripoli in Barbary — Giafer Aga
67 galley of Tripoli — Kara Hamat
68 galley of the same — Rustan Cialmaghi
69 galley of the same — Durmis Ogli
70 galley of the same — Schender Dernigi
71 galley of the same — Mehmet Ali
72 governor of Gallipoli — Aziz Clue Aga
73 galley of Gallipoli — Selim Sciach
74 galley of the same — Heder Bashi
75 galley of the same — Sican Mustafa
76 galley of the same — Sala Reis
77 galley of the same — Deli Iskender
78 *Capitana* of Constantinople — Don Maiva
79 galley of Gallipoli — Pervis Luhumagi Ali Reis
80 galley of Gallipoli — Hasuf Bali
81 galley of the same — Siran Bardaci
82 galley of the same — Yusuf Cinigi
83 *Capitana* of Constantinople — Piri Beg Ogli
84 galley of Constantinople — Deli Osman
85 galley of the same — Piri Sisnam
86 galiot of the same — Demir Chelebi
87 galiot of the same — Dervish Hidir
88 galiot of the same — Sinan Mustafa
89 galiot of the same — Hasirgi Reis
90 galley of Constantinople — Asci Ogli
91 galley of Constantinople — Caia Saraf
92 galiot of Giaur Ali — Agadi Ahmed
93 galley of the same — Osman Sehet
94 galley of the same — Dervish Chelebi
95 galley of the same — Giafer Reis
96 *Capitana* of the governor of the Arsenal — Dargadan

## *Left Wing*

1 (lantern) *Capitana* of the corsair — Kara Hodja
2 galley of the same — Chatali
3 galley of Anatolia — Chiuzel Sinan
4 galley of the same — Chior Mehmet
5 galley of the same — Higna Mustafa
6 galley of the same — Cademli Memi

| | |
|---|---|
| 7 galley of the same | Uschiusli Memi |
| 8 galley of the same | Kara Murat |
| 9 galley of the same | Cumi Memi |
| 10 galley of the same | Passa Dervish |
| 11 galley of the same | Iagli Osman |
| 12 galley of the same | Pisma Reis |
| 13 galley of the same | Tasci Sisman |
| 14 galley of the same | Iesil Hogli |
| 15 (lantern) *Capitana* of the galiots | Kara Chelebi |
| 16 galiot of the same | Sirizi Memi |
| 17 galiot of the same | Magli Reis |
| 18 galiot of the same | Osci Assan |
| 19 galiot of the same | Cumgi Hafus |
| 20 galley of Constantinople | Cadeh Sidir |
| 21 galley of the same | Osman Reis |
| 22 (lantern) *Capitana* of the galiots | Kara Peri, corsair |
| 23 galiot of the same | Giul Pervis |
| 24 galiot of the same | Calabodan Suleiman |
| 25 galiot of the same | Iachuli Ahmed |
| 26 galiot of the same | Sayr Giafer |
| 27 galiot of the same | Chior Memi |
| 28 galley of Constantinople | Giusuel Giafer |
| 29 galley of the same | Ramazzan |
| 30 galley of the same | Calem Memi |
| 31 galley of the same | Giesman Ferhat |
| 32 galley of the same | Zumbul Murat |
| 33 galley of the same | Huipris Assan |
| 34 galley of the same | Sarmusach Reis |
| 35 galley of the same | Tumus Suleiman |
| 36 galley of the same | Calcepi Yusuf |
| 37 galley of the same | Techedel Assan |
| 37 galley of the same[145] | Caiaci Memi |
| 39 galley of the same | Osman Bagli |
| 40 (lantern) *Capitana* of Algiers | Karadja Ali |
| 41 galiot of Algiers | Karaman Ali |
| 42 galiot of the same | Alma |
| 43 galiot of the same | Sinan Chelebi |
| 44 galiot of the same | Agdadi Mustafa |

---

145. Printing error for number 38.

# HISTORY OF THE EVENTS

| | |
|---|---|
| 45 galiot of the same | Dagllia Ali |
| 46 galley of Algiers | Seyth |
| 47 galley of the same | Peri Selim |
| 48 galley of the same | Murat Dervish |
| 49 galiot of the same | Hefus Ogli |
| 50 galiot of the same | Muhuczzur Ali |
| 51 galiot of the same | Iaia Osman |
| 52 galiot of the same | Sali Deli |
| 53 galley of Constantinople | Nasut Fachir |
| 54 galley di Negroponte | Gimongi Mustafa |
| 55 galley of the same | Rustan Cinigi |
| 56 galley of the same | Bali |
| 57 galley of the same | Divit Ali |
| 58 galley of the same | Sitina Reis |
| 59 galley of the same | Caram Hidir |
| 60 galley of the same | Magar Ferhat |
| 61 galley of the same | Arnaut Ali |
| 62 galley of the same | Nafis Reis |
| 63 galley of the same | Curmur Rodh |
| 64 galley of the same | Cos Clueagin |
| 65 galley of the same | Cusli Memi |
| 66 galley of the same | Ballagi |
| 67 (lantern) *Capitana* of the son of Uluj Ali | Karam Bey |
| 68 galiot of Valona | Deli Murat |
| 69 galiot of the same | Abazzar Reis |
| 70 galiot of the same | Scin Schiander |
| 71 galiot of the same | Alman Balli |
| 72 galiot of the same | Assan Sciamban |
| 73 galiot of the same | Seit Aga |
| 74 galiot of the same | Assan Sinan |
| 75 galiot of the same | Cumi Falaga |
| 76 galley of Syria | Osman Ginder |
| 77 galley of the same | Dermur Bey |
| 78 galley of the same | Yusuf Ali |
| 79 galley of the same | Kara Alman |
| 80 galley of the same | Murat Brassan |
| 81 (lantern) governor of Syria | Kara Bine |
| 82 galley of Constantinople | Calam Bastagi |

| | |
|---|---|
| 83 galley of the same | Kara Bey |
| 84 galley of the same | Giafer Hidi |
| 85 galley of the same | Ferhat |
| 86 galley of the same | Memi Beyogli |
| 87 galley of the same | Osman Piri |
| 88 galley of the same | Piri Reis |
| 89 galley of the same | Casam Reis |
| 90 galley of the same | Talitagi Reis |
| 91 galley of the same | Rus Chelebi |
| 92 galley of the same | Tatar Ali |
| 93 (flagship) *Capitana* of Algiers | Uluj Ali, king of Algiers |

*Reserve*

| | |
|---|---|
| 1 (lantern) *Capitana* of Constantinople | Murat Dragut Reis |
| 2 fusta of | Karam Casli |
| 3 fusta of | Hassan Reis |
| 4 galeot of Tripoli in Barbary | Abdulah Reis |
| 5 fusta of | Aligan Assan |
| 6 fusta of | Cus Ali |
| 7 fusta of | Giuzel Ali |
| 8 fusta of | Curtat Chelebi |
| 9 (lantern) *Capitana* of | Deli Bey |
| 10 fusta of | Sandagi Memi |
| 11 (lantern) *Capitana* of Constantinople | Dardagan Reis |
| 12 fusta of | Deli Dormus |
| 13 (lantern) Governor of Chios | Caidar Memi |
| 14 fusta of | Shetagi Osman |
| 15 fusta of | Haedir |
| 16 fusta of | Deli Heder |
| 17 fusta of | Armat Memi |
| 18 fusta of | Sufan Reis |
| 19 (lantern) *Capitana* of | Giafer Bey |
| 20 fusta of | Cabil Sinan |
| 21 (lantern) *Capitana* of | Murat Reis |
| 22 fusta of | Sariogi Giafer |
| 23 fusta of | Mor Ali |
| 24 galiot of Tripoli in Barbary | Piyale Murat |
| 25 fusta of | Karadja Ali Reis |
| 26 fusta of | Murat Ali |
| 27 fusta of | Innuz Ali |

| | |
|---|---|
| 28 galley of Constantinople | Assan Sinan |
| 29 fusta of | Bostandji Murat |
| 30 (lantern) *Capitana* of Constantinople | Deli Suleiman |

## THE BATTLE OF LEPANTO

ON SATURDAY, OCTOBER 6 [1571], they sailed from Lepanto, and at the twenty-second hour the entire armada, arranged as detailed above, arrived at the beach of Galanga, and cast anchor there.

Our Christians, having deliberated and resolved to give battle, decided unanimously to depart as soon as possible from the bay of Alexandria and sail toward Patras[146] and from there to try any possible method to entice the enemy to do battle, and if they held back, to proceed toward the fortresses at the entrance of the Gulf of Lepanto and damage the area as much as they could and continue to deploy every possible means to draw them into battle. Therefore His Highness, who was the person responsible for the execution of issues agreed upon and resolved on, exhorted by Agostino Barbarigo and wishing to please the Venetians by demonstrating his courageous spirit, without further ado, that same night, the eve of Sunday, October 7, during the second guard, even though the wind and the sea conditions were adverse, ordered departure from the said bay. He set his course toward the rocks of Curzolari, a short distance from the mainland, with the intention to attack the enemy the following morning.

The latter, meanwhile, had spent the Saturday and the ensuing night in orgies and celebrations, having it for certain that the capture of our armada is at hand. In due time, on the morning of October 7, they set sail intending to intercept the Christian armada in its own port, not caring and not considering that it was already under way and was advancing against them. Unfolding foresails under favorable tailwinds, the enemy sailed toward a rendezvous off the island of Cephalonia. (The just God with His power had brought the

---

146. A city in western Peloponnese, currently the third largest in Greece, overlooking the gulf of Patras. It was conquered by the Ottomans in 1458 and was thereafter several times attacked and temporarily seized by Venice.

two mighty armadas to a distance of no farther than ten or twelve miles apart without catching sight of each other due to the terrain's cover). Both advancing, at two o' clock of the same Sunday, they sighted each other: our forces about to appear behind the rocks of Curzolari, the armada somewhat disorderly as it had travailed around them, the enemy rounding the tip of Peschiere, called by the Greeks Messolonghi. Shouts reverberated immediately from galley to galley, announcing the happy and audacious encounter.

Elated, our Christians began to take down covers, throw gun ports open, sweep the sterns, and position offensive and defensive weapons over gangways and other places as necessary. Everyone was armed with their favorite weapon, arquebuses, halberds, iron maces, piques, swords, and long swords, and manned their stations at the gunwales, gun ports, the stern, the prow, and midship in good order. On board every galley there were two hundred swordsmen; on the squadron and fleet flagships, according to their rank, there were three or four hundred of them. The gunners had loaded all pieces with chain-linked balls, caltrops, shrapnel, and lead balls, and there were throwers of incendiary grenades, "tubes,"[147] and other similar instruments, everything arranged in perfect order and cared for by those who handled them, the arquebuses positioned above the small shields and the small firearms on the stern.[148] The Christian slaves condemned to be galley-rowers were unshackled and granted perpetual freedom, eager to fight for Jesus Christ, who had been so merciful to free them from their servitude, armed with cuirasses, swords, and shields,

---

147. Contarini's *trombe* are most likely throwers or carriers of incendiary and/or explosive devices, the preparation of which is described by the Sienese author Vanoccio Biringuccio, *De la pirotechnia* (Venice: Venturino Rossinello, 1540), ff. 162–63. Carried on the points of pikes, they discharged projectiles or explosives, frequently also the "artificial fire," the explosive made of a variety of combustible materials used as stuffing for incendiary grenades, including the pottery grenades or *pignatelli* used in the defense of Nicosia and Famagusta, ibidem.

148. Contarini uses the Venetian *canolado*. See Augustin Jal, *Glossaire nautique: Répertoire polyglotte de termes de marine anciens et modernes* (Paris: Firmin Didot, 1848), 398–99.

just like everyone else. In the meantime, the galleys took their battle stations and positions in complete silence and admirable order, and then the galleasses were towed by those detailed to them to their assigned positions.

The enemy, however, continued their advance and arranged themselves in battle order as well. Seeing that the commander of the right wing, Giovanni Andrea Doria, was still far out at sea, followed by other galleys, they assumed that he took to flight. Many of the Christians, observing the enemy, who until that time were navigating under sail, lowering them and spreading out into the sea, similarly concluded that there were fleeing. Thus, their spirits bolstered by a false perception, each side endeavored to go ahead and confront the other. As the two armadas positioned themselves, they valiantly prepared for battle. Having spread out in the sea at a distance that allowed them to face one another without impediments and avoiding the danger to run aground, they slowly sailed into a heads-on collision. All powder holds save the smallest ones were closed so that the wounded men could be brought in there and in the lodgings of the galley scribes, taking into account the munitions that were to be issued. To restore and refresh bodily strength as they advanced against the enemy, bread, wine, and cheese, and whatever else could be quickly prepared, were distributed on the prow-to-stern gangways.

Meanwhile His Highness, together with Don Juan de Cardona[149] and the under-secretary climbed into a swift frigate and made a quick pass in front of the galleys, as befits a courageous and prudent commander, exhorting, encouraging, and comforting captains, soldiers, and others before the battle, affirming that our Lord Jesus Christ would be assisting the Christians, promising certain victory if they fought faithfully for Him. He told them, "Now is the time, valorous brothers, to acquire an immortal name and eternal glory, and in one stroke obtain just vengeance for the many injuries received," dispensing the warm and affectionate words that could be expected from such a courageous prince on occasions like that. At his words and exhortations, many of the troops responded

---

149. Contarini has "Don Luigi di Cardona."

vigorously, "Do not doubt, Your Highness, that we are here for that, and rest assured, that we will not fail in our duty!" Having lavished his affectionate attention on the galleys, His Highness returned to his *Reale*, inflaming the courage of his joint commanders, Colonna and Venier. Fully armed, they stood tall, directing, commanding, and exhorting to all the things that were necessary for such a glorious endeavor. Up went the standards and flags of the galleys. His Catholic Majesty's *Reale* raised the standard of the Holy League with the arms of the three allied powers. Like *Reale*, the other galleys also displayed all kinds of banners, streamers, festoons, and insignia, for joyous adornment and elevation of everyone's spirits. Bugles, wind instruments, as well as percussions, tamboure, and all other kinds of instruments sounded the alert, and a single loud cry reverberated over the armada, invoking devoutly the omnipotent God, the Father, the Son, and the Holy Spirit. All quarters hailed vocally His name and that of the Virgin Mary, His blessed Mother.

Priests and many galley commanders traversed the gangways from prow to stern, crucifixes in hand, exhorting and encouraging everyone with devout and stirring words to praise the One who at this moment had descended from Heaven in person to fight the enemies of His most holy name. Inspired and moved by these appeals, the men became one body, one will, and one desire, neither heeding nor fearing death, eager to fight for Jesus Christ. In this, the great mystery and extraordinary miracle of the supreme power of God was manifested, for in one instant all long-festering hatred, malevolence, and capital enmity caused by many grave offenses, which neither the mediation of friends nor the example and terror of justice were able to negate in any way or time, were suddenly obliterated. Accepting willingly the guidance of the great God, the dispenser of all grace, those who had most cruelly persecuted each other now came to embrace like brothers, holding tight and shedding tears. Oh, blessed power of God, merciful toward the faithful, how miraculous are you in your workings!

The nature and layout of the place where the two armadas met up was such that those who would think of fleeing would be facing imminent danger and total loss, because they caught sight of each other only when they were too close, and within a small segment of the sea no larger than 250 miles in circumference, surrounded by landmasses on almost all sides, the open sea stretching no farther than twenty to twenty-five miles. It is closed on the northern side by the section of the Albanian coast called Natolico,[150] which extends for 80 miles from Santa Maura to Lepanto, on the east, by the coast of the Morea, stretching for 70 miles from the Dardanelles to the cape called Tornese,[151] on the southern side the island of Zante extends for 25 miles, and on the western side are the islands of Cephalonia and Santa Maura, one of which, Cephalonia, is 40 miles long, and the other 15 miles. Almost in the middle of this area of the sea, off the coast of the mainland, raise the three islets of Curzolari, not very large, and differing in size. They are about a mile away from the coast, 35 miles from Lepanto, 45 miles from Santa Maura, 70 miles from Cephalonia, and 80 miles from Zante. For sailors, the islets shield Lepanto from northerlies and north-easterlies. The channel of the island of Zante, oriented east-southeast in the middle, begins at the islets called Strivali[152] and is 25 miles long. The channel between that latter island and Cephalonia, four clicks to the southwest, is 12 miles long. The Viscardo Channel, open to the west at Capoducato, is 7 miles long. Due to all this, both sides, as they came across each other so unexpectedly in this area, were forced to go ahead and fight. That is why, in response to those of his [entourage] who reminded him that one should think it through before rushing to battle, His Highness replied well and prudently that this was neither the place nor the time for discussions and that it would suffice if everyone did their duty and adhered to what had been already decided.

The Turkish armada, numbering two hundred and seventy armed vessels, among them two hundred galleys, fifty galiots, and twenty

---

150. Modern Aitolico, on the north shore of the Gulf of Lepanto, part of the municipality of Messolonghi, Greece.

151. Cape Tornese, ancient Chelonites, the site of a Venetian fortress, is a promontory in the Ionian Sea and the westernmost point of the Peloponnese.

152. Greek Strofadi, an island group in the Ionian Sea, 48 km south of Zante.

fuste, advanced in three squadrons arranged in the same manner as the Christian fleet. Ali Pasha was in the middle, commanding the center with ninety galleys; he had Pertau Pasha on his right side, and on his left, the treasurer of the armada, plus a squad of six galleys, three per division, in his reserve. His right wing of fifty-five galleys, facing our left wing, was commanded by Mehmet Sirocco. His left wing, which advanced to confront our right wing, consisted of ninety galleys under the command of Uluj Ali, the king of Algiers.[153] In the reserve, they had no more than ten galleys and twenty fuste. They advanced against our armada arranged in the same way but with a very different mindset.

Don Juan of Austria, Colonna, Venier, as well as all other captains and mercenaries, and ultimately the entire army, went forward in good spirits and one mind, willing to join battle and determined to vanquish the enemy. For their part, the pashas, captains, corsairs, and their entire fleet advanced in the certain hope that the Christians would take to their heels, persuaded more by the cruel savagery, with which they assessed the accidental and baleful events that had occurred among the Christians in the past and assuming the same for this armada, so different in unity and armament, than by rational consideration and diligent examination of their own capabilities and those of their adversary. For they had not been able to establish either the numbers or the condition of the many forces allied in this League, and when they came to face it, they were shocked and confused. Nevertheless, seeing that the Christian armada closed in on them, and having no longer a chance to escape, out of necessity they did not fail to put themselves together in the manner in which one ought to do it when preparing for battle and facing imminent danger. Thus, they too displayed their splendid standards and their galleys raised an infinite number of their banners, as is their custom, inspired and emboldened as they were by the perspective of the Great Lord's favors and the acquisition of rich booty. Yet, as they gradually became

---

153. Uluj Ali (born in Calabria as Giovanni Dionigi Galeni) (c.1519–87) was at the time pasha, bey of Tripoli, and *beylerbey* of Algiers. In 1574, he became ruler of Tunis as well. See Salvatore Bono, *Corsari nel Mediterraneo: Cristiani e musulmani fra guerra, schiavitù e commercio* (Milan: Mondadori, 1993).

aware of the large numbers of the Christian fleet, they could not but realize that they were now forced to do battle, something they had neither thought of nor expected. The commanders, though, were still delighted and in high spirits, for initially they could only see our center, right wing, and reserve, and had not yet spotted the left wing, which was hidden by the cover of the landmass, and were persuaded that there was nothing more, as Kara Hodja had already reported. But, as little by little the entire left wing revealed itself, and they observed the galleasses nimbly rowed in position, they too, became apprehensive.

On our galleys the tambourines played assiduously, however, as did all other kind of instrument, and they rowed in a splendid order, arranged in a way that did not impede their bearing, advancing together in a half-moon formation, waiting up for one another and aligning themselves so that they maintained the set up stipulated by the commanders. As they approached the enemy armada, the divine Majesty decided to fulfill what it had prescribed for chastisement of those who had for a long time afflicted such cruel wounds on the Christian Commonwealth. Unable to suffer any longer that Christ, his Son and our Lord, would appear to have shed his most precious blood for us in vain, as well as to magnify his glorious name, [the divine Majesty] miraculously worked the sea. Until that moment, it was continuously swelling ever stronger against the Christian armada, constraining it to the inconvenience of tacking all the time. But then, it fell still in an instant, to the great and universal amazement of those with expertise in sea matters. The sea calmed to such an extent that it appeared to be not a mobile element but a hard and firm ground. This occurred at the seventeenth hour, as the armadas entered the straights and the sun rotated so that its rays shone eastwards, against our enemies, and the steady westerly breeze that arose favored the Christians for it was strong enough to carry the gun smoke in the face of the enemy.

Then, the Turkish flagship galley fired a shot, immediately seconded by its two wings, giving the signal to attack. With a courageous spirit and terrifying shouts, they lay on their oars. At this daring move,

Commander Venier called the well-armed galleys of Giovanni Loredan and Caterino Malipiero to his stern as backup for his galley. Similarly, Colonna called another two galleys. As the armadas now faced off at the distance of a cannon shot, the six Christian galleasses in the vanguard opened up in a massive assault on the enemy. The unfailing shots of their brisk and assiduous artillery barrage caused grave and irreparable damage that was the beginning of the ruin of the Turkish enemy. The closer their armada came to the Christian fleet, the greater was its destruction and devastation. The enemy did not know how to evade such harsh and annihilating cannonade. Dispirited and frightened, they began to break formation. Still, they continued their obstinate advance, persuading themselves that the galleasses lacked large-caliber ordnance. Then, as they squeezed in between the galleasses, the latter opened up in earnest, continuously firing large shells that crashed on the enemy galleys, wrecking them completely. The destruction and extermination of the Turkish fleet was the greater because according to their battle order they had to pass through the galleasses in order to approach and attack the Christian armada. The damage was augmented by the contrary wind, which grew stronger by the moment, slowing down their passing through the veritable tempest of large projectiles and blinding them, as it carried all the smoke in their faces, while giving time to the valiant bombardiers on the galleasses to destroy one third of their armada, killing and wounding an infinite number, apart from throwing them in complete disarray.

Our men could now see the terrible mess of masts and yardarms, galleys split in the middle, many sinking to the bottom, others burning, still others immobilized, having lost their tack, capsized, and an infinite number of men floating in the water. The entire sea was now swarming with men, masts, oars, paddles, tuns, casks, and all kinds of weapons. It was an incredible thing that just six galleasses, not tested in naval warfare before, wreaked such destruction. They swerved continually, showing now starboard, now port, now prow, now stern, and unleashing such a continuous and terrible tempest of artillery fire, that Mehmet Sirocco, who commanded the enemy's

## HISTORY OF THE EVENTS

right wing, sought to save it by separating from the center and the rest of the armada and sailed along the coast toward the Christian left wing. But its commander, Agostino Barbarigo, boldly sprang against him and, in perfect formation, took advantage of a reef called Malcantone, prevented the enemy progress and barred his way so that not only a galley but a tiny boat could not have passed through. Marino Contarini, Barbarigo's nephew, who led the reserve of that wing, saw the bulk of the Turkish galleys going against his uncle and, spurred on by excessive valor and driven by a rush of blood, hurled himself forward and joined the savage and deadly encounter and horrible artillery fire from both sides.

Their left wing, commanded by Uluj Ali, and the Christian right wing, commanded by Doria, faced off, but as their valorous captains were experts in naval warfare, both hesitated, each seeking to gain an advantage on the other, although in a different manner. Uluj Ali kept his forces under sail, only waiting to see where and in which point to attack to snatch the victory. Doria treaded carefully, conscious of the disadvantage of having only fifty galleys in his wing against the enemy's ninety. Fearing that he would be split in the middle, he stayed on the alert and, keeping the enemy on their guard, together with several galleys moved aside a mile away from the rest of his wing.

In the center, Juan of Austria, Colonna, and Venier with their squadrons advanced in concert on the center of the enemy. As in the wings, the Christian guns of the center fired two, three, four, and five times[154] before the galleys boarded one another, especially the cannons of the gangway, which caused great terror, grave massacre, and much impediment to the enemy, so much so that they were not able to fire many of their pieces and they were later found still loaded. Of those that opened up, many did not do any damage to the Christians, because the prows of the Turkish galleys were much higher than the Christian ones and even with the cannons lowered down to the rostra shots soared so high as to pass above the gunwales of the Christian galleys. All the same, the maddened enemy proceeded to board the Christians with extreme display of courage.

---

154. The text reads "& chi cinque volte."

The latter sprang back on them spiritedly with shouts of victory. A deadly tempest of arquebus shots and arrows was unleashed. It seemed that the sea was ablaze with the lights and flames of the fires continuously lit up by incendiary pots thrown by "bugles" and other similar instruments. Christian and enemy galleys fastened onto one another, three against four, four against six, and six against one. Everyone fought viciously, giving no quarter to the adversary, and already many galleys of both parties were boarded. Turks and Christians fought in close quarter combat, from which few escaped with their lives. Swords, broadswords, scimitars, iron maces, knives, battle axes, arrows, arquebuses, and incendiary grenades slaughtered an infinite number, apart from those who drowned by being thrown or forced to leap, for various reasons, in the sea that already teemed with men and turned red with blood.

Mehmet Sirocco, the commander of the Turkish right wing, met the fierce and courageous resistance by the Christians' left wing and was unable to execute his design. Seeing masts, yardarms, and rigging shredded to pieces and benches and oars blown up in the air with horrendous casualties of his men, he had to put in a strenuous effort to keep them fighting. In the end, many of his galleys, seeking to save themselves from the carnage, ran precipitously aground on the shore, allowing many to reach the land by swimming. But others, who got wounded, or otherwise impeded, or unable to swim, stayed put, counting on the mercy and clemency of the Christians to save their lives. This is the ancient usage, which has now become part of the nature and customs of the Turks. They go strongly and courageously at first and attack, but if they are met up with valorous and determined resistance, they lose heart and flee. Indeed, as there was no hope of succor by overwhelming numbers of men here, nor was there a large cavalry force to back them up, they could not resist the valor of the Christians, who had already boarded the remainder of the enemy galleys and fell on those who opposed them, massacring and cutting them to pieces. In a short time, the enemy galleys were abandoned by their defenders. The Christians slaves, realizing that our men were now in control, broke down, tore up, and shook off their chains, and with the Turks' own weapons in their hands avenged themselves for their savage abuses.

Marco Quirini and Antonio Canale, who were on the other end of the wing, pressed forward but before they could take over that part of the wing all those who remained alive had jumped in the water and fled. However, all the galleys of that wing were seized by the Christians who, avenging themselves for so many injuries, did not leave alive a single infidel. Of this wing perished Marino Contarini, Vincenzo Quirini, and Andrea Barbarigo. Agostino Barbarigo was mortally wounded in the right eye by an arrow, which struck him dumb instantly; of his death there will be word later. Marco Cicogna was left in a very poor condition, severely burned by fire.

In the center, Don Juan of Austria boarded Ali, the admiral of the Turks, and two other captains of his squad. On board Ali's galley there were three hundred Janissary arquebusiers and a hundred crossbowmen, all carrying scimitars, and they fought ferociously. Don Juan had on the deck of his flagship four hundred arquebusiers, selected from the tercio[155] of Sardinia, under the command of the quartermaster, Don Lopez di Figeroa, apart from many other lords and noblemen. They all jumped into the fight like one, most eagerly and vigorously. Notwithstanding the casualties inflicted by the enemy, Colonna pushed on courageously to take over the galley he had boarded. Venier displayed the highest qualities of a valorous captain, hurling himself boldly on the enemy, setting an example to all his men of how to fight. A squadron of seven galleys ganged up on these three commanders, besides other enemy galleys, which continuously flocked to aid them, and they gave a hard time to our men. Then the flagship *Patrona Reale,* the comendador mayor,[156] and two other galleys, *Loredana* and *Malipiera,* seeing the great numbers

---

155. The *tercio* (Contarini uses the Italianized form *terzo*) was the principal Spanish organizational fighting unit of the period, numbering up to 3,000 men and consisting of three companies of pikemen, swordsmen, and arquebusiers.

156. Luis de Requesens y Zúñiga, comendador mayor of Castile, an official managing a large encomienda estate.

massing to assault their supreme commanders, and many other galleys surrounding them, leaped forward and joined the fray in the center most valiantly, killing a great many of the enemy.

In the end, the two courageous fighters, Loredan and Malipiero, after breaking through to the heart of the battle, were killed on their gangways by a salvo of arquebuses, but the defenders of their [galleys] rallied and, inflamed by desire to avenge them, doubled their effort and seized two galleys. Similarly, Venier and Colonna took over another two. At the same time Don Juan, who alone had withstood the charge of five enemy galleys, took over three of them and, repulsed three times from the galley of Ali [Pasha] with great casualties after advancing all the way to the mainmast, in the end conquered it.

With Ali dead, loud cries were heard from all quarters celebrating victory. The Christians had proclaimed it all along, but it had hung in the balance, due to the great casualties and the courageous valor of both sides in the boarding clash in the center. Now the Turks offered no resistance, and the Christians realized that they were victorious, having vanquished the enemy. From that point on the Christians were more inclined to seize and tie up their enemies rather than fight and kill them. Many of the enemy were dispatched or taken prisoner, a great number of Janissaries and an infinite number of soldiers. Only those saved themselves who in the beginning of the battle, seeing the massacre by the galleasses, took to flight in frigates and small vessels. This is what Pertau did. Aware of the imminent defeat, he boarded a caique as stealthily as possible and found refuge ashore as soon as he could do it. In the part of the armada comprising the center and the reserve the galley captains Giovanni Loredan, Caterino Malipiero, Geronimo Venier, Francesco Bono, Giovanni Battista Benedetti of Cyprus, and Giacomo Tressino of Vicenza lost their lives. Many were wounded, among them Giovanni Bembo, Teodoro Balbi, and the prior of Messina, as well as many other courageous knights, noblemen, and soldiers.

The commander of the right wing, Uluj Ali, realized that the battle was lost. Aware that his adversary Doria had moved in for a daring strike and about to invest him, he seized on his advantage and, knowing well what he needed to do to save himself, fell with several galleys on a few of those who had been with Doria but had broken formation, and unleashed a massive onslaught on them. Our forces bore it valiantly and fought back bravely, counting not so much on their limited resources as on the firm hope that they would be rescued. But the aid did not arrive in time, because Doria had dispersed his galleys at too large a distance, and it was a while before he was able to organize a proper attack with the galley *Pisana* in the lead, with the aim to strike Uluj Ali in the back. The latter saw that Doria was now headed directly for him together with other victorious galleys from the center and the left wing, and abandoned the horrendous and overwhelming massacre of those few galleys, which were not able to resist such a great pressure by themselves and took a bad beating. He fled to the open sea with several galleys, towing along and taking with him the galleys of Pietro Bua of Corfu, the prior of Messina, and Luigi Cippico of Trogir.

In this encounter, Benedetto Soranzo kept fighting notwithstanding the three arrow hits he took to the face. In the end, unable to prevent the enemy from taking over his galley, which he defended for a long time with only a handful of men, he gave up his life, sacrificing it to Christ and his country, and took vengeance on the enemy by setting fire to his munitions, which blasted them in the air and denied them the galley, whose burned-down husk was later seen in the water. Here also died Geronimo Contarini, Marc'Antonio Lando, Marc'Antonio Pasqualigo, Giacomo di Mezzo, Giorgio Corner, and the already mentioned Pietro Bua.

Among the badly injured and mortally wounded was Alvise Cippico[157] of Trogir. He had received seven grave wounds while fighting with several enemy galleys and, having remained with only six of his [men] and much weakened, had been overpowered, but succor arrived in time for him and for the prior of Messina, and the galley of the prior and that of the said Luigi Cippico, which

---

157. In the same paragraph, Contarini uses both the Italianized and the Venetian version of Cippico's name.

were already being towed away by Uluj Ali, were rescued. The two of them were saved, although barely alive. Apart from those already mentioned, a Savoyard, a Florentine, and another Western galley were badly battered by the devastating attack of Uluj Ali, as were several others, both in this attack and in others. Yet even though many men were killed and wounded, the valor of the Christians and the favor of God were such that the galleys were saved, except that of Pietro Bua of Corfu, which was taken away by the enemy. By the divine power, by the twenty-first hour the enemy was completely routed, subjugated, and vanquished in such a manner that the rest of the Turkish armada was taken without a blow of the sword, except for those with Uluj Ali. Because of the great advance that he had gained fleeing in the sea, and because there was little left of the day, he was not pursued. The rest surrendered to whoever approached them first.

## AFTERMATH

IT WAS A FRIGHTFUL AND HORRIBLE SPECTACLE to behold the bloodied sea tossing around infinite dead corpses and a pitiful sight to see many and diverse sorts of craft crisscrossing the sea among the many Christians and Turks still alive, tangled together, swimming in the waters, imploring help, clinging to the same piece of wood, and trying to save their lives. From every quarter shouts were heard, piteous voices cried out for mercy from all sides, and the darker it became the more moving and terrifying the spectacle appeared.

As all Turkish galleys were now in the hands of the Christians, they turned to collecting booty and taking the spoils of the enemy. Before the night fell, they had seized everything. Such was the end of the largest and most famous naval battle since the times of Caesar Augustus. It took place almost in the same spot where he vanquished Marc Antony, which occurred at the promontory of Actium, where at present Prevesa is located. The victorious fleet spent the night in Petala and other ports nearby, triumphing over the Ottoman spoils and dragging through the waters the splendid standards of their enemy. This glorious fact was truly great and miraculous: when least expected, and in mere four hours, the great serpent of the Orient was brought low, and a debilitating blow was dealt to the powerful Selim.

Through the diligent guidance of its leaders, at the first hour of the night the Christian armada was already safely in port when a fierce wind arose, whipping up a terrible and furious sea storm. As the locals said, they had never experienced the like of it before. In safety, they preoccupied themselves with the wounded, which the commanders lodged in their own quarters, using every possible care and remedy. The Venetian admiral, Sebastian Venier, dispatched immediately to Venice the galley of Onfre Giustiniani with missives to the Senate [to report on] the felicitous success granted by the hand of God.

The most sagacious prudence of our commanders, the bravery and dexterity of the captains in putting it into action, and the valor of the noblemen and the soldiers in executing it were crucial for the performance of the fleet, for the fathoming of the enemy's whereabouts and designs, for figuring out and availing themselves of any and all advantage, and for exhorting and urging the soldiers to such a glorious accomplishment.

But other than the fact of this most exalted victory, the memory of Don Juan of Austria, the son of Charles V, the invincible emperor, captain-general of the League of His Holiness, King Philip of Spain, and the Venetians, will remain sanctified for eternity and all ages. The more the picture of this divine victory is contemplated, the greater will be the acknowledgement of the debt that every Christian owes to the Catholic King Philip for having sent his brother.

Marc'Antonio Colonna, the noblest Roman, in this most just war admiral of Pius V, can univocally be called upholder of all Christendom. Pope Pius V [is] the holiest among the pontiffs of many years, and his pontificate will undoubtedly be remembered for eternity. For at a time when the Church of Christ was increasingly oppressed by the mighty forces of Turks and Lutherans and needed defense, his work was most pleasing to God, and he succeeded in keeping together in perpetual unity the above-mentioned Holy League.

Sebastian Venier, the admiral of the happy and devout Republic of Venice, demonstrated as much courage in combat as he did show sound judgment in leadership. In this terrible encounter, he served both as a commander and as a valorous soldier, leaving nothing to be desired to envy. He was indispensable for the victory in this massive battle. Does he not merit a bronze statue to commemorate his valor for eternity as an example of how Venetian noblemen ought to serve their country? Agostino Barbarigo, who learned of the victory he so craved three days later, and although he had lost the power of speech and was unable to articulate a word, raised his arms to the heavens, displaying his invincible heart and his contentment, and in death triumphed in this most exalted accomplishment, carrying along to heaven the palm of victory. The princes of Parma and Urbino, who were in the thick of battle, the former with Ettor Spinola, the latter with Monsignor di Leyni, provided eternal testimony for their great valor and emerged victorious.

The comendador mayor, who never left the side of His Highness, accomplished immortal feats, always shielding and assisting him, and displayed immeasurable gallantry. The marquis of Santa Croce, who led the reserve with such sagacity and promptly lent a hand to all those who were attacked or overpowered, gave a vivid example of his great courage and prudence. What greater courage could be displayed by Paolo Giordano Orsini who, at the spearhead of the center, all by himself in the midst of the enemy, vanquished so many galleys? The prior of Messina, Giustiniani, had he not been severely wounded and forced to retire to his quarters — given that he had provided abundant proof of his courage on other occasions — would not have allowed so many of his men to die if Uluj Ali's assault had not been so overwhelming. Both Marco Quirini and Antonio Canale will remain forever renowned in this world for their glorious feats in the entire war, other than the annihilation of the enemy in this battle. Juan de Cardona, the commander of the right wing, who was on one of the galleys badly battered by Uluj Ali, gave a shining example of his bravery by demonstrating that there was more exalted glory in fighting and saving oneself against overwhelming odds than fighting on an equal footing or with an advantage and gaining the victory.

In conclusion, all those who were in this naval encounter, and fought for our Lord Christ and for their country and survived, ought to exult in contributing to such a glorious feat and gaining such a lofty and immortal victory. Those who died are now among the blessed[158] and rejoice that they had been granted the supreme grace to transform through a quick martyrdom the short hours of the mortal life into eternal attendance of God. This should be a great consolation to their fathers and relatives who, knowing that as mortals they cannot engender immortal sons and wishing them to be men of honor, illustrious in the world, have with one stroke achieved the latter and the former, for their eternal glory will never fade away.

Their number, to the extent it can be ascertained by the roster, was 7,656, of them:

    1 squadron commander, Agostino Barbarigo
    17 galleys governors[159]
    8 galley nobles
    5 chaplains
    6 galley captains
    5 galley patrons
    6 scribes
    7 pilots
    113 gunners
    32 masters
    134 marines
    925 fighting men
    2,274 rowers
    1,333 soldiers

---

158. Contarini uses "*beati*," the first stage on the path of sainthood.

159. Here and below, Contarini uses Venetian and traditional Mediterranean terminology for a variety of galley officers and crew, which can be translated only approximately into their modern English nautical equivalents: "governatori di galee," "nobili di galea," "capelani," "comiti," "patroni," "scrivani," "peotti," "bombardieri," "maestranze," "compagni," and "scapoli." For the variety of personnel thus designated, see Jal, *Glossaire nautique* under the respective headings.

2,000 dead in the fleet of His Catholic Majesty
800 dead in the fleet of His Holiness.

From the enemy, 29,990 were killed or taken prisoner, that is:

34 squadron commanders
120 galley captains
25,000 Janissaries, sipachis, irregulars, and slave rowers
3,846 taken prisoner.

The Christians captured 130 enemy vessels, of which 117 were galleys and 13 galiots. They were all brought into port that night with their munitions and everything, the better part loaded with bread, resins, bacon, butter, rice, beans, and other kinds of provisions and victuals, and fully armed. Apart from these, another 130 vessels were abandoned at sea, about 80 were sunk, and it was estimated that about 40 got away.

The victory was celebrated by the armada with three days of feasting and rejoicing, everyone giving thanks to the great God for His generous grace. Music played on the galleys and all sorts of standards and banners were joyfully displayed. Everyone wanted to overhaul their galley and pursue further the victory that had just been won, but because of adverse weather they were forced to put it off and remain in port until the fifteenth [of October]. Meanwhile the wintry season advanced and men continued to die of their wounds. Hence His Highness, seeing that it was an impossible endeavor, did not want to delay further his departure for Messina, especially as there was good hope that in the following year they could duly get together again. The decision taken, they departed, taking the vessels and the spoils of the enemy to Corfu. There, by common consent they were divided as follows:

*Galleys*
to His Holiness as his portion — 19 galleys and 2 galiots
to His Catholic Majesty — 58 ½ galleys and 6 ½ galiots
to the Most Serene Republic of Venice — 39 ½ galleys and 4 ½ galiots

## HISTORY OF THE EVENTS

*Artillery*
 to His Holiness                                19 cannons, 3 periers,[160]
                                                and 42 small cannons
 to His Catholic Majesty                        58 ½ cannons, 8 ½ periers,
                                                and 128 small cannons
 to the Most Serene Republic of Venice, 39 ½ cannons, 5 ½ periers,
                                                and 86 small cannons

*Slaves*
 to His Holiness                                881
 to His Catholic Majesty                        1,713
 to the Most Serene Republic of Venice          1,162.

In the meantime, on the nineteenth [of October] the galley of Onfre Giustiniani, dispatched by Venier, passed through the two castles of Venice.[161] An infinite amount of people had gathered in Piazza San Marco, wavering between hope and fear. But as the felicitous galley approached firing salvo after salvo, it became clearly visible that it dragged through the waters many Turkish banners and that many Christians on board sported Turkish attire. The euphoria of relief and the certain expectation of some kind of fortuitous outcome took hold of everyone, even though they could not even imagine what an exalted and immortal victory had been just won.

Giustiniani himself, after he had disembarked from his galley with the missives of Admiral Venier, reported in detail to the Most Serene Prince Luigi Mocenigo that the entire Turkish armada had been destroyed and captured with minimal losses for the Christians. Immediately upon that, His Serenity, accompanied by the legate of His Holiness, Patriarch Grimani, two councilors, and Cesare Ziliolo, chancellor of His Serenity, who were currently in the palace on other business, and a few other noblemen, descended into the church of our protector San Marco, where the Senate and the clergy had gathered as well, and began to sing *Te Deum laudamus*. A solemn mass was celebrated afterwards, and everyone rendered their thanks

---

160. A short-barreled gun, about 5' long, for short-distance targets.

161. Part of Venice's maritime defense fortifications, two stone towers, constructed at the mouth of the Lido in the fourteenth century and marking the official entry into the Venetian lagoon.

to our Lord God. Forgiving us all sins with His exceptional mercy, in our hour of need, He had granted through His potent hand such a grandiose victory to His Christian people.

On the same day, His Serenity assigned to Giovanni Battista Rafario, a most learned man, the delivery of the oration. Three days later, he recited it in the same church of San Marco, impressing the Most Serene Senate with the marvels of his talent and leaving the infinite multitude of foreign noblemen stupefied by the glorious triumph and by the eloquence and high erudition of the orator. All over the City nothing else was heard but the jubilating shouts of victory and the tolling of bells, and people were seen embracing each other spontaneously and displaying all other signs of joy, through which everyone praised the Creator for His excessive and most generous grace.

THE END

REGISTER

+ ABCDEFGHIKLMNOP

All are standard, except N & P, which are half [size]

IN VENICE

By Francesco Rampazetto

MDLXXII

# GLOSSARY

*Arsilo:* large naval vessel, usually for transporting horses, but other war materiel as well.

*Bailo:* the Venetian resident diplomatic representative at the Ottoman court.

*Beylerbey:* Ottoman territorial governor with civil and military authority.

*Caique:* also caicco (It.) or kayik (Tr.), a small sailing boat, usually a fishing vessel but used in naval warfare for carrying on communications between the larger vessels in a fleet or sending missives. In the Eastern Mediterranean it was usually a vessel with a sprit mainsail, square topsail, and two or more jibs or other sails.

*Caramuscialin:* large vessel of the Ottomans navy, exclusively for transporting troops and war materiel.

*Chaush:* Ottoman emissary with special authority to relay orders and conduct business on behalf of the sultan.

*Fano:* "lantern" or commanders' vessel, usually with the meaning of flagship or squadron leader's ship.

*Fusta:* also *foist* or *fuste*, galley subclass, shallow-draft, fast lateen-sail vessel with twelve banks of oars.

*Galiot:* galley subclass, oared ship, with sixteenth to twenty banks of oars and two lateen-sail masts.

*Great galley:* also galleass, a large galley developed in the later Middle Ages for both commercial and military purposes, carrying both prow guns and between twenty and forty side cannons.

*Maona:* the Ottoman equivalent of the galleass, large and heavy galley, although not as heavily armed and seaworthy; mostly used as transport.

*Pasha:* high-ranking Ottoman official.

*Palandaria:* lateen-sail merchant vessel, mobilized as transport in war time.

*Podestà:* city governor, usually of foreign origins.

*Procurator:* one of the nine topmost Venetian officials; the procurator of San Marco ranked after the Doge in dignity.

*Provveditore:* Venetian official, superintendent with plenipotentiary powers in a certain matter.

*Reis:* Ottoman captain, or sea commander; often adopted as semi-official cognomen.

*Sanjakbey:* Ottoman provincial governor under the beylerbey.

*Sipachi:* Ottoman regular cavalry, state fief-holders.

*Stratioti:* light cavalry in Venetian service, usually consisting of Albanian, Dalmatian, or Greek fighters.

# BIBLIOGRAPHY

### Editions of the History and the Elegantissima Descriptio

*Historia delle cose successe dal principio della guerra mossa da Selim Ottomano a'Venetiani, fino al di della gran giornata vittoriosa contra Turchi, descritta ... da M. Gio. Pietro Contarini Venetiano.* Venice: Francesco Rampazetto, 1572.

*Historia delle cose successe dal principio della guerra mossa da Selim Ottomano a' venetiani, fino al dì della gran giornata vittoriosa contra turchi. Descritta non meno particolare che fedelmente da m. Gio. Pietro Contarini venetiano.* Milan: Pietro and Francescon Tini, 1572.

*Ioan. Petri Contareni veneti Historiae de bello nvper Venetis a Selimo II Tvrcarvm imperatore illato, liber unvs, Ex Italico Sermone in Latinum conuersus a Ioan. Nicolao Stupano.* Basel: Peter Perna, 1573.

*Historia von dem Krieg / welchen newlich der Türkisch Keiser Selim der ander wieder die Venediger erzeget hat. Fleistig und eigentlich beschrieben von Johanne Petro Contarino einem Rhatsverwandten zu Venedig ... in Welscher und Lateinischen sprach erst ausgangen jetz aber von Georgen Henisch von Bartfeld verteütschet.* Basel: Peter Perna, 1574.

*Historische und gründliche Beschreibung der letzten großen Schlacht so zwischen den Venediern und dem Türcken uffn Meer gehalten worden,* translated by Heinrich Habermehl. In manuscript, 1581; printed with corrections, Dresden: Heinrich Schütz, 1599.

*Historia delle cose successe dal principio della guerra mossa da Selim Ottomano a'Venetiani fino al di della gran giornata vittoriosa contra Turchi, già descritta ... da M. Gio. Pietro Contarini et hora ridata alla luce da M. Gio. Battista Combi Veneto.* Venice: Giovanni and Battista Combi, 1645, reprint of the first edition of 1572.

Ioannis Petri Contareni *Elegantissima totius Europae, ac partis Asiae, nec non littorum Africae descriptio.* Venice: [s.n.], 1564.

## EARLY MODERN WORKS IN PRINT AND MANUSCRIPT

Altomira, Francesco. *Narratione della guerra di Nicosia, fatta nel Regno di Cipro da' Turchi nel' anno MDLXX, al illustre Sig. Conte Pompeo Trissino.* Bologna: Biagio Bignami, 1571.

Anonimous. *Errori notabili commesi da Signori Veneti nella risoluzione et ammistratione della Guerra contro il Turco.* Biblioteca Apostolica Vaticana, Cod. Urb. Lat. 855.

Antinori, Bernardo. *Copia d'una lettera scritta dal sig. cavaliere Antinori ai suoi fratelli. Qual narra la felice, et gloriosa vittoria, che ha hauuto l'armata Christiana contra alli nemici perfidi della fede de Giesù Cristo.* Florence: nella Stampa di Lor' Altezze Serenissime, 1571.

Biringuccio, Vanoccio. *De la pirotechnia.* Venice: Venturino Rossinello, 1540.

Camocio, Giovanni Francesco. *L'ordine delle galere et le insegne loro, con il Fano, Nomi, & Cognomi delli Magnifici & generrosi patroni di esse, che si ritrovano nella armata della santissima Lega, al tempo della vittoriosa & miracolosa impresa ottenuta, & fata con lo aiuto Divino contra la orgogliosa & superba armata Turchescha.* Venice: Giovanni Francesco Camocio, 1571.

Caracciolo, Ferrante. *I commentarii delle guerre fatte co' turchi da D. Giovanni d'Austria, dopo che venne in Italia, scritti da Ferrante Caracciolo, conte di Biccari.* Florence: Giorgio Marescotti, 1581.

Corner, Andrea. *Storia universal dell'isola e regno di Candia, del clarissimo Sig. Andrea Corner q. Giacomo, N.H. Mss di ser Vettor Molin fu Avogador di Comun l'anno MDCCLXX*, in Biblioteca Nazionale Marciana, Venice, BNV MVII 1566, ff. 1–187r.

Della Cornia, Ascanio. *Due discorsi dell'ill.mo s.or marchese Ascanio della Cornia maestro di campo generale della Santissima Lega. Dati da lui al sereniss. s. don Giouanni d'Austria circa al combattere con l'armata turchesca. Con la descrittione dell'esequie fatte in Perugia nella morte del medesimo. Et vna canzone in lode del detto d'incerto autore.* Florence: Antonio Padouani, 1571.

Diedo, Girolamo, in Salvatore Mazzarella, ed., *Onorato Caetani,*

Girolamo Diedo, *La battaglia di Lepanto, 1571*. Palermo: Sellerio, 1995, 177–224.

Diedo, Giacomo. *Storia della repubblica di Venezia dalla sua fondazione sino l'anno MDCCXLVII*. Venice: Andrea Poletti, 1751.

Herrera, Fernando. *Relación de la guerra de Cipre y succèsso de la batalla Naval de Lepanto*. In: *Collectión de documentos inéditos para la historia de España* 21. Madrid: Academia de la Historia, 1852, 243–382.

*Il Successo della navale vittoria christiana contra l'armata turca, occorsa (mercé divina) al golfo di Lepanto, di nuovo ristampato....* Venice and Brescia: [s.n.], 1571.

Lescaut de Romegas, M. *Relazione della giornata delle Scorciolare, fra l'armata Christiana e Turchesca alli 7 d'Ottobre 1571, ritratta dal Commendator Romagasso*. Rome: Heredi di Antonio Blado, 1571.

Longo, Francesco. *Successo della guerra fatta con Selim... Archivio Storico Italiano, Appendice* 4 (1847): 3–58.

*L'ordine che a tenuto l'armata della Santa Lega, cominciando dal di che si partì da Messina, con li nomi di tutte le gallere....* Rome: Heredi di Antonio Blado, 1571.

Manolesso, Emilio Maria. *Historia Nova, nella quale si contengono tutti i successi della guerra Turchesca....* Padua: Lorenzo Pasquari, 1572.

Martinengo, Nestore. *Relatione di tutto il successo di Famagosta; dove s'intende ... tutte le scaramuccie, batterie, mine, & assaltidato ad essa fortezza. Et ancora i nomi de i Capitani, & e numero delle Genti morte... et medesimamente di quelli, che sono restati prigioni*. Venice: Giorgio Angelieri, 1572.

Morosini, Andrea. *Degl'istorici delle cose veneziane i qualli hanno scritto per pubblico decreto, tomo sesto che comprende i sei secondi libri dell'istorie latinamente scritte dal Senatore Andrea Morosini*. Venice: Lovisa, 1719.

Pallavicini, Sforza. *Difesa e narrativa del Signor Sforza Pallavicino sopra tutti i progressi dell' armata Venetiana contra Turchi l'anno MDLXX*. Biblioteca Apostolica Vaticana, Cod. Barb. Lat. 5367.

Paruta, Paolo. *Degl' istorici delle cose veneziane i qualli hanno scritto per pubblico decreto, tomo terzo che comprende gli otto primi libri della prima parte dell'istorie veneziane volgarmente scritte da Paolo Paruta.* Venice: Lovisa, 1718.

Pinargenti, Simone. *Isole che son da Venezia.* Venice: Pinargenti, 1573.

Sansovino, Francesco. *Historia universale dell'origine, et imperio de'Turchi. Raccolta, & in diversi luogi di nuovo ampliata, da M. Francesco Sansovino.* Venice: Altobello Salicato, 1582.

Sanudo, Marino. *Venice, Città Excelentissima: Selections from the Renaissance Diaries of Marin Sanudo.* Patricia H. Labalme and Laura Sanguineti White, ed., Linda L. Carroll, trans. Baltimore: Johns Hopkins University Press, 2008.

Sozomeno, Giovanni. *Narratione della guerra di Nicosia fatta nel regno di Cipro da'Turchi l'anno 1570.* Bologna: Biagio Bignami, 1571.

Valderio, Pietro. *La guerra di Cipro, scritta da Pietro Valderio, visconte della città di Famagosta in quell tempo...* Biblioteca Communale di Treviso, MS It. 505 (S3-105-F).

MODERN STUDIES AND EDITIONS

Ágoston, Gábor. *Guns for the Sultan: Military Power and the Weapons Industry in the Ottoman Empire.* Cambridge: Cambridge University Press, 2005.

Ágoston, Gábor and Bruce Masters. *Encyclopedia of the Ottoman Empire.* New York: Facts on File, 2009.

Alfani, Guido. *Calamities and the Economy in Renaissance Italy: The Grand Tour of the Horsemen of the Apocalypse.* New York: Palgrave Macmillan, 2010.

Arbel, Benjamin. "Cyprus on the Eve of the Ottoman Conquest." In Michalis Michael, Matthias Kappler, and Eftihios Gavriel, ed., *Ottoman Cyprus: A Collection of Studies on History and Culture.* Wiesbaden: Harrassowitz Verlag, 2009, 37–48.

Barbero, Alessandro. *Lepanto: La battaglia dei tre imperi.* Bari: Laterza, 2010.

Battaglia, Salvatore. *Grande dizionario della lingua italiana* 1. Turin: UTET, 1961.

# BIBLIOGRAPHY

Benzoni, Gino. "Contarini, Gianpietro." DBI 28 (1983). Online at: http://www.treccani.it/enciclopedia/gianpietro-contarini_ (Dizionario-Biografico).

Bertoni, Giulio. *Dizionario di marina medievale e moderno.* Rome: Reale Academia d'Italia, 1937.

Bono, Salvatore. *Corsari nel Mediterraneo: Cristiani e musulmani fra guerra, schiavitù e commercio.* Milan: Mondadori, 1993.

Braudel, Fernand. *The Mediterranean and the Mediterranean World in the Age of Philip II.* Siân Reynolds, trans. Vol. 2. "Part Three: Events, Politics, and People." Berkeley: University of California Press, 1995.

Brummett, Palmira. *Ottoman Seapower and Levantine Diplomacy in the Age of Discovery.* Albany: State University of New York Press, 1994.

Bucheno, Hugh. *Crescent and Cross: The Battle of Lepanto 1571.* London: Phoenix, 2004.

Bulgarelli, Tulio. "La battaglia di Lepanto e il giornalismo romano del Cinquecento." *Accademie e biblioteche d'Italia* 29 (1961): 231–39.

Bulgarelli, Tulio. *Gli avvisi a stampa in Roma nel Cinquecento: Bibliografia-Antologia.* Rome: Istituto di Studi Romani Editore, 1967.

Cacciavillani, Ivone. *Lepanto.* Rome: Fiore, 2003.

Canosa, Roberto. *Lepanto: Storia della "Lega Santa" contro i Turchi.* Rome: Sapere, 2000.

Capponi, Niccolò. *Victory of the West: The Great Christian-Muslim Clash at the Battle of Lepanto.* Cambridge, MA: Da Capo Press, 2007.

Carmoly, Eliakim. *Don Joseph Nassy, Duc de Naxos.* Frankfurt-am-Main: George Hess, 1868.

Catizzani, Policarpo, ed. *Narrazione del terribile assedio e della resa di Famagusta nell' anno 1571 da un manoscritto del Capitano Angelo Gatto da Orvieto.* Orvieto: Tosini, 1895.

Cobham, Claude Delaval. *Excerpta Cypria: Materials for a History of Cyprus.* Cambridge: Cambridge University Press, 1908, reprint, New York: Kraus, 1969.

Cobham, Claude Delaval. *Travels in the Island of Cyprus. Translated from the Italian of Giovanni Mariti with contemporary accounts of the sieges of Nicosia and Famagusta.* 2nd ed., Cambridge: Cambridge University Press, 1909, reprint, London: Zeno, 1971.

Constantini, Vera. "In Search of Lost Prosperity: Aspects and Phases of Cyprus's Integration into the Ottoman Empire." In Michael et al., *Ottoman Cyprus*, 49–61.

De la Graviere, Jurien. *La Guerre de Chypre et la Bataille de Lepante.* 2 vols. Paris: Plon, 1888.

DeVries, Kelly and Robert D. Smith. *Besieged Rhodes: A New History.* Stroud: The History Press, 2012.

Dio Cassius. *Roman History.* Earnest Cary, trans. Cambridge, MA: Harvard University Press, 1917.

Dionissoti, Carlo. "Lepanto nella cultura italiana del tempo." In Gino Benzoni, ed., *Il Mediterraneo nella seconda metà del '500 alla luce di Lepanto.* Florence: Olschki, 1974, 127–52.

Fenlon, Ian. "Lepanto: The Arts of Celebration in Renaissance Venice." *Proceedings of the British Academy* 73 (1987): 221–26.

Fisher, Alan. "The Life and Family of Suleyman I." In Halil Inalcık and Cemal Kafandar, ed., *Süleyman the Second and His Time.* Istanbul: Isis Press, 1993.

Gavriel, Eftihios. "The Expedition for the Conquest of Cyprus in the Work of Kâtib Çelebi." In Michael et al., *Ottoman Cyprus*, 25–36.

Gruenbaum-Ballin, Paul. *Joseph Naci, duc de Naxos.* Paris: Mouton, 1968.

Guerrieri, Maria Gabrielli Donati. *Lo stato di Castiglione del Lago e i della Corgna.* Castiglione del Lago: Grafica, 1972.

Guglielmotti, Alberto. *Marcantonio Colonna alla battaglia di Lepanto.* Florence: Felice le Monnier, 1862.

Guilmartin, John F., Jr. *Gunpowder and Galleys: Changing Technology and Mediterranean Warfare at Sea in the Sixteenth Century.* Annapolis: Naval Institute Press, 2003.

Herodotus. *The Histories.* Robin Waterfield, trans. Oxford: Oxford University Press, 1998.

Hess, Andrew. "The Battle of Lepanto and Its Place in Mediterranean History." *Past and Present* 57 (1972): 53–73.

Hill, George. *A History of Cyprus* 3. *The Frankish Period, 1432–1571.* Cambridge: Cambridge University Press, 1948, reprint, 2010.

Hocquet, Jean-Claude. "Venice." In Ricard Bonney, ed. *The Rise of the Fiscal State in Europe, 1200–1815.* Oxford: Oxford University Press, 1999.

Imber, Colin. "The Reconstruction of the Ottoman Fleet after the Battle of Lepanto, 1571–1572." In *Studies in Ottoman History and Law.* Colin Imber, ed. Istanbul: The Isis Press, 1996, 85–102.

Inalcık, Halil. "Lepanto in the Ottoman Documents." In Benzoni, ed., *Il Mediterraneo*, 185–92.

Jal, Auguste. *Glossaire nautique: Répertoire polyglotte de termes de marine anciens et modernes.* Paris: Firmin Didot, 1848.

Jamieson, Alan. *Lords of the Sea: A History of the Barbary Corsairs.* London: Reaction Books, 2012.

Kagan, Donald. *The Peloponnesian War.* New York: Penguin Books, 2004.

Kahare, Henry, Renée Kahare, and Andreas Tietze. *The Lingua Franca in the Levant: Turkish Nautical Terms of Italian and Greek Origin.* Champaign-Urbana: University of Illinois Press, 1958, repr. Istanbul: ABC Kitabevi, 1988.

Kamen, Henry. *The Duke of Alba.* New Haven: Yale University Press, 2004.

Lesure, Michel. *Lépante: La crise de l'empire Ottoman.* Paris: Julliard, 1972.

Levy, M.A. *Don Joseph Nasi, Herzog von Naxos: Seine Familie, und zwei jüdische Diplomaten seiner Zeit.* Breslaw: Scheletter'sche Buchhandlung, 1859.

Losada, Luis. *The Fifth Column in the Peloponnesian War.* Boston and Leiden: Brill, 1972.

Malcolm, Noel. *Agents of Empire: Knights, Corsairs, Jesuits, and Spies in the Sixteenth-Century Mediterranean World*. Oxford: Oxford University Press, 2016.

Manoussacas, Manoussos. "Lepanto e i Greci." In Benzoni, *Il Mediterraneo*, 215–42.

Meeker, Michael. *A Nation of Empire: The Ottoman Legacy of Turkish Modernity*. Berkeley: University of California Press, 2001.

Molmenti, Pompeo. *Sebastiano Venier e la battaglia di Lepanto*. Florence: Barbèra, 1899.

Paruta, Paolo. *Storia della Guerra di Cipro Libri Tre*. Siena: Rossi, 1827.

Peirce, Leslie. *Empress of the East: How a European Slave Girl Became Queen of the Ottoman Empire*. New York: Basic Books, 2017.

Pezzolo, Luciano. "The Rise and Decline of a Great Power: Venice 1250–1650." *Working Papers of the Department of Economic, Ca' Foscari University of Venice* 27 (2006): 1–31.

Pezzolo, Luciano. *L'oro dello stato: Società, finanza, e fisco nella reppublica veneta del secondo '500*. Venice: Il Cardo, 1990.

Preto, Paolo. "Le Grandi Paure di Venezia nel secondo '500: Le paure naturali (peste, carestie, incendi, terremoti)." In Vittore Branca and Carlo Ossola, ed. *Crisi e rinnovamenti nell'autunno del Rinascimento a Venezia*. Florence: L.S. Olschki, 1991, 177–92.

Quarti, Guido A. *La guerra contro il Turco in Cipro e a Lepanto, 1570–1571: Storia Documentata*. Venice: Bellini, 1935.

Ravid, Benjamin. "Money, Love, and Power Politics in Sixteenth-Century Venice: The Perpetual Banishment and Subsequent Pardon of Joseph Nasi." In *Italia Judaica: Atti del I Convegno internazionale, Bari 18–22 maggio 1981*. Rome: Ministero per i Beni Culturali e Ambientali. Pubblicazioni degli Archivi di Stato, 1983, 159-81.

Redolfi, Maddalena. *Venezia e la difesa di Levante: Da Lepanto a Candia, 1570–1670*. Venice: Arsenale, 1986.

Repp, Richard. *The Müfti of Istanbul: A Study in the Development of the Ottoman Learned Hierarchy.* London: Ithaca Press, 1986.

Reznik, Joseph. *Le Duc Joseph de Naxos: Contribution a l'histoire juive du XVIs siècle.* Paris: Librairie Lipschutz, 1936.

Rivero Rodríguez, Manuel. *La batalla de Lepanto: Cruzada, guerra santa e identidad confessional.* Madrid: Silex Ediciones, 2008.

Rhodes, Dennis E. "La battaglia di Lepanto e la stampa popolare a Venezia: Studio bibliografico." In Alessandro Scarsella, ed. *Metodologia bibliografica e storia del libro: Atti del seminario sul libro antico offerti a Dennis E. Rhodes. Miscellanea Marciana* 10–11 (1995-1996): 9–63.

Rodrigues-Gonzales, Augustin. *Lepanto: La batalla que salvo Europa.* Baracaldo: Grafite, 2004.

Rose, Constance. "New Information on the Life of Joseph Nasi, Duke of Naxos: The Venetian Phase." *The Jewish Quarterly Review* 60 (1969–70): 330–44.

Rosell, Cayetano. *Historia del combat naval de Lepanto y juicio de la importancia de aquel suceso.* Madrid: Imprimeria de la Real Academia de la Historia, 1853.

Rozzo, Umberto. "La battaglia di Lepanto nell'editoria dell'epoca e una miscellanea fontaniana." *Rara Volumina* 1–2 (2000): 41–69.

Shuckburgh, Evelyn S., ed. and trans. *The Histories of Polybius.* 2 vols. Cambridge: Cambridge University Press, 2012.

Serrano, Luciano, ed. *Correspondencia diplomatica entre España y la Santa Sede durante el pontificado de S. Pio V.* 4 vols. Madrid: Tipografia de la Revista de Archivos, 1914.

Serrano, Luciano. *La liga de Lepanto entre España, Venecia, y la Santa Sede (1570–1573): Ensayo historico abase de documentos diplomaticos.* 2 vols. Madrid: Tipografia de la Revista de Archivos, 1918–20.

Setton, Kenneth. *The Papacy and the Levant, 1204–1571.* 4. *The Sixteenth Century: From the Reign of Julius III to Pius V.* Philadelphia: American Philosophical Society, 1976.

Soucek, Svat. "Certain Types of Ships in Ottoman-Turkish Terminology." *Turcica* 7 (1975): 233–49.

Stockhamer, Avishai. *Don Joseph Nasi: A Marrano's Rise to Power.* New York: Mesorah, 1991.

Stouraiti, Anastasia. "Costruendo un luogo della memoria: Lepanto." In *Meditando sull'evento di Lepanto: Odierne interpretazioni e memorie, Convegno storico. Venezia, 8 novembre 2002. Raccolta delle relazioni.* Venice: Studi Veneziani, Series Storia di Venezia, 2002.

Thucydides. *History of the Peloponnesian War.* Oxford: Oxford University Press, 1960.

Tusa, Sebastiano, and Jeffrey Royal. "The Landscape of the Naval Battle at the Egadi Islands (241 BC)." *Journal of Roman Archaeology* 25 (2012): 7–48.

Vargas-Hidalgo, Rafael. *La Batalla de Lepanto: Segun cartas ineditas de Felipe II, don Juan de Austria y Juan Andrea Doria e informes de embajadores y espias.* Santiago: CESOC, 1998.

White, Elizabeth, Sarah Spence, and Andrew Lemons, ed. and trans. *The Battle of Lepanto.* Cambridge, MA: Harvard University Press, 2014.

Yermolenko, Galina, ed. *Roxolana in European Literature, History, and Culture.* London: Ashgate, 2016.

Yıldırım, Onur. "The Battle of Lepanto and Its Impact on Ottoman History and Historiography." In Rosella Cancila, ed. *Mediterraneo in armi (Sec. XV-XVIII).* Palermo: Associazione Mediterranea Quaderni-Mediterranea, *Ricerche Storiche* 4 (2007): 533–56.

Zilfi, Madeline. "The Ottoman *ulema.*" In Suraiya Faroqhi, ed. *The Cambridge History of Turkey* 3. *The Later Ottoman Empire, 1603–1839.* Cambridge: Cambridge University Press, 2006.

Zupko, R.E. *Italian Weights and Measures from the Middle Ages to the Nineteenth Century.* Philadelphia: American Philosophical Society, 1981.

# INDEX

We have indexed all proper names, from the greatest families to the lowliest knights. The index offers a valuable snapshot of Christian military aristocracy and forms of service, of the Venetian colonial aristocracy, of the provenance and positions of the Ottoman serving elite. Contarini derived his information from several sources; and neither he, nor his publisher, nor subsequent editions and translations regularized the differing spelling and transliteration of Italian and foreign proper names, place names, and titles. To avoid confusion, the following transliteration system has been adopted. Italian and other Western names are rendered in their modern form, with the dialect (mainly Venetian) form in which they occasionally appear in the text in parentheses. The Ottoman Turkish names, with a few exceptions, are rendered as Contarini has them in the text, with his phonetic transliteration, Romanized and/or converted to avoid the special characters of modern Turkish, according to the systems adopted by Eleazar Birnbaum, "The Transliteration of Ottoman Turkish for Library and General Purposes," *Journal of the American Oriental Society* 87.2 (April–June 1967): 122–56; and Halil Inalcik, *The Survey of Istanbul 1455: The Text, English Translation, Analysis of the Text, and Documents* (Istanbul: Ege Yayinlari, 2012).

## A

Abazzar Reis 111
Abruzzo 21
Accoramboni, Camillo 39
Actium, battle of 126
Adami, Bonifacio 38
Adamo, Aniballe 76
Adrianopolis 8
Adriatic Sea 14, 15, 71. *See also* the Gulf.
Aegospotami, battle of 4
Agadi Ahmed 109
Agadi Rustan 106
Aga Pasha 106
Agdadi Mustafa 110
Agdadi Reis 108
Agubio 76
Aintap, sanjakbey 76
Aitolico. *See* Natolico.
Albania 22, 60, 69, 70
Albarino, Ottaviano 39

Albini, Pietro 29
Alcazar xv
Alcicogli 108
Aleppo 75, 76
Alexander the Great 3
Alexandria: Egypt 105; Greece 95, 98, 99, 113
Algagia Sinan 106
Algiers 97, 110, 111, 112, 118
Aligan Assan 112
Ali Pasha (Müezzinzade) xiii, 12, 18, 22, 26, 28, 34–36, 52, 59, 62, 96, 104, 108, 118, 123–24; strategy 43
Alma 107, 110
Alman Balli 111
Alma Reis 107
Altomira, Francesco xix
Amadei, Francesco 94
Ambracian Gulf. *See* Gulf of Arta.
Amphilochia 95
Anatolia 22, 43, 44, 75, 76, 106, 109

Ancona 25
Andrada, Gil 86–88, 91
Andrea, Giovanni 27, 31, 33, 41, 77, 79, 81, 85, 86, 90–94, 115
Angelo, Giovanni 90
Antikyra 96
Antipaxos 95
Antivari 71
Aquaviva family 21
Aquileia 3, 5, 19
Arab Ahmad Pasha 54
Arabia 76
Arbe 41, 93
Archangelo, Alfonso 38
Archipelago 10, 14, 19, 23, 29, 46–48, 52, 54
Armat Memi 112
Arnaut Ali 111
Arnaut Chelebi 107
Arnaut Ferhad 106
Asci Ogli 109
Ascoli 61, 76, 95
Aspropiti 96
Assam Bey 107
Assan Sciamban 111
Assan Sinan 111, 113
Astypalaia. *See* Stampalia.
Athens 3, 4
Atlantic Ocean 64
Atri 21
Attalus, king 3
Attavanti, Pandolfo 20
Augustus, emperor 4, 126
Averaldo, Ferrante 20
*avvisi* xix–xx
Avogadro: Alvise 21; Rambaldo 39
Avonal, Nicolò 23, 42, 90
Aziz Clue Aga 109

## B
Baccio of Pisa 91
Bachini, Cesare 38
Bachla Reis 107

Badoer: Francesco 21, 42; Piero (Pietro) 15, 22, 40, 55, 91, 94
Bagdar Reis 108
Baghdad Assan 106
Baglione (Baglioni): Astorre 21, 28, 37, 76; Francesco 41, 56, 57, 60, 66; Frederico 76
Bagli Saraf 105
Bagnato, Josef 39
Bagnese, Simone 76
Balbi: Alvise 42, 94; Teodoro (Todaro) 15, 42, 50, 92, 124; Zuan 21, 42
Balci (Balzi), Giovanni (Zuan) 15, 42, 91
Baldinazzo, Giovanni Maria 38
Bali 108, 109, 111
Ballagi 111
Baluhji Ogli 107
Bar 71, 102. *See* Antivari.
Barattier, Camillo 38
Barbarigo: Agostino 52, 53, 82, 85, 86, 89, 113, 121, 123, 128, 129; Alvise Barbaro 16; Andrea 17, 39, 42, 55, 89, 123; Christoforo 39; Giorgio (Zorzi) 24, 42, 89; Giovanni 93; Lorenzo 21, 42; Marco Antonio 16; Michiel 16, 41, 70; Piero (Pietro) 23, 42
Barbaro: Barzotto 66, 72; Daniele I, patriarch 19; Francesco 17; Zaccaria 21, 42
Barbarossa, of Algiers 97, 100, 107
Barbary 99, 101, 104, 109, 112
Barbetta, Onorio 39
Bardach Chelebi 106
Barila, Federico 38
Barise, Giacomo 39
Barone, baron 38
Basio, the renegade 81
Bastian of Sole Fiorentino 76
Battaglino, captain 93
Bayazid Siman 105

# INDEX

Bayezid, sultan 7, 8
Bazarci Mustafa 108
Belvi, Giovanni Alvise 90
Bembo: Alvise 21, 34, 41; David 16, 42; Giovanni (Zuan) 15, 22, 41, 94, 124; Luigi 44
Benedetti, Giovanni Battista 15, 40, 64, 77, 94, 124
Benitses 88
Bentivoglio, Cesare 38
Benzati, Piero 39
Bergamo 20, 39, 91
Bernardino of Agubio 76
Bernardo, Lorenzo 25, 43
Bertolazzi, Piero (Pietro) 15, 42, 70
Bevilacqua, Bonifacio 39
Bienzini, Ortensio 38
Birejik 75
Bisali, Angolo 94
Bisante, Girolamo 94
Bizanti, Marian 41
Black Ali. *See* Kara Ali.
Boccabella, Giovanni Bartolomeo 39
Boccapodoca, Tiberio 39
Bodinello 41
Bogone, Francesco 57
Bollani, Constantin 55
Bon: Antonio 23, 42, 50, 93; Francesco 15, 23, 42, 50, 90, 91
Bonacelli, Camillo 21
Bono, Francesco 124
Bonvecchio, Francesco 89
Borsh 69
Boschetto, Baldistera 40
Bosnia 76
Bostandji Murat 113
Bottino, Paulo 91
Bragadin: Ambrogio 25, 43, 86, 89, 90; Andrea 16, 56, 57, 60, 68, 73, 74, 75; Antonio 25, 43, 86; Giulio 16; Marc'Antonio 37; Vettor 52
Brescia 19, 20, 40, 76, 90

Brindisi 80, 84, 85
Brunello, Camillo 39
Brus Ali 108
Brusali Piri 106
Bua, Pietro 94, 125, 126
Budva 71, 78, 102
Bugon, Francesco 76, 77
Buonrizzo, Alvise 16
Bureter, Rosano 39
Butrint 69, 70, 81
Buyuk Kasapoglu 105
Buzzacarini, Pataro 55, 93
Byzantion 3. *See also* Constantinople.

## C

Cabi Heit 108
Cabil Sinan 112
Cadeh Sidir 110
Cademli Memi 109
Caia Beg 99
Caia Celebi 37, 40, 43, 99
Caia Chelebi 106, 108
Caiaci Memi 110
Caia Saraf 109
Caidar Memi 112
Calabodan Suleiman 110
Calabrese: Marco 40; Moretto 40
Calabria 78, 118
Calafat Cheder 105
Calafat Ogli 107
Calam Bastagi 111
Calcepi Yusuf 110
Calem Memi 110
Calergi: Andrea 23, 42, 93; Giacomo 23, 42; Giorgio 90; Mattio 16, 41
Calesano, Giovanni 38
Calesati, Daniel 90
Calipei Memi 106
Callassa 28
Calogiero. *See* Soassera.
Cameti, Andrea 38

Camocio, Giovanni Francesco xx, 27
Canale: Antonio 59, 63, 64, 77, 78, 80, 82, 86, 89, 123, 128; Fabio 17
Candia 15, 18, 24, 25, 28, 29, 30, 31, 33, 34, 37, 40, 42, 43, 45, 47–52, 54, 58, 59, 61, 62, 63, 64, 66, 68, 69, 72, 73, 77, 78, 79, 80, 89, 90, 91, 92, 93, 96, 102, 105. See also Crete.
Canea (Chania) 23, 40, 42, 47, 48, 50, 59, 62, 63, 89, 90, 92, 93
Caneval, Agostin 89
Caocolonne 47
Cape: Drepano (Drepanum) 59; Ducato 64; Gramvousa 33; Matapan 24; Meleca 59; Salomon 40, 50; Schilaci 87; Tornese (Chelonites) 117
Capizuco: Biagio 39; Giorgio 37
Capo d'Istria 42, 89
Capello: Piero 59; Polo 64
Capoducato 117
Caracciolo, Metello 91
Carafa, Cesare 20, 39
Caramania 35, 46, 75
Caraman Pasha 35
Caram Hidir 111
Carchiopulo, Stelio 93
Carissimi, Francesco 38
Carpasso 20
Carthaginians 4
Casam Reis 112
Casli Caia 105
Cassius Dio 4
Castel: Bianco 87; Nuovo 71, 78, 87; Rosso 54; Tornese 53
Castile 86, 123
Catalonia 69
Catholic king. See Philip II, king.
Catholic majesty. See Philip II, king.
Cavalier de Volti 57
Cavalier Goito 56
Celan, Guerrier 38
Celio, sargeant-major 61

Celsi: Bartolomeo 16, 42; Giacomo 14, 22, contingents & numbers 42; Lorenzo 42
Centurione, Giulio 94
Cephalonia 64, 69, 89, 95, 96, 102, 103, 105, 113, 117
Cereteli, Alessandro 38
Cerigo 63, 102
Ceruto, Tiberio 77
Cesare of Adversa 76
Charles V, emperor 83, 101, 127
Chatali 109
Cheder Aga 106
Cheder Siman 106
Chiappe, Giacomo 93
Chior Mehmet (Memi) 109, 110
Chios 3, 52, 53, 112
Chiugeve Mustafa 106
Chiuzel Sinan 109
Chlemoutsi. See Castel Tornese.
Cicogna (Cigogna): Marco 16, 89, 123; Zuan 41
Cicuta, Lodovico 15, 42, 90
Çihangir the Hunchback 7
Cilicia 26
Cimera, Marco 89
Cinoguera, Bernardo 91
Cippico: Alvise (Luigi) 41, 93, 125; Christofalo 15
Città di Castello 76
Ciurano, Benetto 39
Cividale 20
Civran, Benedetto 20
Clement VII, pope 5
Cleopatra, queen 4
Cocco (Coco): Bernardino 76; Lorenzo 31
Cochin, Georgio 94
Colach Reis 107
Coleoni (Colleone) Giovanni (Zuan) Antonio 55, 91
Colomba, Giovanni Battista 29, 33
Colonna: Marc'Antonio 31, 33, 39,

# INDEX

45, 47–49, 69, 78, 82, 86, 92, 116, 118, 120, 123, 124, 127, contingents & numbers 41–42; Pompeo 41; Prospero 41
Colsi, Matteo 73
Condocolli, Cristofolo 90
Congoli, Roberto 38
Constantinople: Arsenal 108, 109; battle of 3; High Porte 75; hospices and madrasas 8; Jews 10; news 52, 78; Ottoman military base 14, 18, 46, 48, 49; Pera 18; Venetian bailo 16
Contarini: Alessandro 15, 22, 40, 50, 92; Bertuzzi 42, 91, 55; Carlo 42; Francesco 18, 42; Geronimo 25, 43, 55, 91, 125; Giovanni (Zuan) 18, 42, 90; Giovanni Battista 15, 22, 40, 45, 88, 94; Giovanni Pietro: causality xxii, *Elegantissima descriptio* xviii, xxv, life and works xvii–xxi, publication history xxv, sources xx–xxi; Girolamo 16, 25; Marino 15, 40, 88, 121, 123; Paolo 95
Conte, Piero (Pietro) 40, 57, 60, 61, 76
Corfo, Santo 38
Corfu 19, 21–23, 25–28, 40, 45, 48, 53, 54, 59, 64, 65, 69, 70, 81, 84, 87, 88, 90, 93–96, 102, 105, 125, 126, 130
Cornaro: Andrea 89; Francesco 21, 24; Georgio 16; Girolamo 93
Corner: Francesco 41, 42, 93; Giorgio (Zorzi) 41, 90, 125
Corniglia, Antonio 93
Corsica 19
Cortese, Andrea 29, 30
Cos Clueagin 111
Coz Ali 107
Crema 39, 93
Cremona 76
Cres 15, 22, 40, 64
Crete 14, 23, 28, 29, 33, 37, 48, 49, 53, 54; Ottoman conquest xiv
Crissa, Cristofalo 89
Crivelatore, Marco 76
Croton 80, 87
Cuiran, Pietro 16
Cumgi Hafus 110
Cumi Falaga 111
Cumi Memi 110
Curbali 108
Curmur Rodh 111
Curtat Chelebi 112
Curzola 71
Curzolari xi, 3, 4, 95, 113, 114, 117
Cus Ali 112
Cusli Memi 111
Cyprus: archbishop 20; Carpass 20, 28; Gardens 36; Ottoman conquest xiv, xxiv, 26–29; Ottoman strategy xii, xiii, 9, 11, 12–15, 14, 17; Venetian administration 26
Cytaeum (Paleocastro). *See* Fraschia.

# D

da Bazán: Alonzo 41; Álvaro 41, 85, 94
da Caglie, Antonio 38
da Canal: Antonio 16, contingents & numbers 42; Gabriel 16, 41, 91; Geronimo (Girolamo) 18, 42, 91; Vecenzo (Vincenzo) 18, 42
da Colalto, Antonio 40
da Costa, Nicolò 93
d'Ada, Ludovico 39
da Dulcigno, Bruto 39
da Fabiano, Agostino 38
da Fabriano, Giacomo 61
da Fermo: Erasmo 61; Marchetto 65
Dagllia Ali 111
da Lezze: Giovanni 17; Priamo 16, 41

dalla Cornia, Ascanio  79–80, 82
dalla Cuevas, Giovanni  90
dalla Lata, Paolo  38
dall'Asta, knight  76
dalle Cernole, Bartolomeo  76
dalle Haste, knight  74
dall' Nero, knight  39
Dalmatia  17, 49, 70, 71, 78–80
da Lonà, Vido  39
da Luvan, Nicolò  92
dal Vin, Antonio  38
Dami, Ottaviano  38
da Molin: Francesco  23, 42, 50; Marco  18, 41, 94; Paolo  31
da Monte, Vicenzo  38
da Mosto: Giacomo  21, 43; Nicolò  25, 42
da Napoli, Celsi  39
Dandolo: Bartolomeo  55; Francesco  91; Giovanni (Zuan)  24, 42; Marin  15, 40; Nicolò  28
da Padua: Bonifacio  39; Ludovico  39
da Pesaro: Andrea  25, 43, 93; Girolamo  21
da Pola, Sergio  39
da Porto, Lodovico  59, 94
Dardagan Bali  108
Dardagan Bardambeli  105
Dardagan Reis  112
Dardanelles  117
Dargadan  109
da Sacile, Girolamo  74
d'Ascoli, Antonio  61, 95
da Seffa, Ugolino  39
d'Asti, Georgio  91
da Thiene, Antonio  38
da Torre, Lorenzo  93
Davalo, Giovanni  87
da Velasco, Bernardino  41
da Veletri, Horatio  57
da Vepi, Galeazzo  21
Davit Yusuf  106

de Accaves, Teribio  90
de Aguilar, Emanuel  92
de Aschale, Giovanni  94
de Benavides, Francesco  92
de Busto, Pietro  93
de Caide, Martino  92
de Cardona, Juan  77, 85, 86, 89, 92, 115, 128
de Contrarii, Hercole  21
de Coronado, Vasquez  95
de Dominis, Giovanni (Zuan)  15, 41
degli Alessandri, Vincenzo  18
de Glianos, Diego Lopes  92
de Heredia, Luis  95
Delagia, Pietro  94
de la Graviere, Jurien  xx
Delfino, Giovanni  20
Deli Aga  105
Deli Assan  107
Deli Bey  112
Deli Chelebi  107
Deli Chiafer  107
Deli Dormus  112
Deli Heder  112
Deli Ibrahim  108
Deli Iskender  109
Deli Murat  111
Deli Osman  109
Deli Piri  107
Deli Suleiman  113
Deli Yusuf  108
della Corbara, Jacopo  76
della Penna, Cesare  21
della Riva, Federico  39
del Tacco: Dominico  89; Giovanni Battista  15, 42
de Machada, Giovanni  94
de Marin, Stefano  41
de' Medici, Thomaso  92
de Medrano, Diego  93
de Mezo, Giacomo  93
Demir Bali  108

# INDEX

Demir Chelebi 109
de Morilo, Giovanni Pietro 94
de Neillino, Giovanni de Riva 94
de Osedo, Francesco 93
Dermigi Peri 105
Dermur Bey 111
de Roig, Pedro 95
Dervish Aga 105
Dervish Chelebi 109
Dervish Hidir 109
Dervish Sach 108
de Toledo, Fernando Alvares 83
de Valascho, Giovanni Rufis 94
de Vergas, Eugenio 92
di Capis, Vincenzo 39
di Capua, Ottavio 38
di Carasse, Giovanni 93
di Casal, Giacomo 92
di Castello, Prospero 39
di Cavalli: Antonio 16, 42, 54, 90; Marino 95, 96
di Dominis, Giovanni 93
Diedo, Girolamo xx–xxi
di Fano, Colonel 32
di Figeroa, Lopez 123
di Grimaldi, Giorgio 41
di Leyni, monsignor 86, 92, 128
di Lobi, Francesco 76
di Lucito, marquis 39
di Mari, Ciprian 91
di Massimi: Domenico 41, 45; Fabio 38; Lelio 39
di Medina, Gabriel 93
di Mezzo, Giacomo 125
di Mongiva, Cristofalo 90
di Monte de l'Ormo, Cornelio 38
Dinati, Francesco 39
di Negro, Ambroggio 41
Diodorus Siculis 4
di Prioli (Priuli): Antonio 29, 42; Giacomo 18, 41; Marc'Antonio 29; Vincenzo Maria 15, 22, 34
di Rocadi, Occava 89

di Rossi, Antonio 38
di Ruggiero, Prospero 38
di San Giovanni, Francesco 38
di Sermonetta, Honorato Gaetano 39
di Somma, Andrea 41
d'Istria, Giovanni 61
di Tessera, Alvise 92
Dium Promontory 49
Divit Ali 111
di Vorgara, Garzia 90
Divrigi 76
Dodecanese 47
Dolfin: Francesco 21, 42; Girolamo 16; Piero (Pietro) 16, 42
Donado: Andrea 21, 42; Marco 42; Nicolò 15, 42, 45, 48, 54, 55
Donaldo, Nadal 41
Donato: Alessandro 71; Bartolomeo 90; Marco 21; Nicolò 21, 93
Don Juan of Austria xiii, 68, 77, 78, 82, 91, 101, 118, 121, 123, 127
Don Maiva 109
Doria: Filippo 92; Giovanni Andrea 27, 31, 33, 45, 77, 79–82, 85, 86, 94, 115, 121, 124–25, contingents & numbers 41; Nicolò 41, 93, 94
Drascio (Drasco), Colane 15, 22, 40, 64, 89
Dressano, Giacomo 55, 91
Dromus Reis 107
Dubrovnik. See Ragusa.
Ducco, Carlo 38
Dulcigno 39, 71
Duodo: Francesco 21, 86, 92, contingents & numbers 43
Durazzo (Durrës) 70, 71
Durmis Ogli 109

E

Echinades 95
Egadi (Favignano) 4

Egypt 4, 9
Elis 53
Emmo: Alvise 16, 42; Gabriel 21, 42; Piero (Pietro) 16, 42, 45, 47
Enchinades. *See* Curzolari.
Epirus 69, 81
Erasmo of Fermo 76
Eroto, Livio 38
Ettore of Brescia 76
Eudomeniani, Antonio 90
Euphrates River 75

F
Falier, Giovanni 29
Famagusta: Andruzzi 57, 59, 60, 65, 67; Arsenal 56, 57, 59, 60, 61, 65, 68, 72; Campo Santo 57, 59, 60; Castel 56; Constanza 51; Gardens 43, 46, 55; Limasol Gate 66; Precipola 55; Santa Nappa 57, 59, 60, 65, 67; siege xii, xix, 28, 29, 33, 36–77, 80–81, 88, 96, 102, 114
Fantuzzi: Camillo 20; Passotto 20
Fauri, Malvezzo 21
Ferath Bhali 108
Ferazzo, Pietro Avogadro 21
Feretti, Alessandro 45
Ferhat, sanjakbey 75, 76, 108, 112
Fermo 40, 61, 65, 76; Tomaso 40
Ferretti, Alessandro 41
Fiaterra, Lazaro 38
Fineka 22, 25, 44
Fiskardo 95
Fisogno, Horatio 55, 90
Flaminio of Florence 76
Florence 11, 20, 31, 79
Fornaretti, Lorenzo 76
Foscarini: Andrea 54; Battista 16, 42; Marc'Antonio 15, 16, 18, 41; Marco 93
Fossa di San Giovanni 87
Fradello, Nicolò 24, 42, 50, 89
Francesco, Arsenal 57

François, duke de Guise 82, 83
Frangipani: Giacomo 39; Mattio 41
Fraschia 49

G
*gabella* 107
Gabrielli, Giulio 39
Galanga 28, 113
Galeni, Giovanni Dionigi. *See* Uluj Ali.
Gamba, Luigi 94
Gambara: Lucrezio 20; Nicolò 20, 21
Gambella 51
Garibaldo, Nicolò 94
Gatto, Angelo 55
Gazaruolo 41
Gaziantep 76
Gazi Reis 107
Genoa xi, 69, 77, 86, 91, 93
Genovese, Ali, corsair 106
Geronimo of Pesaro 42
Ghelso, Giulio Cesare 76
Giafer Aga 107, 109
Giafer Bey 112
Giafer Caran 108
Giafer Chelebi 107
Giafer Chiagia 105
Giafer Reis 109
Giambelat Bey 60, 75
Giaur Ali 108, 109
Giegior Ali 106
Giesman Ferhat 110
Gimongi Mustafa 111
Gioachini, Ottaviano 39
Giuliano, abbot 20
Giul Pervis 110
Giustinian (Giustiniani): Bernardo 16, 18, 41; Giacomo 55; Giustiniano 25; Lorenzo 31; of Cyprus 20; Onfre 16, 41, 90, 127, 128, 131; Pietro 47

# INDEX

Giusuel Giafer 110
Giuzel Ali 112
Gomeniza 88
Gonzaga, Orazio 39
Goro, Giovanni Francesco 60
Gradenigo: Piero (Pietro) 42, 92
Greco, Georgio 93
Griffante, Girolamo 15
Grimaldi, Giorgio 92
Grimani: Antonio 5; Domenico 5; Geronimo 5; Giovanni 5; Giovanni, patriarch xviii, 3, 19, 131; Marco, cardinal 5, 52; Marino 5; Ottaviano 20; Pietro 5; Victor 5
Grisanto, Geronimo 45
Gritti: Francesco 21, 42; Geronimo (Girolamo) 16 42, 45
Grivellatore, Marco 61
Grotto, Cesare 39
Guardiola, Monserat 90
Guasches, Christofolo 91
Gulf, the. *See* Adriatic Sea.
Gulf of: Aiazzo 26, 28 Argolis 107; Arta 95; Corinth 96; Kotor 49; Lepanto 88, 95, 113, 117; Patras xi; Satalia 26, 28, 44; Taranto 87
Guoro: Giacomo 43, 86; Simon 18, 42, 45, 90
Guoto, Giacomo 91
Gurucli Ogli 107
Gyuzel Allib 106

# H
Hadji Kalfa xx
Haedir 112
Haluaghi Mustafa 108
Hapsburg: xiv, Ernest 68, 69, 77; Rudolf. *See* Rudolf II, emperor.
Hasirgi Reis 109
Hassan Pasha 35, 97–99, 107. *See also* Caraman Pasha.
Hassan Reis 112

Hasuf Bali 109
Heder Bashi 109
Heder Lumett 106
Hefus Ogli 111
Hellespont 4
Herbetci 107
Herceg Novi. *See* Castel Nuovo.
Herculiano, Antonio 38
Herodotus 3
Hettor of Brescia 74
Hierosomilitano, Francesco Brutto 41
Higna Mustafa 109
Himarë 69
Holy League xi–xiii, xvi–xvii, 31, 49, 63, 77–88, 116, 127; contingents and numbers 37–43; finances 19–21; forces 72, 88–96; unity xxiii
Honorio Cioti 21
hour systems 35
Huipris Assan 110
Hungary 7, 13

# I
Iachuli Ahmed 110
Iagli Osman 110
Iaia Osman 111
Iaran Shaban 106
Ibrahim, captain 106
Iesil Hogli 110
Imperiale (Imperiali): David (Davide) 41, 89, 92; Nicolò 94
Innuz Ali 112
Ionian Sea xi, 24, 64, 95, 117
Istanbul. *See* Constantinople.
Istria 42, 61, 76, 89
Ithaca 9, 64

# J
Jacopo of Fabiano 76
Janissaries 22, 25, 26, 28, 55, 70, 73, 75, 96, 108, 124, 130

Jerusalem 41
John Frederick I, elector 83

## K
Kara Ali xxi, 62, 64
Kara Alman 111
Kara Bey 112
Kara Bine 99, 104, 111
Kara Chelebi 110
Kara Deli 108
Karadja Ali 110, 112
Karadja Reis 107
Kara Hamat 109
Kara Hodja 71, 78, 96, 98, 100, 108, 109, 119
Kara Kubad 105
Karaman Ali 110
Karam Bey 111
Karam Casli 112
Kara Murat 110
Karamursal 18
Kara Mustafa 106, 107
Kara Peri 107, 110
Karpathos 44, 54
Kas. *See* Caramania.
Kassiopi 49, 70, 87
Kastellorizo 44, 46, 47
Knights Hospitaller xi
Korčula. *See* Curzola.
Kotor 15, 21, 41, 45, 71, 87, 94, 105
Kres 89
Krk 15
Kubad, chaush 15, 16, 17, 18
Kythera (Kythira). *See* Cerigo.

## L
Lacedemonians 4
Laconian Gulf 24
La Goleta 19
Lala Mustafa Pasha xii, 12
Lando: Alvise 18, 42, 45; Marc'Antonio 16, 41, 93, 125
Lasagna, Giovanni Giorgio 93

La Spezia 81
Lefkada 64
Leon (Leone, Lione), Filipo (Filippo) 15, 40, 50, 94
Lepanto; battle of xii–xvi, xx, 1, 3, 31, 81, 95, 96, 113–24; aftermath 126–30; booty 130–31; casualties 129–30; contemporary accounts xvi; historiography xiv–xvi; primary sources xvii
Lesbos 107
Leschino 88
Lesina 16, 71, 78, 91
Levant 6, 11, 12, 17, 19, 72
Limasol 26, 43, 56, 57, 61
Lipoman (Lippamano, Lippomani, Lippomano): Nicolò 15, 22, 41, 90; Pietro 20
Lomellini, Pietro Battista 86, 91, 93
Longo, Zuane 29
Longos 47
Loredan: Giovanni (Zuan) 64, 94, 120, 124; Pietro 16, 19
Lošinj 15
Lotta, Hercole 92
Lucich, Christofolo 94
Lumagh Yusuf 106
Lutherans 83, 127
Lysander, general 4

## M
Magar Ali 107
Magar Ferhat 111
Maggi (Maggio): Geronimo 29, 61, 65, 77; Honofrio 19; Magrino 29
Magli Reis 110
Mahmut Saider Bey 108
Maina 24, 26
Malaguzzi, Alfonso 41
Malaspina: Camillo 38; Giacomo 38; marquis 39
Malatesta: Ercole 61, 76; Roberto 20

INDEX

Malatya 76
Malcantone reef 121
Malfatto, Antenore 39
Malgaritini 27
Malipiero: Bernardo 17; Caterino 15, 22, 40, 45, 94, 120, 124; Gasparo 92; Nicolò 42; Piero (Pietro) Francesco 21, 42, 89; Zuan 72
Malta 47, 69, 82, 86, 92
Malvezzi (Malvezzo), Roberto 57, 65, 76
Mamur Reis 108
Mandia 28
Manolesso, Emilio Maria xvii
manuscripts: Rome, Biblioteca Alessandrina, Rari, 215/4 xxv; Venice, Biblioteca Nazionale Marciana, BNV MVII 1566 xxv
Marash 35, 75
Marc Antony 4, 126
Marcello, Geronimo 55
Marches 23
Martelli, Hieronomo 39
Martinengo: Alvise 20, 40, 74, 76; Antonio 38, 71; Francesco 21; Girolamo 20; Hector 57; Hercole 61, 73, 74, 76; Luigi 57, 66; Marc'Antonio 20, 39; Nestor xix, 51, 56, 57, 60, 61, 65, 73, 74, 76, 77
Marul Mustafa 106
Mat Assan 105
Maximilian II, emperor 68
Mazatosto, Angiolo 39
Mecca 9
Megil Reis 106
Mehmet Ali 109
Mehmet Bey xxi, 78, 80, 96, 99–104, 104, 106
Mehmet II, sultan 8
Mehmet Pasha, vizier 8, 11, 12, 13, 18
Mehmet Suluç (Sirocco) 99, 104, 105, 118, 120, 122

Melfi 27, 41
Memi Beyogli 112
Memin Durmis 106
Mengano, Francesco 89
Messina 27, 31, 64, 69, 77, 78, 79, 80, 82, 86, 87, 92, 124, 125, 128, 130
Messolonghi 114, 117
Michele, Giovanni 10, 11
Michetto, Piero (Pietro) 15, 22
Michiel: Antonio 16, 42; Luca 59; Marco 25, 43; Piero 42; Tomà 18, 41
Mignanello, Pietro Paolo 38
Mignano of Perugia 76
Milan 20
Milos 59
Mingrelia 13
Minotto: Andrea 42; Geronimo (Girolamo) 41, 45
Mocenigo: Alvise, doge 19; Giacomo 39; Giovanni (Zuan) 18, 42, 92; Luigi 131
Modon 29, 88, 95
Molin, Francesco 90
Mondin, Nicolò 90
Mont'Albero 76
Montebello 21
Montenegro 71
Monte Santo 39
Mor Ali 112
Morea 24, 117
Moretto, Ottaviano 93
Mormori: Giovanni 58, 77; Manolis 22, 70
Moro, Daniel 59, 92
Morosini: Andrea 11, 20; Antonio 25, 39; Giacomo 21, 42; Marc'Antonio 25, 43; Tomà 31
Moschetti, Domitian 20
Muazzo (Mudazzo), Francesco 24, 42
Müezzinzade Ali Pasha. See Ali Pasha (Müezzinzade).

Mühlberg, battle of 83
Muhuczzur Ali 111
Murad III, sultan 11
Murat Ali 112
Murat Brassan 111
Murat Chorosan 108
Murat Dervish 111
Murat Dragut Reis 112
Murat Reis 16, 106, 112
Murat Trasil 108
Mustafa Bey 76
Mustafa Esdei 108
Mustafa Genovel 105
Mustafer Pasha 75
Muzaffer (Muzzafer) Pasha, sanjakbey of Valona, first Ottoman governor of Cyprus 35, 36, 37
Mytilene (Mytilini) 107, 108

## N

Nafis Reis 111
Nafplio (Nauplion). *See* Naples in Romania.
Naldo: Alvise 40; Carletto 76; Fabio 40
Nani: Fausto 43; Ferigo 16, 42; Polo 16, 42, 90
Naples 19, 41, 77, 78, 81, 82, 83, 89, 90, 91, 92, 93, 94
Naples in Romania 22, 107
Nasi, Joseph. *See* Michele, Giovanni.
Nasut Fachir 111
Natolico 117
Naupactus, battle of 3
Navarino 63, 64
Negroni: Alessandro 92; Giovanni Ambroggio 94
Negroponte 21, 52, 53, 54, 59, 99, 106, 111
Nicomedia 18
Nicosia: Carafa 30; Costanza 30, 32, 35; Davila 30, 32, 35; fall 44, 48; Margheritti 30; Podocataro 30, 32, 35, 58; Santa Maria 30; siege xii, xix, 26, 28, 29–36, 37, 44, 46, 52, 55, 75, 114; St. George di Magnana 30; Tomandia 30; Tripoli 30, 32, 35
Noce, David 65, 76
North Africa xiv

## O

Occi Reis 107
Orchan Reis 107
Order of Saint John of Malta 47, 82
Orlando, Giovanni 38
Orsini: Horatio 41; Paolo 20, 38; Paolo Giordano 82, 86, 91, 128
Osci Assan 110
Osman Ali 105
Osman Bagli 110
Osman Chelebi 105
Osman Ginder 111
Osman Occan 105
Osman Piri 112
Osman Reis 108, 110
Osman Sehet 109
Osmo, Dario 38
Otranto 31, 87
Ottone, Renuccio 21

## P

Padua 20, 39, 93
Palavicini (Palavicino, Pallavicino): Ettore 38; Giovanni Mattio 41; Sforza 20, 21, 27, 38, 45, 48, 49, 52, contingents and numbers 42–43
Palazzo, Ortensio 29, 36, 39
Palermo 81
Paliano 31, 41
Panormo 87
Papacoda, Alfonso 38
Paphos 37, 56
Parga 81
Parma xi, 82, 86, 91, 128

# INDEX

Paros 47
Pascalo, Vincenzo 91
Pasqualigo: Agostin 71; Alvise 18, 42; Antonio 15, 29, 40, 93; Daniel 72; Luigi 92; Marc'Antonio 125
Pasquini, Stefano 38
Passa Dervish 110
Pathos, bishop of 36
Patras 113
Paul IV, pope 83
Paxi 95
Paxos 95
Pazinardo, Sigismondo 38
Pelleran, captain 91
Peloponnese 53, 107, 113, 117; ancient 3; Peloponnesian War 3, 4
Penelo, Camillo 38
Pepoli, Fabio 20
Perignano, Giacopo Antonio 91
Peri Selim 111
Persio, Francesco 38
Pertau Pasha 53, 54, 59, 96, 104, 108, 118, 124
Peruis Sinan 108
Pervis Luhumagi Ali Reis 109
Pervis Reis 105
Pesaro: Andrea 86; Francesco 64; monsignor 20
Peschiere. *See* Messolonghi.
Petala (Petalas) 95, 126
Pezano, Alvise 76
Philip II, king xiii, 15, 27, 69, 101, 127; contingents & numbers 38; Holy League 77, 82; war preparations 19, 68
Philip of Hesse, landgrave 83
Phillip of Macedon, king 3
Piga 44
Pignatello: Lucio 38; Marco 38
Pinargenti, Simone 27
Pio, Hercole 38
Piovene, Captain 29, 32
Piri Beg Ogli 109
Piri Reis 112
Piri Sisnam 109
Pirola, Martin 89
Pisani (Pisano): Giorgio (Zorzi) 16, 41, 92; Lorenzo 31; Marc'Antonio 15, 42, 50, 90; Piero (Pietro) 16, 29, 42, 86, 92, 94
Pisma Reis 110
Pius V, pope xii, 15, 19, 25, 29, 31, 33, 34, 37, 39, 40, 41, 45, 49, 63, 69, 77, 82, 86, 92, 127, 130, 131
Piyale Pasha 12, 13, 18, 21, 25, 26, 28, 33, 34, 43, 47, 48, 53, 112
Platanias 62
Plutarch 3
Pocopani, captain 29, 32
Pola, Sergio 20
Polani: Filippo 23, 42, 89; Paolo (Polo) 23, 42, 93
Polidoro, Pandolfo 93
Polybius 3
Porcelaga, clan 20; Scipione 39
Porto, Hippolito 20
Porto Kagio 24
Porto Picorna 29
Portuguese 64
Potamo 37
Preuil Aga 107
Prevesa (Preveza) 4, 95, 100, 102, 126
Priuli 18, 20, 22, 29, 34, 41, 42, 46, 47; Matteo 20, 48; Vincenzo Maria 46, 47
Prostunagli Ogli 107
Provaio: Annibale 39; Marco 39
Puglia 23

# Q

Quaglie 24
Quesada, Michiel 90
Quirini: Carlo 16, 42, 45; Gian (Giovanni) Antonio 37, 58, 60, 74; Giovanni Battista (Zuan Battista)

21, 42, 90; Marc'Antonio 15–17,
42; Marco 23, 24, 26, 29, 33, 34,
44 54, 59, 63, 64, 66, 69, 77, 80, 82,
86, 90, 123, 128, contingents and
numbers 40; Vicenzo (Vincenzo)
21, 25, 41, 43, 50, 88, 123

## R

Rab 15
Rafario, Giovanni Battista 132
Ragazzoni, bishop 48
Ragonasco, Carlo 74, 76
Ragusa 16, 70, 71
Ramazzan 110
Rangone: Giulio 21; Palavicino 20
Renier, Federico (Ferigo) 55, 90
Requesens y Zúñiga, Luis de 123
Retimno (Rhetymno) 23, 42
62, 90, 93
Rhodes 16, 21, 22, 29, 33, 43, 44,
47, 52, 55, 66, 76, 77, 107
Riminaldi, Giovanni Maria 39
Rimini 77
Rivarolo 76
Rocca, Giovanni Maria 38
Roccaful, captain 91
Rodlu Ali 106
Romania (Peloponnesus) 22
Rome 4, 83
Rondacchi, commander 72
Roxolana, sultaness 7
Rubbio, Giulio 93
Rudolf II, emperor 68
Rus Chelebi 112
Rustan Cialmaghi 109
Rustan Cinigi 111

## S

Sagredo, Bernardo 16, 41
Salach Fachir 108
Salamis, battle of 3
Salamone, Girolamo 18
Sala Reis 109

Sali Arnuar 107
Sali Deli 111
Salih Reis Pasha 99
Salines 26, 28, 33, 34
Salò 39, 40
Salomon: Giacomo 42; Pietro 16;
Zaccaria 43, 53
Sandagi Memi 112
San Fedra, Francesco 90
San Marco 131
San Nicolò 63, 89, 90
San Quentin, battle of 83
San Severino, Filippo Angelo di 38
Sansovino, Francesco xxv
Santa Croce: Fabio 41; Ludovico
39, 82, 128
Santa Iuliana, Marc'Antonio 55
Santa Maura 117
Santoni, Roberto 38
Santubi, captain 92
Sanudo: Agostin 21, 41; Marino
xviii
Saraf Reis 107
Sarandë 69
Sardinia 19, 123
Sarmusach Reis 110
Saseno 78, 80, 81
Sauli, Bendinelli 91
Saulo, Hercole 21
Savona 69
Savoy xi, 86, 92, 93
Sayr Giafer 110
Sazan 78
Schender Dernigi 109
Schmalkaldic War 83
Scin Schiander 111
Scipione, knight 76
Scotto, Alberto 29, 32
Seit Aga 111
Selim II, sultan xii, 7, 10, 11, 104;
diplomatic demands 18; motives
for war 7–12; war preparations
15

# INDEX

Selim Sciach 109
Setecai 46
Seyth 111
Shaban, captain 106
Shehrizur 35
Shender Selim 106
Shetagi Osman 112
ships: brigantine 53; caramuscialin 18; fanò 14; foist 53; fusta 18, 53; galea grossa 89; galiot 18, 53; galleass 18, 89; galleys 26; lantern galley 14; large galley 89; maona 18
Šibenik 15, 22, 42, 94
Sican Mustafa 109
Sicily 41, 78, 89, 92, 94, 100
Sicuro, Marin 92
Sigismondo of Casoldo 76
Simoneta, Curzio 38
Simonetti, Giulio 20
Sinan Bali 108
Sinan Chelebi 110
Sinan Dervish 106
Sinan Mustafa 106, 109
Sinan Reis 107
Sinclitico, Eugenio 28
*sipachis* 26, 28, 55, 96, 130
Siran Bardaci 109
Sirizi Memi 110
Sitia 37, 40, 45, 47
Sitina Reis 111
Sivas 75, 76
slaves & slavery 6, 15, 16, 24, 25, 26, 28, 36, 37, 42, 43, 46, 48, 50, 52, 53, 59, 70, 71, 74, 75, 76, 77, 78, 96, 97, 102, 104, 105, 114, 122, 130, 131
Smyrna 99
Soassera 48
Solac Reis 106
Soldatello, captain 61
Solomon, Zaccaria 25
Sopot 22, 69, 70, 102
Soranzo: Benedetto 16, 42, 93, 125;

Vettor 39
Soriano, Anzolo 34
Souda 29, 33, 45, 47, 59, 62
Sozomeno, Giovanni xix, 32
Spinola: Ettor 86, 91, 128; Zuan Battista 91
Spolverino, colonel 20
Stalla, Fulvio 39
Stampalia 47
St. Clement 28
Stracco, Francesco 74, 76
Strafoldo, Zuan 59
Straight of Otranto 78
Strambali, Giacomo 72
Strivali (Strofadi) 117
Strozzi, Pandolfo 94
St. Theodore, island 62
Sufan Reis 112
Suleiman Bey 76, 106
Suleiman Chelebi 108
Suleiman the Magnificent, sultan xii, 7, 8, 11
Suriano: Angelo 15, 16, 46, 47; Nicolò 16, 41
S.Vliana, Marc'Antonio 91
Syria 9, 75, 99, 106, 111
Szigetvar 7, 8, 13

T
Tafer Mustafa 106
Taffone, Hercole 39
Talitagi Reis 112
Tasci Sisman 110
Tatar Ali 112
Techedel Assan 110
*tercio* 123
Themistocles 3
Tiene, Ottavio 21
Tiepolo: Almoro 25; Andrea 21, 41; Donà 42; Donado 18; Geronimo (Girolamo) 21, 42; Lorenzo 37, 56, 57, 72, 73, 74; Sebastian 16

Tinos 19
Torcello, bishop 20
Torre Magra 38
Tramontana Reis 108
Travel, Alessandro 40
Trecha, Lorenzo 93
Tressino, Giacomo 124
Trevisan: Francesco 31; Giovanni, patriarch 20; Piero (Pietro) 18, 42
Treviso 20
Tripoli 30, 32, 35, 75, 106, 109, 112, 118
Tristamo 44
Trogir 15, 41, 93, 125
Tromba, Vido 38
*trombe* 114
Tron: Andrea 18, 42, 93; Daniel 94; Francesco 15, 16, 30, 42, 49, 64, 70; Geronimo (Girolamo) 15, 40; 50; Hector 17; Piero 43, 50, 52; Santo 16, 50, 52, 53
Troncavilla, Francesco 76, 77
Tron, Santo 42
Tumus Suleiman 110
Tunis xiv
Turco, Lodovico 38
Turlurù 62, 63
Tuscany xi

## U
Ugone, Ludovico 39
Ugubio, Bernardino 61
Ulcinj 71, 102. *See* Dulcigno.
Uluj Ali xi, xx, 62, 70, 71, 78, 95, 99, 104, 111–12, 118, 121, 124–26, 128
Uluj Rais 107
Urbino xi, 82, 86, 92, 128
Uschiusli Memi 110

## V
Valaresso, Valerio 59, 92
Valciati, Fabio 89
Valier: Agostino 20; Zaccaria 21, 42
Valignano, Giovanni Vicenzo 38
Valona 78, 80, 87, 108, 111
Veglia 15, 45, 90
Veletri 57, 76
Vendramin, Francesco 16, 42
Venice: Arsenal 10, 11, 12, 14, 15, 25, 56, 57; contingents & numbers 38–40; Crete 14; historiographical tradition xviii; Holy League xi; lagoon 131; Lido 131; Ottomans xii; patriarch 20; Piazza San Marco 131; piracy 9; San Antonio 5; San Francesco 5; San Marco 5, 16, 17, 19, 22, 41, 132; Senate 16, 17, 18, 49, 52, 54, 77, 127, 131, 132; Signoria 10, 20, 21, 28, 82; Tapana 15; taxes 20
Venier: Agostin 16, 42; Geronimo 71, 91, 124; Lorenzo 41; Sebastian 19, 22, 27, 45, 50, 52, 53, 59, 64, 65, 69, 77, 78, 82, 86, 88, 91, 116, 118, 120, 123, 124, 127, 128, 131; Stefano 16, 41
Verona 20, 39, 40, 76, 77
Vetturi, Marco 25
Vicenza 20, 29, 32, 91, 94, 124
Vicomercato, Hieronimo 39
Vienna 69
Villano, Fabrizio 39
Viscardo Channel 117
Vitelli, Alfonso 21
Vizzamano: Alessandro 23, 42, 50, 92; Giovanni (Zuan) Michiel 23, 42, 90
Vlati 71, 72
Vlorë 78
Vonitsa 95

## W
weights & measures 88

# INDEX

## X
Xenophon 3, 4
Xerxes, king 3

## Y
Yumurtalık 26
Yusuf Aga 105
Yusuf Ali 111
Yusuf Chelebi 106
Yusuf Cinigi 109
Yusuf Magar 105
Yuzel Memi 106

## Z
Zadar 15, 16, 17, 22, 23, 42, 70
Zakynthos (Zante) 53, 64, 69
Zambeccari: Alessandro 21, 38; Flaminio 37; Paolo 38
Zamboti, Geronimo 38
Zampesco, Brunoro 20
Zancaruol: Antonio 23; Francesco 23, 90; Giovanni Francesco 23; Vicenzo (Vincenzo) 23, 42
Zane (Zanne): Girolamo 16, 17, 22, 23, 27, 29, 30, 44, 48, 49, 52, 53, contingents and numbers 41; Piero (Pietro) 16, 41, 45
Zante 53, 88, 90, 92, 95, 102, 103, 105, 117
Zara 21
Zen: Francesco 42, 89; Renier 93
Zeno, Giovanni 91
Ziliolo, Cesare 131
Zonchio 63
Zorzi: Alvise 41; Geronimo (Girolamo) 23, 42, 93
Zumbul Murat 110
Zurla, Evangelista 64, 93

*Production of This Book Was Completed
On 10 July 2019 at Italica Press,
Clifton, Bristol, United Kingdom.
It Was Set in Adobe Bembo,
Adobe Bembo Expert &
Columbus Ornaments*

www.ingramcontent.com/pod-product-compliance
Lightning Source LLC
Chambersburg PA
CBHW030111170426
**43198CB00009B/575**